Nuclear Flashpoint

"Institutionalized systemic racial persecution … against the people of Kashmir has pushed the world to the edge of nuclear conflict. Torture, unlawful killings, and the denial of basic human rights and freedoms are well-documented by Amnesty, Human Rights Watch, and others. Dr. Chak's skillful analysis explains just how this unresolved crisis threatens global peace."

—Ilyasah Shabbazz, educator and author of *Growing Up X: A Memoir by the Daughter of Malcolm X*

"An urgent and trenchant examination of Kashmir. Beautifully meshing history with modern political analysis, Chak masterfully interrogates … the intersecting flashpoints that make the Kashmir crisis one of the most politically sensitive issues in modern world history. Beyond intellectual examination, Chak injects first-hand insights as a scholar, advocate and ancestral Kashmiri to offer a richness that few other books provide—bringing intimacy and empathy to words that spring colorfully from the pages."

—Khaled A. Beydoun, Law Professor and author of *The New Crusades: Islamophobia and the Global War on Muslims*

"Repeated clashes between India, Pakistan, and China over Kashmir threaten to erupt into a nuclear conflict that might kill as many as 120 million in India and Pakistan, and perhaps several thousand million worldwide. These disputes need to be resolved, which requires understanding their origins, the people of Kashmir and their struggles, and recent changes in the region. *Nuclear Flashpoint* provides essential insight into these issues for all who are concerned."

—Professor Brian Toon, Department of Atmospheric and Oceanic Sciences, University of Colorado Boulder

Nuclear Flashpoint

The War Over Kashmir

Farhan M. Chak

First published 2024 by Pluto Press
New Wing, Somerset House, Strand, London WC2R 1LA
and Pluto Press, Inc.
1930 Village Center Circle, 3-834, Las Vegas, NV 89134

www.plutobooks.com

British Library Cataloguing in Publication Data
A catalogue record for this book is available from the British Library

ISBN   978 0 7453 4616 8   Paperback
ISBN   978 0 7453 4620 5   PDF
ISBN   978 0 7453 4618 2   EPUB

This book is printed on paper suitable for recycling and made from fully managed
and sustained forest sources. Logging, pulping and manufacturing processes are
expected to conform to the environmental standards of the country of origin.

Typeset by Stanford DTP Services, Northampton, England

Simultaneously printed in the United Kingdom and United States of America

Contents

CONTENTS

Abbreviations

AFSPA	Armed Forces Special Powers Act
AINC	All Indian National Congress
BRI	Belt and Road Initiative
BJP	Bharatiya Janata Party
CAA	Citizenship Amendment Act
CASO	cordon and search operation
DAA	Disturbed Area Act
J&K	Jammu and Kashmir
KC	Kashmir Civitas
KSCAN	Kashmir Scholars Consultative and Action Network
LAC	Line of Actual Control
NGO	Non-Governmental Organization
NHPC	National Hydroelectric Power Corporation
NSA	National Security Act
OIC	Organization of Islamic Cooperation
QUAD	Quadrilateral Security Dialogue
RSS	Rashtriya Swayamsevak Sangh
SAARC	South Asian Association for Regional Cooperation
SASB	Amarnath Shrine Board
SWK	Stand With Kashmir
UN	United Nations
UNSC	United Nations Security Council
UAPA	Unlawful Activities Prevention Act
VHP	Vishnu Hindu Parishad
WKAF	World Kashmir Awareness Forum

1
Introduction

The disputed territory of Jammu and Kashmir (Kashmir) remains the longest unresolved conflict on the United Nation's agenda.[1] It is also the most militarized space on the planet.[2] Even worse, this international conflict—certainly not bilateral, since it involves Kashmir, Pakistan, India, and China—can be described as a *nuclear flashpoint*, especially after the Sino-Indian border erupted into the bloody Galwan Valley clash of 2020.[3] Also, since 2019, the reputable non-governmental organization Genocide Watch has issued two genocide alerts over Indian government designs in Kashmir.[4] In spite of that, no matter how frightening the stakes, little is understood about this conflict outside the region, and its resolution is nowhere in sight. More often than not, the history, culture, identity, and, most importantly, the will of the people of Kashmir have been deliberately obscured, particularly by the post-colonial Indian state, which uses a sophisticated network of misinformation to control the narrative on Kashmir. In fact, there is an irrefutable strategy to silence indigenous Kashmiri voices, imprison their bodies, curtail their agency, and even take their lives—all under the uninterested eyes of the world. India's aim is to avoid international attention on its ongoing violations of human rights, settler-colonist agenda, and increased militarization. How many people worldwide know that the Valley of Kashmir is riddled with thousands of armed checkpoints? How many realize that Indian soldiers guard the entrance and exit of almost every village? How many people understand that Kashmir has thousands of mass graves and has had at least 337,000 deaths since 1947? The seriousness of this crisis threatens not only Kashmiri life but also wider global peace.

Today, the strategy employed by the post-colonial Indian state is denial, deflection, and destruction. This is in order to incapacitate the will of an oppressed Kashmiri populace and skew world opinion. India desperately wishes to devitalize the spirit of resistance and enact harsh punitive measures to dissuade dissent. Worse, the Indian state enacts its agenda unrestrainedly on the men, women, and children of Kashmir under the cover of obscurity.[5] Of course, this is the playbook for every colonial regime throughout human history: break the spirit of the fraught public; exploit their will; fracture society; delude the rest of the world; and distort reality by bribing handpicked operatives unrepresentative of the reality on the ground. Indeed, the post-colonial Indian state has always followed this playbook in Kashmir. Despite this, it has been unable to control the people. As a result, it becomes increasingly frantic in its attempts to forcibly manufacture consent and dubiously project normalcy.

This precarious situation took a turn for the worse with the 2014 electoral victory of the Bharatiya Janata Party (BJP), a political party founded on a Hindutva ideology that is violent, Islamophobic, and supremacist. Since then, the erosion of Muslim, Christian, Sikh, and Dalit rights has rapidly escalated not just in Kashmir but throughout India.[6] Furthermore, the lengths that the BJP-led government goes to project a false normalcy include doctored images showing Kashmiris waving and smiling at Indian soldiers.[7] Still, whether it is the red herring of terror, instrumentalizing women's emancipation, or dangling promises of economic development, Indian attempts to contain Kashmir are futile. Indian intelligentsia who support the settler-colonial policies remain clueless on how to manage Kashmir. Consequently, Prime Minister Narendra Modi's government unilaterally abrogated Articles 370 and 35A of the Indian constitution on August 5, 2019, erasing the disputed region's special status. What followed was a harrowing call for a "final solution."[8] Basically, India annexed the disputed territory in direct contravention of United Nations (UN) resolutions and international law and threatened genocide. That unilateral, illegal act threw the entire region into disarray, bringing China into the conflict, and considerably raising the likelihood of a war.[9]

The abrogation of Articles 370 and 35A of the Indian constitution as it pertained to Kashmir was a gross miscalculation by the Indian government. It inadvertently internationalized the conflict, and what followed was global denunciation. Several major international newspapers such as the *Washington Post*, the *Guardian*, the *New York Times* and *Le Monde Diplomatique* criticized the abrogation. Major international non-governmental organizations (NGOs), such as Amnesty International and Human Rights Watch, expressed shock at the levels of "repression" in Kashmir and denounced the "arrest of prominent Kashmiri human rights activist, Khurram Parvez, on political motivated charges under the so-called counter-terrorism law, the Unlawful Activities Prevention Act (UAPA)."[10] Responding to the heightening tensions, the European Union, the Organization of Islamic Cooperation (OIC), and the UN condemned the abuses. The United Nations Security Council (UNSC) also held two closed-door meetings on the evolving crisis, which were the first in decades.[11] Ignoring worldwide censure, India chose to double down and imposed a communications blockade in Kashmir in August 2019. This angered former UN Special Rapporteur on Freedom of Opinion and Expression David Kaye, who called it "draconian."[12] Yet, most importantly, as a result of the Modi government's punitive measures, Kashmiris were put in a corner. The annexation of the disputed territory provoked Kashmiris from all over the world to assert their rights.[13] Ethnic Kashmiris in several cities in the West, whether writers, artists, musicians, academics, or activists, freely began speaking their mind and condemned India's human rights violations and political suppression.[14] Today, those indigenous Kashmiris worldwide are leading the resistance against what they describe as the occupation, militarization, and settler-colonialism taking place on their ancestral land. Several organizations have formed, such as World Kashmir Awareness Forum, Justice for Kashmir, Critical Kashmir Studies, Stand with Kashmir, Kashmir House, Kashmir Scholars Consultative and Action Network (KSCAN), and Kashmir Civitas. Kashmiri voices will not be silenced, and this book aims to contribute to bringing forth a sophisticated indigenous Kashmiri narrative that represents the primary religious/ethnic demographic.[15]

THEATER OF WAR

From the onset, it should be noted that what is commonly referred to as Kashmir has become a convenient but misleading shorthand for the five distinct regions of the erstwhile 1947 princely state of Jammu and Kashmir.[16] Part of the problem is that historically the borders of the princely state included ethnically diverse peoples. This complicates our understanding of this dispute since the words Kashmir/Kashmiri may refer to either a specific people—the largest but not the only ethnic group in the disputed territory—or to every citizen of the disputed territory regardless of ethnicity. Collectively, the five regions are now divided into Indian Administered Kashmir, which consists of three areas: 1) the Valley of Kashmir (15,948 km²) with a population of 8 million people—the heart of Kashmiri culture and language, and the focal point of the uprising against Indian hegemony; 2) Jammu (26,293 km²) with a mixed ethnic population of 5,350,811 people comprising Kashmiri Muslims, including Bakerwal Muslims and Gujjar Muslims; Kashmiri Pandits; Dogra Hindus and Sikhs; Punjabi Sikhs, Hindus, and Muslims; and an unregistered, sizable minority of Indian citizens who migrated there; and 3) Ladakh (59,146 km²) with a small population of 274,289 that is divided between Buddhists, Kashmiri Muslims—including Balti, Bakerwal and Gujjar Muslims, and a tiny population of Indian Hindus. On the other hand, Pakistan Administered Kashmir is nearly entirely Muslim and includes two areas: 1) Azad Kashmir (13,297 km²) with a population of 4.6 million; and 2) Gilgit-Baltistan (72,971 km²) with a population of 1.8 million, which is actually two ethnically distinct areas of Gilgit and Baltistan. Together, this amounts to a total population of approximately 21 million people, 86 percent of whom are Muslim. Also, one must not forget the forcibly uprooted Kashmiris who reside in cities such as Lahore, Gujranwala, Sialkot, and elsewhere.

Now, India's attempts to aggressively alter the demographics through a settler-colonial project has threatened to further destabilize the region. The most recent statistics from Indian sources indicate 4.1 million domicile certificates were granted to non-ethnic

Kashmiris, in a clear instance of demographic change.[17] Kashmiris are not exaggerating when they claim India is resorting to "demographic flooding" to dilute the Muslim-majority demographic.[18] Kashmiri artist Suhail Mir has produced beautiful work criticizing the manner in which the Indian state is "inventing Kashmiris" of their own liking.[19]

It is critical to emphasize that what many think of when hearing about Kashmir in the media—beyond the lush valleys and snow-capped mountains—pertain to the human rights violations, rapes, mass graves, widows, orphans, and ongoing violence that is exclusively occurring in Indian-controlled Kashmir—well documented by the UN.[20] This is the geographical expanse morbidly described as "the theater of war" by many of those studying the conflict. Violence occurs, largely, but not exclusively, in the Indian-controlled Valley of Kashmir. Of course, parallel violence continues to occur in the Muslim-majority areas of Jammu, such as Rajouri, Poonch, Doda, Kishtwar, Ramban, and Reasi. Actually, the Jammu area has the unfortunate legacy of being home to one of the worst atrocities committed during the last days of the British Raj, which was a genocide in which at least 237,000 Muslims were mercilessly butchered, and several hundred thousand forced to flee, including surviving members of my family, with my maternal and paternal grandparents among them.[21] Nevertheless, when referring to the ongoing repression in Kashmir, this book is specifically referring to the geographical space of Indian-Occupied Kashmir, which includes the Valley of Kashmir, Jammu, and Ladakh. Unquestionably though, the impact of this crisis is global.

The post-colonial Indian state is responsible for human rights violations and settler-colonial violence in Kashmir. Yet, it is not singularly responsible. The United Kingdom has displayed a remarkable indifference to the plight of Kashmiris, even though it is responsible for their current predicament, which shall be elaborated later. Likewise, the European Union, the OIC, and UN—even while issuing two Office of the United Nations High Commissioner for Human Rights (2018, 2019) reports, have all failed to address the violations of international law. Concerning Pakistan, while there is much to be desired in regard to the rule of law, due process, and representative governance, it does not operate as a settler-colonial power in relation to areas of the disputed territory it controls, such as Gilgit-Baltistan or Azad Kashmir. This is substantiated by the following reasons: 1) the regions of Azad Kashmir and Gilgit-Baltistan are almost exclusively Muslim, but have their own unique ethnic composition, with a minority ethnic Kashmiri population; 2) neither Gilgit-Baltistan or Azad Kashmir has any serious independence movement, since the major religious, ethnic, and linguistic groups that reside in these areas overwhelmingly identify with Pakistan; 3) both Gilgit-Baltistan and Azad Kashmir launched their own, indigenous armed resistance against the British-supported Dogra rulers, vanquishing them in armed combat.[22] In Gilgit-Baltistan it was the Gilgit Scouts[23] and in Azad Kashmir the heroics of Sardar Muhammad Ibrahim Khan, as well as Ghulam Abbas—the leader of the Muslim Conference—which booted out the Dogra forces.[24] In other words, these two regions of the erstwhile princely state fought for their freedom, willfully joined the Pakistan movement, and kicked out the foreign Dogras in 1947.[25] Therefore, there are strong historical reasons for considering India's treatment of the people of Kashmir differently from that of Pakistan.

Interestingly, there are indigenous Kashmiri narratives that emerge from Azad Kashmir, but more importantly from the cities of Sialkot, Wazirabad, Lahore, and Gujranwala in Pakistan. This book includes these overlooked narratives, since they are the principal agitators of the Kashmir cause in Pakistan. In fact, the Kashmiris residing in those cities are steering the Pakistani state towards their oppressed kith and kin across the ceasefire line, as much as the people of Azad Kashmir. While this is all critically important, and will be included, it will not be the focus of the book, as that would distract from its main impetus: India's settler-colonial project in Indian-Occupied Kashmir and its impact on regional and global instability.

CONTESTED IDENTITIES

Undoubtedly, the people of Kashmir—their ethnic origin, culture, and language—are unique. They are a fascinating fusion of the original Semites, and, then later of Greeks, Central Asians, Persians, Afghans, and Turks, among others. For that reason, Kashmir and what it means to be Kashmiri have become contested terms. In fact, for over a millennium a majority of the inhabitants of the Valley of Kashmir were Buddhist—not Hindu, as wrongly asserted by Hindutva propagandists.[26] Still, let there be no mistake, Kashmiri people are just that—their own people with a sense of past, present, and future.[27] In fact, the idea of India has never resonated with Kashmiris. India finds this unconscionable. And India's approach to this unthinkable situation is to adopt the logic of settler-colonialism, which seeks to forcibly label a population, hijack their agency, and compel them to concur. This reasoning relies on the mendacious claim of normalcy,[28] when at least 93,000 people have been killed over the last 30 years.[29] As Mir and Raafi describe, the projection of normalcy simultaneously involves arresting journalists, stifling freedom of expression, and compelling people to chant *Bharat Mata* in a faux display of nationalist sentiment.[30]

Behind this strategy of enforcing identity is the complex, deeply entrenched obstacle towards peace. This is the peculiar logic of all settler-colonial states whose dispossession of land, erasure of indigenous culture, coercive patriotism, and consequent crimes against humanity are rationalized in every way imaginable. It was Golda Meir who said that "We can never forgive Arabs for forcing us to kill their children."[31] After all, Palestinians were purportedly given a choice: submit, or else. Such is the resentment exhibited by settler-colonial powers who are enraged at resistance to their settler-colonial policies. Actually, Kashmiris endure the same. This is the profound idiosyncrasy that explains the post-colonial Indian state's insistence that Kashmiris are Indians. This, too, in front of Kashmiris—who look on in disbelief, vehemently responding they are not. Such is the absurdity, where "falsification of history," myth, insecurities, identity crisis and post-colonial fixations coalesce with complexes of color and desirability.[32] This is the irrationality of post-colonial India's infatuation with Kashmir—the largest democracy in the world is unwilling to allow the people of Kashmir the opportunity to exercise their democratic rights. Imagine someone insisting that you must love them, carry their flag, sing their songs, and chant their anthem. As Christopher Snedden writes, India's policy in Kashmir is: "Damn you. Come here."[33]

This pathology was elucidated by one of the largest Indian Muslim organizations, *Jamiat-Ulama-i-Hind*, with tens of millions of followers, when chastising Kashmiris for demanding the right of self-determination.[34] The president of this organization, Mahmoud Madani, who has partnered with Prime Minister Modi, stated in a live TV interview that if Kashmiris started carrying the Indian flag and singing *Jai Hind* then they would be neither cursed or shot.[35] In other words, Madani is blaming Kashmiris, since they do not celebrate Indian identity in a way the post-colonial state would like. Post-colonial India's attitude towards Kashmir implies a choice between compliance and punishment.

This book directly deals with the question of identity and cultural violence in addition to the potential global nuclear catastrophe looming before our eyes. In fact, if there is ever to arise a narrative of mutual respect it must unravel the dystopic reality taking place on the ground, and the profound psychological obstacles and deep-seated fixations of shame that hinder the chance for peace. Similarly, that false imaginary of a monolithic Indian identity—*Akhand Bharat*—that swallows individuality, diversity, and pluralism must be challenged.[36] In fact, in India's new parliament building a map of "Greater India" is clearly on display, which has riled its neighbors.[37] In a way, *Akhand Bharat* aims to "Orientalize" Kashmir, or, as Homi Bhabha puts it, to "not allow for native agency," to muddle it up to the point of becoming undecipherable.[38] The "native," or Kashmiri, is thus only permitted a voice once they have been epistemologically, culturally, and ideologically conscripted. Only then are Kashmiris allowed a "voice," so long as it underwrites the manufacture of pacified "Indian" subjects.

BRITISH RAJ, PARTITION, AND HINDUTVA FASCISM

During the last days of the British Raj, conflicting narratives/identities were a major point of contention between all stakeholders. This debate has all but disappeared, but this book revisits it. Winston Churchill was quoted to have said India is "no more a country than the equator."[39] Naturally, then, divergent conceptualizations of identity were bound to emerge. On the one hand, the charismatic Muhammad Ali Jinnah proposed a non-ethnic, non-denominational Muslim identity when declaring his infamous two-nation theory.[40] That narrative was, and remains, in competition with the Indian National Congress' one nation theory. However, both are somewhat misleading. There were neither one nor two identities in the British Raj, but many. It was home to several dozen nations, with distinct languages, cultures, and traditions. And, in recognition of that, it is unsurprising that the overwhelming majority of the people of Kashmir refused to accept the post-colonial imaginary nation called India. Yet, this does not diminish India. Nor should Indians consider it as shame or a rejection. What diminishes India is the manner with which it deals with Kashmir—the torture, rape, and murder documented by international human rights organizations.[41] Nonetheless, approaching the quagmire of Kashmir from a perspective of false imaginaries, contested identities, and conflicting/combative narratives allows us to challenge prevalent discourses that frame the conflict in a particular way.

This brings us to another point of contention that goes to the heart of the acrimony between India and Pakistan: the misleading and poorly studied phenomenon of the partition of the British Raj in 1947. At that time, the emerging narratives were unable to tolerate pluralism. The inability to manage diversity and accept the existence of alternative identities resulted in the use of physical power to pulverize them. Unraveling this contestation over identity provides a deeper understanding of the ethos of the post-colonial Indian hegemonic state in relation to Kashmir.[42] Pakistan, too, has fared little better in this regard. However, after the break-up of the country and creation of Bangladesh in 1971, there seems to have been a slight course correction. In contrast, in India a majoritarian intolerance has arisen that may justifiably be called fascism. No longer interested in persuading, and unwilling to concede, Hindutva India insists on brute force. And, embedded within that is the Hindutva idea of a monolithic Indian identity built upon historical revision-ism that is exclusionary and demonizing.[43] It is important here to consider how Prime Minister Modi responded to President Donald Trump's offer for mediation over Kashmir. Modi responded that Pakistan and India were formerly "one nation" and so they under-stand one another and do not require third-party mediation. This false image of India as a single country has proliferated since the end of the British Raj to the present day. This is why I argue that the British Raj, rather than India, was divided in 1947. In fact, it is illog-ical to regard India, Pakistan, Afghanistan, Bangladesh, Nepal, or Bhutan as single countries when the majority of people cannot com-municate in a mutually intelligible way. Without question, this holds for Kashmir. And why is this so important? Because by recogniz-ing how the concept of "one country" is weaponized, it unravels the deeper pathology of loss, theft, and robbery that Hindutva fascists preach against Kashmiris, and generally all Muslims, as a result of partition.[44]

Truschke insightfully describes fascist Hindutva ideology as teaching a type of "pain of theft" ethos to its followers that claims "Muslims stole *Indian* land."[45] In that Hindutva narrative, the sacred borders of India were sullied by Muslims who forcibly converted the local people to Islam and then, eventually, dissected the land to create a new country, namely Pakistan.[46] Now, Muslims are asking for those sacred boundaries to be ripped apart again, that is, by Kashmiri Muslims who aim for their own country or autonomy with Pakistan. This sentiment was explicitly made clear by the late Kuldip Nayar in Washington, DC, on July 29, 2010, when he told me "India will never accept another partition. Kashmiris will not parti-tion India. We allowed it once, and will not again."[47] In these words are the deeper assumptions that many uncritically hold. What did he mean when he said, "India will never accept another partition?" Exploring that led me to understand the ways that Hindutva pro-pagandists conveniently ignore any history that is problematic to their narrative building. Leave aside that the majority population in the territory of Pakistan were Buddhists prior to the advent of Islam,[48] or how Kashmiri Muslim oral traditions trace the origins of their culture to the lost tribes of Israel,[49] or how several Buddhist stupas scattered throughout Kashmir are inaccurately described as Hindu.[50] This is the irrationality of Hindutva fascism that is averse to facts, not unlike other populist, nativist trajectories as described by Jeremiah Morelock's analysis of authoritarian populism.[51]

MOTIVATION FOR THE BOOK

This book approaches the ongoing crisis in Kashmir by centering the voices of the primary religious, ethnic demographic of Kashmir, foregrounding their beliefs, and critically engaging with the literature. Its aim is to tell our story. Consequently, it has been written to put forward the Kashmiri Muslim narrative on dispossession of land, falsification of history, and erasure of identity. To accomplish that, it dissects history, myth, and identity to reveal how Kashmir has been forcibly manufactured to fit into a particular mold where it doesn't belong—that of post-colonial India.

I am also motivated by a sincere will for peace in the vast, diverse region of South Asia. Consider how, on February 14, 2019, a suicide bombing took place in Indian-Occupied Kashmir, in the restive town of Pulwama. It resulted in the killing of 40 Indian soldiers.[52] Immediately, without any actionable intelligence or transparent investigation, India targeted Pakistan with an airstrike in the town of Balakot, Khyber-Pakhtunkhwa.[53] This bombing culminated in emptying the fighter jet's payload in a deserted, forested area, with the only sign of death being a lifeless crow. Yet this was no laughing matter. Responding fiercely, Pakistan retaliated by bombing several locations in Indian-Occupied Kashmir. While claiming to have inflicted no loss of life, Pakistani authorities stated this was a clear signal to India "that we can target you at will," and any military adventurism will be responded to with full force.[54] Yet, rather than dissuade India, the situation rapidly escalated. India sent two military fighter jets to attack the intruding Pakistani aircraft. This resulted in both Indian jets being shot down, an Indian helicopter destroyed and Indian Wing Commander Abhinandan captured.[55] The dramatic turn of events cooled only after Pakistan's prime minister at the time, Imran Khan, in a goodwill gesture, freed the captured Indian pilot.[56] However, even as tensions subsided, the message was clear: two nuclear armed countries had engaged in a dogfight and were on the brink of a full-scale war. For a moment, the world shook.

Commenting on the ongoing crisis, the UN High Commissioner for Human Rights Michelle Bachelet called on India and Pakistan to give "access that is unconditional" in divided Kashmir.[57] India refused, and Bachelet expressed "deep concern" at the human rights violations in Kashmir and the snub to international observers. Perversely, the BJP government doubled down. They created a hyper-nationalist, warlike frenzy in India and chastised the UN for its "bias."[58] Undoubtedly, it's to India's advantage to solemnly address this issue, but we see the opposite occurring. The rhetoric, the crackdown on civil liberties, and violence on the ceasefire line between India and Pakistan worsens day by day. Now, more than ever, a roundtable including Pakistan, India, China, and the legitimate representatives of the Kashmiri people under the auspices of the UN should commence. This can only come about by embracing radical new thinking, especially in regard to identity, social contestations, and social imaginaries, because those competing ideological trajectories prevent reconciliation. Indeed, it is in the failed social imaginary and contested identity of contemporary post-colonial India where Kashmir's quest for peace is located.

Third, this book is motivated by setting the record straight concerning the diversity in the region referred to as South Asia. It aims to dissect how fear of rival identities aggravate the vitriol between India and Pakistan, which poisons relations with Kashmir. This is because diversity is seen as a threat. But, being different need not necessitate war. India does not need to possess Kashmir to exist or thrive. Society does not need to be homogenous to function well. On the contrary, it is not homogeneity, but the management of diversity that is vital.[59] Ultimately, these are matters of choice and persuasion, not coercion. Unfortunately, rather than acknowledge Kashmiri rights, India illegally and unilaterally revoked Articles 370 and 35A of the Indian constitution on August 5, 2019.[60] By doing

so, they effectively annexed the disputed territory in contravention of UN resolutions and international law. Then, they sent tens
of thousands of Hindutva mercenaries to Kashmir and imposed a
draconian communications blockade, further suffocating society.
Today, the famed mountainous wonderland of Kashmir is witnessing one of its most turbulent moments in years. Despondency is
perceptible everywhere; its unhappy children, resigned elderly, and
enflamed youth.[61]

Still, there are no indications that India is changing strategy.
Even Kashmiri politicians who were warm to India, such as Farooq
Abdullah, Omar Abdullah, Mehbooba Mufti, and Shah Faisal, have
been arrested.[62] Only after spending several months in jail were
they released. In addition, an unprecedented number of youth, civil
society activists, and even children (under the age of 14) are imprisoned too—upwards of 13,000.[63] This was reported by conscientious
Indians who traveled throughout the Valley during September
17–21, 2019, for a factfinding mission.[64] Admittedly, some of the
detained Kashmiri youth and children had been released, but only
to be rearrested on flimsy charges, leading to Kashmiri journalist Ashiq Peerzada to describe this tactic as the "revolving-door"
of arrests.[65] Consequently, the Valley of Kashmir reeks of despair.
Despite this, the official Indian response continues to be abjura-
tion, painting the situation in Kashmir as normal. This has been
debunked by Reuters, the BBC, and Aljazeera. Glaringly, though,
New Delhi's ongoing confrontation with China, with at least 20
Indian soldiers killed on June 15, 2020, has seriously transformed
the dispute into an even larger threat.[66] The truth is that the fabled
Valley is out of control, and the Indian government remains out of
touch—both with the Kashmiris and the reality on the ground.

Fourth, this book wishes to reach out in solidarity to those brave
Indians who in principle recognize Kashmir's right of self-determination. After all, India is a country with abundant resources and
tremendous potential and people power. It harms itself by its actions
in Kashmir. And why does it need Kashmir? Why does it falsely caricature the Kashmiri struggle for self-determination as separatist?

Kashmir cannot be considered a separatist movement because it is officially recognized as a disputed territory by the UN and has never been a part of India. Misrepresenting Kashmir history by relying on unrepresentative voices to support the Hindutva position will not resolve this nuclear flashpoint. Importantly, a small, brave section of Indian intelligentsia are questioning their government's logic. The Indian scholar Pankaj Mishra wrote, "once known for its extraordinary beauty, the Valley of Kashmir now hosts the biggest, bloodiest and also the most obscure military occupation in the world. With more than 90,000 people dead in an anti-India insurgency backed by Pakistan, the killing fields of Kashmir dwarf those of Palestine and Tibet."[67] In addition, the arbitrary arrests, curfews, raids, and checkpoints enforced by upwards of a million soldiers, paramilitaries, and mercenaries form nothing short of a war crime.[68] Recently, in a stunning admission, senior Indian Congress leader Jyotiraditya Scindia said, there should be "plebiscite" in Kashmir, only to be compelled to recant shortly thereafter.[69] Others, such as the renowned Indian writer and Booker Prize winner Arundhati Roy, stated, "Kashmir has never been an integral part of India."[70] In solidarity with her, Swaminathan Aiyar, Gautam Navlakha, Angana Chatterji, and Vir Sanghvi have all been asking India to rethink their game plan in Kashmir. These voices need to be supported.

Lastly, this book emphasizes the real possibility of this region turning into a nuclear flashpoint. Pakistan and India have fought four wars, and skirmishes across the ceasefire line are an everyday matter.[71] This poses an imminent threat to global peace. Worse, an extremist Hindutva government holds the reins of power in India. As such, the danger of a nuclear exchange is terrifyingly close. After all, the recent "accidental" misfiring of an Indian Brahmos missile into Pakistani territory could have easily led to a hostile military reaction.[72] Imagine how any country would react if a neighbor launched a missile towards it and claimed it was "accidental." This should have been international news and condemned the world over. Instead, there was almost no response from the interntional community.

ORGANIZATION OF THE BOOK

To begin, Chapter 2 introduces the design behind the manufacture of a vast, post-colonial monolithic Indian identity that appropriates Kashmir. It begins by asking the question, "Who are the Kashmiris?" and approaches the discussion of Kashmiri identity by foregrounding the beliefs of the primary ethnic/religious community—the Kashmiri Muslims, who for far too long have been marginalized. It also explores how many post-colonial Indian scholars, especially those with Hindutva proclivities, have propagated false narratives to misconstrue the history of Kashmir. What we realize is that post-colonial Indian interpretations of Kashmir's history are part of a political project that has given greater weight to the Sanskrit texts rather than Kashmiri Muslim oral tradition, and has attempted to forcibly erase the Kashmiri Muslim counternarrative.

Chapter 3 briefly deals with the history of the last indigenous ruler of Kashmir—Yusuf Shah Chak—this author's direct ancestor, who was tricked, imprisoned, and forced to live out his final days away from Kashmir. Thereafter, it concisely describes Mughal and Afghan rule, but goes on to focus on the wretched 1846 Treaty of Amritsar. By that treaty, the British "sold" Kashmir—its land, people, and livestock—to a non-Kashmiri Dogra family, and provided them with military support. This culminated in the cruelest era in Kashmir's history as the foreign Dogra rulers treated the people of Kashmir as slaves. Eventually, this led to a popular revolt and much of what is conflictual in Kashmir today has its origins in that era.

Chapter 4 investigates the conditions in the state of Jammu and Kashmir prior to the Jammu genocide, thereby laying the foundation for how violence was operationalized. In addition, it analyses the systematic and state-sponsored nature of the genocide. Relatedly, it then goes on to explore what happened to the leadership of the Muslim community and how it responded to the violence. Next, this chapter scrutinizes how genocide continues to impact the memory of Kashmiri Muslims—not just in Indian-Occupied Kashmir, but especially for the millions of Kashmiri descendants in Pakistan, and elsewhere throughout the world. Little is known about the genocidal violence that engulfed this region and few attempts have been made to uncover its barbarity. How could upwards of 500,000 people simply disappear?

Chapter 5 takes a unique approach to dissect some of the deep-seated, pathological impediments towards peace in South Asia. It does so by deconstructing the conceptualization of "partition" and unraveling those embedded ideas that fuel demonizing narratives and dispossession of Kashmir. There is a sophisticated process involved in the perpetuation of what I describe as the *partition industry*, which encompasses three intersecting variables: 1) myth; 2) demonization; 3) dispossession. Altogether, each variable of the partition industry interconnects to deny agency, demonize, and erase alternative identities in order to possess Kashmir. Also, in order to uncover the workings of the partition industry, this chapter examines the last days of the British Raj. A pertinent question remains, "What was being partitioned?" Which ethnic groups/ identities were claiming independence? Looking closely, this book brings forth a contentious assertion that there was no partition of India in 1947. Instead, the British Raj was divided, creating two new, political entities—India and Pakistan—led by competing identities/ ideological trajectories.[73] Eventually, this led to the pervasiveness of the Hindutva social imaginary in India that weaponizes false history to claim a monolithic ancient India.

Chapter 6 charts the progression of Islamophobia in both India and Kashmir, and focuses on the electoral victory of the BJP in 2014. At that point, Islamophobia in India took a dramatic turn.[74] Islamophobia in India continues to inform post-colonial Indian intelligentsia and policymakers. And we will go into greater detail within the chapter on what this means for the region and global peace.

Chapter 7 explores the background, origins, and significance of India's abrogation of Articles 370 and 35A. It explains the immediate impact of its abrogation on the Simla Agreement signed between India and Pakistan on July 2, 1972, which has essentially been nullified. It also details how the abrogation has led to a flurry of Indian settler-colonial policies in Kashmir operationalized by seven policies: 1) inventing Kashmiris through issuance of domicile/citizenship certificates (so far, nearly 4.1 million fake citizenship certificates have been issued);[75] 2) land theft; 3) altering maps and changing the names of public institutions, schools, and places of interest to enforce "Indianization"; 4) misrepresenting Kashmir on official government websites to falsely show it as having a Hindu majority; 5) coercive patriotism; 6) removing all Kashmiris from top bureaucratic positions to solidify the occupation; and 7) a delimitation process to project normalcy.

Finally, Chapter 8 explores the complex intersections of the Galwan Valley clash, Sino-Indian border relations, and the future consequences of that rivalry on Kashmir. It explores the history of Sino-Indian border relations, India's forward policy, the impact of abrogating Article 370 on China, and the macro-level Indo-Pacific rivalry that involves the US. More specifically, this includes the Quadrilateral Security Dialogue (QUAD) that binds India into a particular camp. Together, these factors explain how Sino-Indian relations deteriorated and clarify its impact on Kashmir.

The chapter ends with an evaluation of the developments from the time period June 15, 2020, to October 2021. As a result, three main developments come to the fore: 1) there have been 13 military-to-military engagements, which have not produced any serious reduction of tension;[76] 2) on September 23, 2021, India was alleged to have crossed the Chinese border, which elicited a response by China, sending 100 troops across the border—in a tit-for-tat move[77] (conveniently, this incident coincided with the QUAD meeting on September 24, 2021[78]); 3) as recently as October 4, 2021, both countries are increasing their border patrols, troop activity, and war preparations.[79] Recently, the US-India war games near the Chinese border further exacerbated an already enflamed region.[80] We should all be on edge.

2

Who Are the Kashmiris?
Resisting Post-Colonial Identity
Theft and False Narratives

The history of Kashmir is contested. There has been a deliberate attempt by modern, post-colonial Indian historiography to appropriate Kashmiri history in order to make it fit into a carefully crafted idea of what India is. Moreover, this ideologically driven movement to *imagine* India largely grew in the backdrop of the last days of the British Raj. Obviously, the process of nation-building, or manufacturing an Indian identity, had to be done, especially for post-colonial states.[1] That process often involves myth or, as Anderson describes, "imagining communities."[2] This goes hand in hand with the invention of tradition.[3] Likewise, the erasure of conflicting identities as an effort to build a single national self-image has been discussed in post-colonial Ireland too.[4] Often, imagining nations as political projects involve some degree of erasure, however, there is some level of consensus between diverse constituent parts. In India, the manner in which the post-colonial Indian state crafted its self-image was by erasing others, coercive manufacture of consensus, and projection of acceptance where in reality it was not the case. This led to hostility from those ethnic groups marginalized or erased, such as those in Punjab, Kashmir, Nagas, Goan, and others. And, any attempt to resist that hegemonic imposition of an Indian identity, such as in Kashmir, resulted in accusations of being "separatists," "anti-national," or, even worse, a "terrorist."[5] In other words, contesting the newly formed post-colonial Indian identity became equivalent to violating the false imaginary of India, and treason.

It is important to analyze how Indian historiography usurps Buddhist history—its temples and iconography—hyphenating the two divergent ideologies together and using them for soft power purposes.[6] Or, how many Indian writers misidentify Vedic and Indus civilizations—again, for purposes of appropriation, identity-shaping, and political posturing?[7] All this is important when describing the nation-building process in India that rewrites history, denies space to alternative identities, and justifies an irredentist narrative.[8] This process of myth and falsification of India's past needs to be rigorously exposed, especially in the ways it intensifies animus and rationalizes dispossession.[9] Just take a look at how ideologues of the Rashtriya Swayamsevak Sangh (RSS)—a paramilitary Hindu nationalist organization working closely with the BJP—openly threaten academics who criticize their version of history.[10] Most troubling is the way Kashmir has been *framed* as an integral part of India. In fact, the "integral part of India" trope is so often repeated, as Arundhati Roy analyzes, that many accept it unquestionably.[11] Going further, the subjugation of Kashmiris is then justified based on that pointed framing of Kashmir's history. Obviously, this cannot be explained away as fortuitous, since there are clear instances of the word India being used for grander hegemonic purposes or massive cultural appropriation. The reasons for this, too, are clear: Indian intellectuals involved in the nation-building enterprise were manufacturing history and inventing a nation. However, they quickly realized that neither the areas that became Pakistan nor, as is the focus of this book, Kashmir had a substantive, cultural link to the geographical expanse of present-day India. With the exception of Punjabi, no indigenous language of Pakistan is spoken in India. Because of that, links needed to be created, invented, almost whimsically out of thin air. Why? Because there is a deep-seated awareness of the fragility of the post-colonial Indian union. It is this insecurity that compels the subjugation of the Kashmiri people, or any contrary identity, and poisons the regional atmosphere.

To reiterate, Kashmir is not an integral part of India, and never was—at least not in the opinion of the primary ethnic, religious demographic in Kashmir—the Kashmiri Muslims. This is the way they feel, and cannot be ignored. While acknowledging that sentiment, Arundhati Roy has said, "Kashmir has never been an integral part of India," for which she received death threats.[12] The monolithic Indian identity project is operating in high gear, especially under Prime Minister Modi. It does so in many ways, but first among them is the disingenuous claim that "we (all South Asians) are all the same (Hindu)"—a claim used as a clever way to appropriate different ethnic groups under the appealing, morally high-sounding garb of universality. This, too, all while enforcing Hindu dominance.[13] Razing mosques, lynching Muslim traders, threatening to rape dead Muslim women, and then calling for peace is the Hindutva *modus operandi*.[14] The perennial question remains: Why does India feel the need to go to such great lengths to own Kashmir? Why does it not lay the same claim to Nepal or Bangladesh?

During the time of British rule, several historians asserted that India is more an idea than an identity. However, for some that assertion was not only injurious but treasonous. And, to blur reality, falsification of history was necessary. In the house that post-colonial India built, led by Brahmanical ethno-fascists, there was little room for genuine plurality, which has steadily decreased with the passage of time. Admittedly, the Indian intelligentsia tried to manufacture their own expansive, post-colonial identity that paid lip service to diversity. By doing so, the hope was to swallow up everything in their midst—Kashmir, Afghans, Punjabis, Baluchis, Sindhis, Brahuis, Baltis, Buddha—everything and everyone, including the Indus civilization.[15] Yet, the irreconcilable ongoing fissures between caste, class, and economic privilege in India made it impossible. This is because all post-colonial states impose a hegemonic identity, and India was no different.

Lastly, this chapter explores how the operationalization of a hegemonic post-colonial Indian identity falsely projects Kashmir as an integral part of India. It does so by deconstructing the narrative put forward by Indian scholars who tenuously connect Kashmir to the

Hindu Rashtra.[16] This framing is revealed through a meticulous reading of medieval texts, interviews, and other well-referenced documents. Specifically, four primary examples are examined that highlight how Kashmir is framed as a part of India: 1) a misrepresentation of the origins of the Kashmiri people; 2) deliberate falsification of history, especially concerning the role of Sanskrit in Kashmiri culture; 3) appropriation of Buddhist remains in Kashmir, conflating it with Hinduism, to exaggerate Hindu presence; and 4) erasure of Kashmiri Muslim oral traditions. All in all, this chapter approaches the discussion of Kashmiri identity by foregrounding the beliefs of the primary ethnic/religious community—the Kashmiri Muslim. Also, this chapter confronts the way many post-colonial Indian scholars—especially those with Hindutva proclivities—have used language, false narratives, and deliberate obfuscation to misconstrue the history of Kashmir, its people, and the aspirations of its people. Thereafter, it argues that irrespective of the internal cultural diversity of the disputed territory of Jammu and Kashmir, the question "who is an ethnic Kashmiri?" is secondary to "who is a political Kashmiri." In other words, the UN resolutions on Kashmir explicitly recognize the political rights of all those state subjects who reside in the geographical consigns of the disputed territory. Those rights have been consistently denied by the Indian state.

KASHMIR, NOT INDIA

The physical boundaries of Kashmir, from the earliest recorded times to now, are primarily an area between the main Himalayas range in the northwest and the Pir Panjal mountains in the southwest.[17] Throughout history, this area has been unequivocally described as the heartland of Kashmiri culture, language, and civilization.[18] In short, this can be referred to as the Valley of Kashmir, or simply the Valley. More interestingly, this coveted area has always had the mountains as natural boundaries—which prevented outsiders from easily entering, and locals knew this well.[19] These natural borders protected the Kashmiri population for several centuries, with only one main pathway to enter the famed Valley, from the southern

Poonch district. Even now, this natural roadway is referred to in Kashmiri as the "road from where outsiders enter" or the "Mughal" road. Overall, the Valley of Kashmir has maintained an overwhelming Muslim presence for the last several centuries.

Admittedly, what complicates matters is that the boundaries of Kashmir have shifted over the centuries. Also, successive waves of Kashmiri migrants left the Valley and began inhabiting adjacent areas—most evidently, in the Chenab plains, Jammu, and elsewhere on the lower or upper hilly terrain surrounding the Valley. Then, after the end of the British Raj and Dogra titular rule, hundreds of thousands of Kashmiris were forcibly relocated to the newly created country of Pakistan as a result of the Jammu genocide.[20] Of course, leaving the Valley did not necessarily mean that those Kashmiris lost their culture and language. Certainly, many did, and became culturally and linguistically immersed in the dominant cultures they found themselves in. However, many Kashmiri families tenaciously held onto their identity in remarkable ways—through marriage, custom, and food. Eventually, this meant that those adjacent areas began to be included into the cultural repository of Kashmir even though they were populated by other ethnicities and outside the Valley.

Today, it should be understood that what is commonly referred to as Kashmir describes the five distinct regions of the erstwhile 1947 princely state of Jammu and Kashmir.[21] It is important to reiterate that the category of ethnic Kashmiris is disputed. The word Kashmir/Kashmiri may refer to either a specific ethnicity—the largest but not the only ethnic group in the disputed territory—or, alternatively, every citizen who resides in the disputed territory regardless of ethnicity. Collectively, the five regions of the former princely state of Jammu and Kashmir are divided into Indian-controlled Kashmir and Pakistan Administered Kashmir. Indian-controlled Kashmir consists of three areas: 1) the Valley of Kashmir (15,948 km^2) with a population of 8 million people—the heart of Kashmiri culture and language, and the focal point of the uprising against Indian hegemony; 2) Jammu (26,293 km^2) with a mixed ethnic population of 5,350,811 people comprising Kashmiri Muslims—including Bakerwal and Gujjar Muslims—Kashmiri Pandits, Dogra Hindus and Sikhs, Punjabi Sikhs, Hindus and Muslims; and 3) Ladakh (59,146 km²) with a small population of 274,289 that is divided between Buddhists, Kashmiri Muslims—including Bakerwal and Gujjar Muslims—and Balti Muslims. On the other hand, Pakistan Administered Kashmir is nearly entirely Muslim and includes two areas: 1) Azad Kashmir (13,297 km²) with population of 4.6 million; and 2) Gilgit-Baltistan (72,971 km²) with a population of 1.8 million, which is also two distinct socio-cultural areas (Gilgit and Baltistan). Together, this amounts to a total population of approximately 21 million people, 86 percent of whom are Muslim. As will be discussed in this book, India's attempts to alter the demographics of the region has heightened fears of settler-colonialism in the local population. The most recent statistics, from Indian government sources, indicate at least 4.1 million domicile certificates were granted to non-ethnic Kashmiris, in the most blatant instance of demographic change.[22] Kashmiris are not exaggerating when they claim India is resorting to "demographic flooding" to dilute the Muslim-majority demographic. However, to start, let's talk about the contested origins of the people of Kashmir, and the political project behind it.

ORIGINS OF KASHMIR

When it comes to researching, documenting, and producing a Kashmiri historiography, two competing mythical narratives come to the fore—Pandit and Muslim. It is here where great efforts are made by many post-colonial Indian writers to obfuscate Kashmir's past and compel a single reading of history. For Kashmiri Pandits, the emergence of the Valley of Kashmir is the result of their folk hero, named Kashyapa, who drained the flooded terrain to enable settlement.[23] On the other hand, Kashmiri Muslims entirely reject that myth and present a different account. Kashmiri Muslim oral traditions believe that the water of the lake was drained by "Prophet Solomon who visited Kashmir ...."[24] This fable is corroborated by Bernier who described it as an "old legend among the people of Kashmir."[25] What is clear, and still current, is the way the beliefs of the Kashmiri Muslim—the overwhelmingly majority ethnic/religious demographic—are ignored. Instead, a tiny Pandit minority, accounting for approximately 3 percent of the Kashmiri population, have attempted to compel their interpretations on the origins of Kashmir through their mythical lore.

When explaining the origins of the Kashmiri people, Pandits rely on the *Nilamata Purana*, which was written in Sanskrit by an anonymous author sometime in the eighth century.[26] This mythical, non-historical text is lauded by the minority Pandit community and is taken as a primary source of Kashmir's identity even though the overwhelming majority of Kashmiris could not read it, as it would have been in a foreign language for them. Interestingly, the controversy of this document begins even in its descriptive name— whether it is "*Nilamata Purana*" or "*Nilamata Mahatyma*."[27] Pandit scholars broadly concede that it does not conform to the strict definition of a Purana as loosely upheld by the infamous 18 Puranas.[28] Instead, the *Nilamata* is often described as a *mahatyma*, which is essentially a book of prayers for a specific religious community that usually praises a deity or natural, earthly force. And, in no way are the hymns in the text categorically Hindu. Neither the word Hindu nor Bharat is found in the text. In fact, K. M. Panikkar, who writes the introduction to Ved Kumari Ghai's translation of the *Nilamata Purana*, alludes to it being a *mahatyma*, which is a literary form that engages in embellished glorification of sacred localities, often contriving fairytales, and preferring certain deities over others.[29] As Ahmed describes, citing Panikkar, a "good many of them" are valueless, except as propaganda literature for places of pilgrimage.[30]

On the other hand, a Purana is something considered by Pandit scholars, such as Kanilal and Zadoo (1924), as much more authoritative and convincing.[31] Perhaps this explains why Pandit scholars prefer to describe the *Nilamata* as a *purana*, rather than *mahatyma*, in order to give it more legitimacy. As a literary genre, a *purana* is meant to express historical, cultural, and religious sensibilities. It documents folklore. Yet, post-colonial Indian historiographers, in their manufacture of monolithic India, have arrogated any form of idol worship under the heading Hindu. This process then goes on to justify Kashmir's association with India. In other words, the misleading description of the *Nilamata* as a Purana is meant to more authoritatively use it to project the Hinduness of Kashmir, or the idol-worshipping heritage of the original Kashmiris.

Furthermore, the *Nilamata* describes the origins of the people of Kashmir as being from either a ghost-like people, half-human and half-serpent, called Pisacas or ethnic Nagas. Obviously, descriptions of the origins of Kashmiris as a type of non-human entity called Pisacas cannot be taken seriously and are definitely not historical. Still, much of the Pandit community and Hindutva ideologues elevate this text as an unquestionable source of identity for their community, and proof of the Hindu origins of Kashmir. Even though the author of the *Nilamata* never described him-/herself as a Hindu or Indian.[32] Zutshi pivots away from accusations of disingenuousness by suggesting different societies had different ideas on what constitutes truth.[33] The problem with Zutshi's line of reasoning is that it does not address the core issue of the misrepresentation of the primary religious-ethnic demographic. Hence her claim that Eurocentric standards of veracity that would discount such sources are not applicable to Indian historiography is unjustified.

The controversy goes deeper when studying the Nagas, who inhabited parts of present-day Pakistan and parts of Northern India. Certainly, there is some evidence of Aryan and Naga presence in some parts of present-day Pakistan, but not in Kashmir. For that reason, Professor Gulshan Majeed categorically states that "no Nagas existed in Kashmir."[34] In addition, renowned scholar on Kashmir, Sir Aurel Stein describes the *Nilamata* as being "in a very bad condition, owing to numerous lacunae and textual corruption of all kinds ... [It is] by no means improbable that the text has undergone changes and possibly additions at later periods."[35]

Furthermore, another widely recognized treatise relied on by Pandits, compiled by an author named Kalhana, in the twelfth century, is the *Rajatarangini*.[36] Its account spans over four millennia and, as Ahmed writes, is "strikingly precise but generally incredibly fictional."[37] The *Rajatarangini* has attained a lofty status of fascinating repute because it contains a bewildering repository of fiction and fact, intertwined in storytelling, with both humans and super-natural beings. Furthermore, the *Rajatarangini* was not written in the language of Kashmiris, but in Sanskrit. As mentioned, this was certainly not a language spoken or understood by the overwhelming majority of the Kashmiri people. This indicates that the *Rajatarangini* was not meant to be widely shared outside a certain select group. Also, the words Hindu, India, Brahmans or Pandit are not men-tioned in the text. In addition, Kalhana mentions and relies upon several ancient texts, most of which are now extant, but verbatim quotes the *Nilamata*.[38] As Ahmed writes, an "examination of the *Rajatarangini* reveals that it elevates mixing myth and history to an art form."[39] What is important to acknowledge is that for the vast majority of Kashmiri Muslims the *Rajatarangini* is not a trustworthy source of their history or identity. Nor do they support the claims of Naga presence in the Valley. In essence, it is a historical treatise that generously intermixes myth with storytelling, which affects its veracity. Again, the issue is that these community founding myths in the *Nilamata* and *Rajatarangini* are presented as representative of the primary religious-ethnic demographic and as authoritative. Admittedly, community founding myths often conflate myth with storytelling. However, if that process of mythmaking erases the majority primary religious-ethnic demographic and is complicit in coercively forcing the interpretation of mythical texts as authorita-tive then it is part of a greater hegemonic project and complicit in cultural oppression.

IMPOSING SANSKRIT

Another way that many Indian scholars project Kashmir as an integral part of India is by falsely associating the Kashmiri language with Sanskrit. Sanskrit was the elitist *lingua franca* of a small Shaivite religious minority community in Kashmir, as was Persian for the overwhelming majority of Kashmiri Muslims.[40] Therefore, neither the misnamed *Nilamata* or *Rajatarangini* represents the indigenous Kashmiri language. As Ahmed poignantly writes, "Interpolation and contextual corruption further chipped at the recorded history of Kashmir. While the account of the earliest period was a free run of imagination, textual corruption in the account of the medieval period was not uncommon."[41] Notwithstanding their questionable historical veracity, both these ancient texts—the *Nilamata* and *Rajata-rangini*—have been passed off as incontestable sources of information on Kashmir. If anything, they can point to the precursor traditions of a minority Shaivite community, possible forebears of the present-day Kashmiri Pandit community—but certainly not all Kashmiris. And, by solely relying on these mythical accounts of Sanskrit literature to read Kashmiri historiography, scholars from the Pandit community such as Kaul (2018) indulge in a major form of cultural violence on the majority community—the Kashmiri Muslims.

Post-colonial Indian historiographers have invented narratives in order to rationalize the colonization of Kashmir. Take, for instance, K. N. Pandit's poor translation of the ancient Persian chronicle on Kashmir—*Baharistan-i-Shahi*. In it, he admits to translating the Persian words *"ba qalam Kashmiri,"* or "the written Kashmiri word," as Sanskrit.[42] Why would he commit such a glaring error, when undeniably Kashmir has its own language—Kashmiri? Why would he incorrectly translate those Persian words as Sanskrit? By mistranslating the Persian phrase *"ba qalam Kashmiri,"* the Indian author is engaging in whitewashing Kashmir's history, undermining the dominant ethnic/religious demographic and facilitating the post-colonial Indian hegemonic project of appropriating Kashmir. In another instance, without providing any references whatsoever, he describes the origins of Kazi Shah Chak—my ancestor and direct family relative—as Kanchan Chakra.[43] Again, K. N. Pandit offers no evidence and admits much of his analysis is simply "surmise."[44] Another Indian writer, related to K. N. Pandit, also falsely projected Sanskrit as the totality of early Kashmiri culture based on speculative reasoning.[45] This is what Ahmad refers to as "creative history-writing," but, more accurately, should be described as an outright lie.[46] In another instance, Ahmed cites Pandit Anand Koul, whom he challenges for the claim that Pathar Masjid in Srinagar was partially built on the ruins of a Hindu Temple: "The sole evidence the 'historian' relies on to make this sweeping conclusion was the three-letter assumption 'it is said.'"[47] All this reveals how many Kashmiri Pandits who subscribe to the Indian identity project are orchestrating a campaign to distort the history and origins of Kashmir. In fact, every single historical piece of writing on Kashmir—including the sixteenth-century Persian treatise *Baharistan-i-Shahi*, refers to "*Hind*"—the Arabic word for areas south of the Indus River—as a foreign country. This simply just reinforces the idea that Kashmir is not, and has never been, an integral part of India.

Moreover, not only is Sanskrit inaccurately projected as the original language of Kashmiris, but the word India or associated Indic terms have been deliberately inserted into English translations of ancient Persian, Kashmiri, and Sanskrit texts, when no such word was used. As mentioned, neither the word Hindu, Pandit, Brahman, or India can be found in either the *Nilamata* or *Rajatarangini*. The use of these words is not incidental. Arguably, it is a deliberate attempt to support the imaginary of a perennial monolithic Hindu India. This myth then goes on to inaccurately incorporate Kashmir as a part of India. Not only this, there are several books authored by Indian authors that perpetuate this link between Kashmir and Sanskrit without providing any references.[48] By claiming Sanskrit as the original Kashmiri language, many post-colonial Indian intellectuals not only undermine the cultural heritage of the Kashmiri Muslim but also ignore the evidence that linguistically links Kashmiri to the Dardic branch of languages.[49]

BUDDHISM IN KASHMIR

Another way in which post-colonial Indian scholars attempt to appropriate Kashmir is by confusing/conflating Kashmir's Buddhist history with Hinduism. Soon after the establishment of Buddhism, in the sixth century BC, many adherents traveled to Kashmir. In fact, Buddhists have inhabited the Valley of Kashmir for over a millennium.[50] Interestingly, most ancient Buddhist relics found in Kashmir can be traced to the second and third century AD.[51] And, by the sixth century AD, Buddhism was deeply rooted in Kashmir.[52] The popularity of the religion is borne out by the fact that Kushan ruler, Kanishka, held the Fourth World Buddhist Conference here, marking the birth of a new and progressive Buddhism known as the Mahayana.[53] Further, the arrival of Buddhist scholars such as Xuanjang (Hiuen Tsiang) from China attest to the prevalence of Buddhism in Kashmir.[54] Also, Kashmiri Buddhist scholars and monks spread the message of the Buddha throughout Central and South Asia.[55] At that time in history, it is quite reasonable to suggest that the land referred to as Kashmir, until the sixth century AD, had a majority Buddhist population. There is no recorded evidence for the existence of Hindus or Muslims at this time.

In the sixth century AD a transformative event took place with the arrival of a tyrannical White Hun named Mihirakula. His beliefs may be characterized as a type of Shaivism, which was a form of militant worship that diverged from the views of Kashmiris. What is known is that he oppressed the Buddhist population and demolished their religious places and symbols.[56] This is corroborated in Xuanjang's account, who stated that Mihirakula tyrannized the Buddhist population.[57] This controversial figure also emerges as a liberal patron of Shaivism who extended courtesies to and distributed land and property to the Brahmans. And, in support of this new faith, Mihirakula brings thousands of Brahmans to Kashmir.[58]

With the arrival of Mihirakula, and the ensuing influx of thousands of Brahmans, the Kashmiri landscape altered. Stein, too, acknowledges that in all likelihood Shaivism grew from that point onwards.[59] This also put the newly arrived Shaivites and the Buddhist community at odds. Importantly, there is no caste system in Buddhism. In fact, Buddhism differs from Shaivism and, later, Hinduism, chiefly in the latter not allowing for social mobility. Not just that, it is also important to recognize that Buddha's anti-caste teaching was in direct opposition to the prevalent Shaivite racial supremacist beliefs. Perhaps this is one of the factors that led to intense hostility between the two groups. Nevertheless, the key point here is that Buddhism predates Hinduism in Kashmir, and, while Ashoka established his rule in Kashmir later, there was certainly a strong presence even before his rule.[60] This is further verified by several Buddhist archeological findings—the stupas, temples, and ancient monuments— that have been unearthed.[61] However, it is important not to confuse or conflate a large Buddhist presence with a large Hindu presence—especially when they were inimical to one another. There is no evidence to suggest that Brahmans, Shaivite Huns, or Hindus were ever a majority community in Kashmir at any point in history. This, too, I believe post-colonial Indian historiography has misrepresented to perpetuate the myth of a monolithic India.

LOST TRIBES OF ISRAEL: MUSLIM ORAL TRADITION

According to Kashmiri Muslim oral traditions, a story passed down in many Kashmiri Muslim families from the Valley asserts that the original, indigenous Kashmiris were from the lost tribes of Israel. My grandmother Sughra Bibi Butt clearly told me, in my cherished moments with her, that the original Kashmiris were monotheists—believers in one God—and from Bani Israel. Corroborating that, Al-Biruni's eleventh-century classic mentions that the people of Kashmir, curiously, only allowed Jews to enter their lands.[62] Later, during the time of Mughal Emperor Akbar, a Portuguese Jesuit named Monserrate described the inhabitants of Kashmir as being Jewish by race and custom: "their type of countenance, general physique, style of dress and manner of conducting trade are all similar to those of European Jews."[63] However, as he goes on to acknowledge, while being ethnic Jews, Kashmiris had accepted Islam.[64] Moreover, François Bernier's seventeenth-century account *Travels in the Moghul Empire* describes the Kashmiri people as unambiguously Jewish.[65]

There is some indication of the presence of Muslims in Kashmir as early as the eighth century.[66] Yet, how the Muslim community gradually transformed into the majority community is somewhat unclear. One may reasonably conclude that the process took centuries and that until the eleventh century—at the time of Al-Biruni's book—Kashmir had a Jewish population and was not predominantly Muslim. Similarly, they certainly could not be classified as Hindu—since that terminology was not even in use at the time. Moreover, simply having some people who use Sanskrit does not qualify as characterizing the entirety of Kashmiri society as Hindu. However, Ahmed (2017) recognizes that by the twelfth century a large number of Buddhists, a growing Muslim population, and a smaller minority of Shaivites resided there. Evidently, three communities were inside Kashmir by the thirteenth century (Buddhist, Muslim, and Shaivite), when eventually Islam became the dominant religion of the people and gained political supremacy.

According to several medieval Kashmiri chronicles, the first Muslim ruler of Kashmir was Rinchaan—who was originally a Buddhist.[67] Upon killing a rival claimant to the throne of Kashmir, he assumed power, accepted Islam, and adopted the name Sadruddin Shah in AD 1320.[68] From the eleventh century to the fourteenth century, it is presumed that no ruler of Kashmir was Muslim, however, neither the *Nilamata* nor *Rajatarangini* is reliable for many Kashmiri Muslims. During this time, the clearest evidence indicates the presence of three communities: Buddhists as the major ethnic/ religious majority of the people in Kashmir, a sizable Muslim community—many of whom had Semitic roots—and a small minority of militant Shaivites. However, in the twelfth century, there was the arrival of at least 1000 Muslim Turkic fugitives from among whose progeny was the famous Islamic scholar Sharaf-ud-Din, known as Bulbul Shah.[69] Importantly, he was instrumental in spreading Islam throughout Kashmir and is credited with the conversion of Rinchaan to Islam.[70] Looking closely, by the 1300s in Kashmir, it is reasonable to assume that Rinchaan's conversion may have also been for political expediency, and that his conversion to Islam was meant to solidify his rule. It would make no sense for a foreigner— as Rinchaan was—to adopt a religion that was not followed by the majority of Kashmiri people and expect political legitimacy. People would have resisted, since minorities ruling over majority populations do so only by the use of force or fear. And we do not find evidence for that during Rinchaan's rule. Instead, we find overwhelming support for him. In all likelihood, this meant he was supported by the primary religious/ethnic demographic—the Kashmiri Muslim. One thing is for certain, the Shaivites in Kashmir who opposed both the Buddhist and Muslim communities did not take kindly to these developments.[71]

Furthermore, Kashmiri Muslim oral tradition refers to the Valley of Kashmir in their own language as *Bagh-I-Suleman* or the Garden of Solomon.[72] This coincides with another Kashmiri Muslim oral tale that states the Prophet Solomon made the Valley inhabitable. And, as Ahmad writes, since that time Kashmiri Muslims describe the shrine on the hill as "Takht-e-Sulaiman (Solomon's Throne), the hill as Koh-i-Sulaiman (Solomon's Hill) and Kashmir as Bagh-e-Sulaiman (Solomon's Garden)."[73] There is also a Kashmiri Muslim oral tradition that after 40 years of wandering some Jewish tribes eventually made their way to Kashmir—their promised land. Exiled in 722 BC, it was believed that they had traveled to Kashmir by taking the historic Silk Route. Moreover, several villages in Kashmir bear some resemblance to place names in the historic land of Palestine, including Bandpoor as Beth Peor; Naboo Hill, comparable to Mount Nebo; Pishgah, similar to Mount Pisgah; and regions in both lands named Mamre. In Vigne's account, he expresses astonishment at the great resemblance of the old buildings in the Valley to places in Jerusalem. Looking at his surroundings, he wrote, "it became for a moment a question whether the Kashmirian temples had not been built by Jewish architects."[74]

In addition, the word Kashmir in the Kashmiri language is referred to as being derived from the Hebraic "Kash" tribe or possibly as "pure" from the Hebrew word *Koshur*.[75] There are several other linguistic parallels as well. In the Kashmiri language the suffix *Joo* is attached to several names, and itself is a last name. The Star of David is also used frequently in Kashmiri arts and craft.[76] Together, all this corroborates Kashmiri Muslim oral tradition that claims the original Kashmiris were descendants of the lost tribes of Israel—albeit one that became predominantly Muslim. When? It is not exactly clear. But probably between the eleventh and twelfth century. By the reign of Sadruddin in AD 1320 it is likely that Kashmir was a Muslim-majority area.

Interestingly, early Kashmiri society had Buddhist, Muslim, and Shaivite religious communities coexisting. In essence, these three communities shared space and, eventually, the Buddhist community in the Valley largely disappeared. Thereafter, the Shaivite and

Muslim communities developed divergent narratives about their shared space. Yet what is particularly troubling is the manner in which the Shaivite community, the precursor to the Pandit community, attempted to erase Kashmiri Muslim (Valley 96.4 percent) oral tradition. Not only that, the Pandit community then replaces it with their own, while being merely 3 percent of the population. Furthermore, the Pandit community now attempts to appropriate the Buddhist community in order to further entrench their own peculiar Kashmiri narrative that delegitimizes and disempowers the majority community.

From 1320 to 1846, Kashmir was exclusively ruled by Muslim kings and gradually over the centuries became almost exclusively Muslim. Over the course of these centuries, several other ethnic peoples came to inhabit the region, including Greeks, Central Asians, Persians, Turks, Afghans, and Mughals,[77] and, more recently, Tibetans and Biharis.[78] Internally, Kashmiri society became an amalgamation of several diverse ethnicities and managed to reconcile that diversity. It possessed a cultural power that was able to do this and project unanimity. Certainly, Islam, as the overwhelming faith of Kashmiris, provided the main unifying factor. Of course, the Pandit community were part of the tapestry of Kashmiri society. However, it was not until the fracturing of the Durrani empire that ruled Kashmir, by British colonialists, that Kashmiri society began to deeply splinter.[79] In fact, the Dogras—in collusion with the British—gained supremacy and ensured that splintering. Not only did the Dogras exacerbate differences but they capitalized on the exacerbation of difference and the resulting division. Dogra rule has been described as tyrannical in its use of measures including banning the call to prayer, destroying mosques, and targeting Muslim religious processions.[80] Such measures undermined the historical tolerance of Kashmiri society.

WHO IS KASHMIRI?

The question "who is Kashmiri?" is complex and is perhaps not as important to answer definitively as it is to consider from an ethnographic, anthropological, and political angle. Kashmiris from all walks of life will invariably respond differently based on a wide range of assumptions. History, too, attests to the arrival of several different races and peoples to Kashmir over the last several centuries. Some may say, as did my late grandmother Sughra Bibi Butt, that all those who trace their lineage to the original Semitic tribes of the Valley are *bona fide* Kashmiri. But who are those now? Initially, she disapproved of my mother Khalida Yasmeen Butt's marriage to my father, Mujahid Akhtar Chak—claiming the Chaks were outsiders. Interestingly, my paternal family, the Chaks, who once ruled Kashmir and were one among the medieval noble families of the time, are still considered as "outsiders" by some in Kashmir.[81] This even though the Chaks have had a presence in the Valley for several centuries. Compare this with the Kashmiri-American poet Agha Shahid Ali. His family—Qizilbash Shia Muslims—migrated to Srinagar in the nineteenth century from Qandahar, at the behest of the Dogra regime.[82] His Kashmiriness is never questioned. Why? This has much to do with how education in the Valley, largely in the control of Kashmiri Pandits, deliberately corrupted Kashmiri history to exclude those it considered a threat. And an unwritten policy of the Dogra rule was to co-opt Shia Muslims and other minorities into the Dogra powerbase, hoping to use them against the majority Sunni community. In 1872, severe Sunni–Shia rioting erupted when the Sunni weavers revolted against the Shia industrialists.[83] This weaponized strategy of pitting different religious/ethnic communities against one another continues unabated by the post-colonial Indian hegemonic state, becoming an acrimonious part of Kashmir's cultural milieu.

Bhan compellingly writes that "the politics of identity in Kashmir, much like elsewhere, is deeply imbricated with the everyday operations of statecraft. Such operations take on more urgency in occupied zones as governments create new or intensify existing divisions to build their legitimacy, one identity at a time."[84] Essentially, Bhan goes on to describe the processes through which the Indian state governs through "fragmentations" and then deliberately makes the Kashmir dispute an "intractable" one.[85]

Today, attempts to obfuscate Kashmiri political agency under the garb of religious-ethnic plurality is weakening. The attempts by Indian occupational forces to foster divisiveness in Kashmir are not having the same impact, as seen by leading Kashmiri Shia and Sunni clerics denouncing Indian policies in the disputed territory.[86] The severity of the threat to their life and livelihood, extent of Indian atrocities, and growing awareness of society of the overt and subtle forms of oppression have seen a new political consciousness emerge among Kashmiris—irrespective of ethnic/religious persuasion. And the denial of basic rights for the peoples in Kashmir has completely exposed the totality of India's occupation. As a result, sectarianism—ethnic/religious chauvinism—is no longer as relevant as it was for several decades before. Perhaps this is the clearest indication that the occupier's grip is slowly weakening, as Kashmiri society coalesces—that and the revival of an authentic, inclusive, and pluralistic Islamic practice, which has given solid shape to Kashmiri identity. In fact, Islam remains the most significant unifying factor in Kashmir today—encompassing nearly 96.4 percent of the Valley,[87] almost all of Gilgit-Baltistan and Azad Kashmir, and more than half of the districts in Jammu and Ladakh. India has attempted to weaponize the Muslim majority as being connected to fanaticism, and, by doing so, delegitimize the Kashmiri right to self-determination. That, too, will not work. Kashmiris are anything but extremists— it goes against their very pluralistic socio-cultural nature, evinced in the diversity of Kashmir under historical Muslim rule—even to a fault. Further, this religious extremism has nothing to do with the seething rage that Kashmiris feel against their Indian occupiers. After all, Kashmir is a political, anti-colonial issue based on a denial of human rights—not a religious war.

STATE SUBJECT

It is important to explore the question of who a state subject in the disputed territory of Jammu and Kashmir is. All those who have state-subject status are legally able to vote in any future UN Mandated plebiscite. There are millions of ethnic Kashmiris and their descendants who call Pakistan home, or who are living across the world, but who are no longer state subjects. In fact, many are culturally every bit Kashmiri—some arguably even more so, since they have not had to endure attempts to alter their own culture by the post-colonial Indian state. Yet, if and/or when a UN-authorized plebiscite ever materializes then who qualifies as a state subject is paramount. As a result, India, Pakistan, and Kashmiris have much at stake. With the revocation of Article 370 and Article 35A, India has essentially told the world that it no longer cares about who is a state subject.[88] And, by issuing dubious domicile certificates, they continue to oppress Kashmiri people and erase their identity.[89] Nevertheless, India may be compelled to rethink these machinations if international pressure continues to mount, war crimes are brazenly committed, or war breaks out. India's claim over the region of Aksai Chin further aggravates the situation. For Pakistan, in order to remain true to the principles of several UN resolutions, maintain the moral high ground, and ensure that the will of the people of the disputed territory is assessed, maintaining records on who is a state-subject is vital.

The idea of the state subject was first put forth by the non-Kashmiri Dogra regime, under Maharaja Gulab Singh, in order for the Dogra rulers to be able to legally clarify who counts as a Kashmiri—but especially for purposes of bureaucratic employment allotments entailing economic privileges.[90] The term state subject is basically a substitute for citizen, and, as Ashai writes, "the primary distinction being that the term 'subject' is used generally to describe permanent residents of a monarchical state."[91] Yet, who qualifies as a *Kashmiri*, and how does this relate to ensuing privilege? This question has been a longstanding peculiarity in Kashmir's social fabric, which has been manipulated by foreign powers. The term state subject characterizes and describes Kashmiris into four separate classes:[92] Class I—All persons born and residing within the state before the commencement of the reign of Maharajah Gulab Singh in 1885; Class II—All persons who settled within the state before 1900 and who have since acquired property and resided permanently; Class III—All persons who have acquired immovable property under a *rayatnama* or *ijazatnama* [royal decree or grant], and have ten years of continuous residence; Class IV—Companies registered with the state in which the government has a financial interest or which provide economic benefits to the state.[93]

Ashai writes that the present-day boundaries of the disputed territory of Jammu and Kashmir materialize as a result of the Treaty of Amritsar in 1846, "through which an amalgamation of various small territories were gifted to a Dogra lord as a reward for his cooperation with the victorious British in the Anglo-Sikh War."[94] Following the treaty, in 1927 the Dogra Maharajah Hari Singh proclaimed the first of several orders that defined and divided state subjects into the above classes. This definition was later incorporated into the Jammu and Kashmir constitution. Hence these definitions have nothing to do with culture, but everything to do with politics.

Furthermore, another interesting aspect related to the state-subject laws is that they partly arose in response to Kashmiri Pandit resentment at the arrival of foreign civil servants from Punjab into the Dogra administration. This resulted in poor representation of Kashmiri Pandits in the civil service.[95] Consequently, Kashmiri Pandits campaigned for the state-subject definition to secure their political and economic privilege. Here, it is important to highlight how the Kashmiri Muslims were completely ignored. Essentially, as Ashai writes, the Kashmiri Muslims were shut out of the bureaucratic employment pool due to the racist, colonial nature of Dogra rule.[96]

Both India and Pakistan have slightly different procedures to verify those who qualify for state-subject status.[97] Now, in India, with the abrogation of Article 370 and Article 35A, this no longer has any meaning—at least for them.[98] Nevertheless, in Pakistan, the process is long, arduous, and complicated. It requires documentation, land deeds, and two adult witnesses who are able to verify the authenticity of properties and original residency. The author's father ensured that all the necessary paperwork was done so that all his children and grandchildren would qualify as Class I. That was an immensely emotional day for my family. Of course, Pakistan claims to maintain the highest level of veracity in order to not be accused of any type of demographic manipulation. Actually, the demographics already ostensibly favor them, since Kashmir has an overwhelming Muslim majority. This means that in any vote that restricted options to Pakistan and India they would likely win. Also, a recent survey undertaken to assess Kashmiri youth clearly mentioned that not only do Kashmiris want Indians out of Kashmir, but largely view Pakistan favorably.[99] Of course, the option of independence for the peoples of the disputed territory cannot be ruled out. However, this would raise the issue of the five distinct regions of the disputed territory and how one would manage them in any plebiscite. Nonetheless, it should be included in any eventual plebiscite, following an agreement on internal borders. The Dixon plan is important to raise here.[100] To explain, the Dixon plan recognized that the princely state of Jammu and Kashmir was an artificial state and, consequently, should be divided along religious/ethnic lines that loosely translated as Gilgit-Baltistan and Azad Kashmir to go to Pakistan, Jammu to be split between India and Pakistan, Ladakh to go to India, and the Valley of Kashmir to have a plebiscite.[101] Australian academic Claude Rakisits has proposed a slightly modified version of the Dixon plan to break the current impasse.[102] Yet, as of now, there seems to be no support for this initiative.

CONCLUSION

Post-colonial India, led by Brahmanical supremacists, has attempted to appropriate Kashmir through cleverly orchestrated misrepresentations of history, mythical narratives, and outright erasure of Kashmiri Muslim oral tradition and agency. Similarly, Indian intelligentsia falsely project Kashmir as an integral part of India by connecting it to the Hindu Rashtra.[103] The means employed to do so include misrepresenting the origins of the Kashmiri people, falsifying history, exaggerating the role of Sanskrit, appropriating Buddhist history to conflate it with Hinduism in order to inflate Hindu presence, and erasing Kashmiri Muslim oral traditions. Altogether, this amounts to incorrectly describing Kashmir as a former Hindu-majority area that was forcibly converted to Islam. This chapter has presented evidence to contest those assumptions. It has underlined how all ancient texts attest to the fact that Hindus were never a majority in Kashmir. In fact, Buddhists were among the first inhabitants in Kashmir. Soon thereafter, between the eleventh and thirteenth century, Islam emerged as the majority community. Nevertheless, the evidence is quite clear that Kashmir is home to three diverse communities—Buddhist, Muslim, and Hindu. However, each has its own narrative about the region and there is a competition on who gets to own Kashmir. This rivalry set in motion the rival histories and mythical narratives that we have before us today. Specifically, two primary clashing narratives emerged—Kashmiri Pandit and Kashmiri Muslim. Although, the minority 3 percent Kashmiri Pandit community has monopolized history and attempted to speak for 96.4 percent of the population—the Kashmiri Muslim.

Furthermore, concerning the historiography of Kashmir, this chapter has explained the ways that the Kashmiri Pandit community began to project total ownership of Kashmiri identity and used the *Nilamata* and *Rajatarangini* as the medieval sources to do so. Both medieval texts were presented as authentically Kashmiri and representative of *all* the Kashmiri people when no evidence for such a claim exists. Moreover, both texts are written in a language—Sanskrit—that the majority of the people could not understand. Furthermore, there is no credible evidence to suggest that Sanskrit was ever the language of Kashmiris, especially since Kashmiris have their own language. That language is more accurately described as being from the Dardic branch of languages, rather than Indo-Aryan.[104] Yet, there is a reason for this projection. Tying Sanskrit to Kashmir and insisting the Kashmiri language is Indo-Aryan are both part of the broader project of manufacturing the idea of an irredentist, monolithic India that usurps Kashmir. In fact, there is an entire industry associated with orchestrating the possession of Kashmir. The most glaring instance of this is through the falsification of historiography—for instance, when the translation of the ancient Persian treatise *Baharistan-i-Shahi* dubiously mistranslates "*ba qalam Kashmiri*" as Sanskrit, when Koul dishonestly claims the presence of a temple at the Pathar Masjid,[105] or through the invention of Hindu traditions in Kashmir such as the Amarnath Yatra.[106] All in all, there is a preponderance of evidence to support the contention that there have been deliberate attempts to misrepresent Kashmiri history in order to rationalize its links to India, deny Muslim oral tradition, and erase Kashmiri Muslim understandings of their own history. Hence, what this chapter argues is that none of this historical revisionism is incidental. In fact, there is an ongoing deliberate attempt to misconstrue Kashmiri history in order to project it as part and parcel of an imagined India.

It is no easy feat to claim a land without its people. As ambitious as it is to talk about Kashmir without its primary religious-ethnic demographic—the Kashmiri Muslims—it is bound to falter. Foregrounding Kashmiri ethnic and religious differences is used as a means to stall a political awakening. But, no matter how many ethnic, religious, and cultural contestations exist and are exacerbated by colonial apparatuses of power, Kashmiris refuse to accept Indian settler-colonization. After all, what kind of nationalism is promoted by coercively raising Indian flags or distorting curriculum to project a Hindu past?[107] How brittle is an identity built on coercion? And, for what gain? To serve the broader impulses of an insecure Indian union, which rid itself of colonial power only to commit the same on the Kashmiris they subjugate.

What makes the Kashmiri Pandit and Kashmiri Muslim divide more unfortunate is that the distrust between the communities has led the former to work alongside foreign powers, including the Indian state, to undermine the Kashmiri Muslim agency. By AD 1320 Muslims were the majority in Kashmir and since then ruled it until 1846.[108] In fact, the Valley has always been almost exclusively Muslim since the rulership of Rinchaan or Sadruddin Shah—the Buddhist convert to Islam who ruled Kashmir in AD 1320. Since that time until now, the Valley of Kashmir has remained overwhelmingly Muslim—upwards of 96.4 percent.[109] It was only after the British colonialists sold Kashmir to the foreign Dogras that new narratives emerged that attempted to undermine Kashmiri Muslim agency, which will be discussed in the following chapter.[110]

"Who is a Kashmiri?" has been a perennial question. It is an internal quirk quite unique to the original indigenous Kashmiris no matter if living inside Indian-Occupied Kashmir, Pakistan, or elsewhere. Foreign occupiers have weaponized the historical ethnic diversity of Kashmir in order to obfuscate reality and dilute the ability of the majority community to establish a stable polity. However, now it is undeniable that over the centuries many other peoples and tribes have settled into the region. Therefore, the question of who a *bona fide* Kashmiri is should be approached from a political point of view, rather than an ethnic/racial one.

Interestingly, as will be discussed in following chapter, the Dogra state did introduce a law that has become critical in today's quest for a plebiscite in Kashmir. For that reason, all those who qualify as state subjects of the former Dogra princely state are political Kashmiris and should be able to participate in any future plebiscite. Yet, this has always frightened post-colonial Indian apologists who know that any plebiscite will most certainly go against joining India. Arguably, that is why India abrogated Articles 370 and 35A, erased the state-subject laws, and introduced the new dubious domicile certificates.[111] Despite the overwhelming Muslim majority in Kashmiri society, India has engaged in a multivalent effort to usurp Kashmiri identity and to replace it with the cultural hegemony of the post-colonial Hindu state.

3

The Long Life Cycle of Resistance

In the final resting place of King Yusuf Shah Chak—the last indigenous sovereign ruler of Kashmir, who was betrayed, imprisoned, and sent to live out his last despondent days in Bihar—we find a compelling metaphor for Kashmir.[1]

In uncanny ways, the trials and tribulations of my fifth great grandfather, King Yusuf Shah Chak, continue to impact the Kashmiri social imaginary. In 1586, with aspirations of sparing his people undue bloodshed, he accepted a peace overture from Mughal Emperor Akbar.[2] On two previous attempts, the Mughals had tried to conquer Kashmir but were decisively defeated and routed in hand-to-hand combat by Kashmiri warriors.[3] Consequently, Emperor Akbar concluded that direct warfare was not feasible, and then sent several peace propositions to King Yusuf Shah Chak, inviting him to Delhi for deliberations. Eventually, King Yusuf Shah Chak agreed, assuming Akbar would honor his word. His *wazir*, Muhammad Butt, pleaded with the king not to go.[4] Paying no heed, King Yusuf Shah Chak set out for Delhi. What happened afterwards has forever scarred the Kashmiri psyche. Prior to his arrival at the Mughal Imperial Court, King Yusuf Shah Chak was arrested, imprisoned, and forced to live out his final days in Bihar—far away from his beloved homeland. Since that day, this tale of dispossession and treachery has been retold in every Kashmiri household and woven into the very tapestry of Kashmiri society.

The imprisonment of King Yusuf Shah Chak led to a short-lived guerilla resistance by his eldest son Yaqub Shah Chak, aided by his first cousin Ali Dar. Both carried on with a guerilla warfare campaign against the Mughals, until encouraged to submit to their sovereignty. The Mughal Emperor Akbar, hoping to appease the

Chak clan, even took a Chak bride and betrothed his son Prince Saleem to a daughter of an important Chak noble.[5] What happened thereafter is difficult to accurately follow. Only months after the agreement, Yaqub Shah Chak was poisoned to death, breathing his last in the presence of his confidante and relative, Miran Sayyid Shah Abul Ma'ali, a leading Sunni nobleman from the Baihaqi Sayyids, Ali Dar, and other family members.[6] Following his murder, his body was taken to be buried next to his father outside Kashmir in Bihar.[7] There is evidence to suggest that adjacent to King Yusuf Shah's grave is also that of his famous wife, the poetess Hubba Khatoon, who, after years of sorrow, had been finally permitted by Mughal authorities to travel to her husband.[8]

The Mughals' consolidation of their control over Kashmir led to the massacre of all the leading Chak nobles—so much so that those who escaped changed their names, fled to the mountainous surrounding areas, and went into hiding.[9] This incident has been corroborated by the elders of my family, who described the Mughal purge of the Chak family as cruel, relentless, and unforgiving. Chaks disappeared, left the Valley, and hid in the plains. Other leading members of Kashmiri nobility—Raina, Lone, Shahmiri, Magrey, Baihaqi Sayyids, Dar, Butt/Bhat—were targeted in a total annihilation of Kashmiri Muslim aristocracy from which Kashmiri society has still not recovered.[10]

With that context, this chapter begins with a brief outline of both Mughal and Afghan rule. While doing so, it explores the intersectionality of resistance and withdrawal in Kashmir. Interestingly, neither the Afghans nor Mughals were entirely seen as outsiders by Kashmiri Muslims. They established their writ but contributed to the maintenance of law and order and intermarried with locals. In contrast, the arrival of the Dogras was disastrous. For that reason, this chapter focuses on the atrocious consequences of the British East India Company's immoral and illegal sale of Kashmir to the foreign Dogra family, and the eventual emergence of a resistance narrative. Explicitly, this began with the illegitimate Treaty of Amritsar, signed in 1846.[11] From that moment onwards, the ebb and flow of defiance appeared, resisting the Dogra imposition of a

Hindu Raj over an overwhelming Muslim population. This chapter explains how Dogra rulers appropriated Kashmiri land, resources, and agricultural output. The foreign Dogra rulers weaponized the agricultural sector to the great disadvantage of the Kashmiri Muslims and fractured society by co-opting select religious and ethnic classes. Meanwhile, the Dogras began a Hinduization process in Kashmir that included inventing traditions in order to assert ownership of land and rationalize their presence. Of course, that was not enough. The fragile Dogras exacerbated socio-cultural and religious tensions such as the first major Sunni–Shia riot in order to pit different communities against one another. Next, when that failed, they resorted to outright brutality. Lastly, this chapter sheds light on a major catastrophe and defining moment that shook Dogra rule to its core and transformed the Kashmiri Muslim social imaginary: July 13, 1931—known as Martyrs' Day. Altogether, the intersections of foreign colonial rule, the ebb and flow of resistance, and the Kashmiri Muslim social imaginary of freedom is interwoven into the analysis.

MUGHAL AND AFGHAN RULE

Notwithstanding the initial brutality of Mughal rule, their supremacy lasted for 166 years from 1586 to 1752. During that time, the Mughals did not alter the socio-cultural or religious composition of Kashmir. Society remained largely untouched, and the Mughals were incidentally Muslim, rather than explicitly.[12] In many ways, Kashmiris throughout history have always calculated the viability of resistance upon the level of autonomy they were granted by larger foreign occupying powers, maneuvering to allow nominal control. This all while maintaining de facto power in local hands. Nevertheless, Mughal rule brought organization, administration, and a wealth of knowledge on managing different societies and peoples. Hassnain writes that the "Mughals, though conquerors of Kashmir, added to our cultural heritage, in the shape of various Mughal gardens around Dal lake and at various places in the Valley."[13] Also, Mughals were "patrons of learning" and it was during their period of rule that great literary works were produced, including Mulla Tahir Ghani's *Diwan*.[14] They adopted a watchful yet distant relationship with Kashmir—a live and let live attitude. And, curiously, they left most administrative day-to-day affairs to Kashmiri Pandits.[15] It seems important to connect the relatively hands-off Mughal rule to the increasing resentment of Kashmiri Muslims.

Such was the conflictual nature of Mughal rule: wiping out Kashmiri Muslim aristocracy, employing minority communities to administer the territory, but judiciously attending to the needs of Kashmiri society. In fact, Emperor Akbar visited Kashmir in 1588 and personally traveled to major villages, such as Pampore, Bijbihara, and Islamabad, to win over the people.[16] Ancient manuscripts reveal that the Mughal rulers forbade soldiers to enter into Kashmiri homes, they appointed three Kashmiris as intermediators, abolished aggressive taxation, and made peace overtures with several prominent Kashmiri families.[17] Essentially, during the lengthy Mughal rule, the socio-cultural fabric of Kashmiri society was left intact. There was no demographic change or attempt to repopulate Kashmir with foreigners. There was an appreciation of Kashmiri culture, norms, and spirituality. There was also a recognition that the people of Kashmir cherished their autonomy and freedom. And, even though Kashmiri Muslims were sidelined from the corridors of power, they were not dehumanized. For these reasons, many local Kashmiris did not consider the Mughals entirely as an occupying power.

After the Mughals lost control of Kashmir due to internecine warfare, the Afghan Durrani Empire ruled Kashmir from 1752 to 1819. During that time, all of present-day Pakistan, Afghanistan, and Kashmir were united by the Pushtoon chieftain Ahmad Shah Abdali.[18] Generally, the Afghans followed the same detached rulership style as the Mughals, leaving the bulk of society unchanged. Yet, the period of Afghan rule has been characterized as one of bigotry, violence, and intolerance by several Indian/Pandit chroniclers, such as Zutshi, Kaul, and Bamzai.[19] In fact, when perusing the English literary sources on Afghan rule in Kashmir it is worthwhile to note that almost the entirety of what is written is by Kashmiri

Pandits, or those who rely on their sources, which is overwhelmingly negative.[20] Considering what has been previously explained about attempts to Indianize and misrepresent Kashmiri history and identity, it is worthwhile to revisit Afghan rule in Kashmir and scrutinize the literature in the field. What makes this perplexing is that Pandits benefitted as intermediaries between the rulers and the majority Kashmiri Muslim community, and Kashmir's administration was almost singularly in the hands of the Pandit community due to the absentee landlord style of the Afghan rulers.[21] Dar acknowledges that many historians have been unkind to the Afghan rulers.[22] Undoubtedly, it was an important time in the collective history of the region and more scholarly work needs to be done because of the lack of critical Afghan or Kashmiri voices speaking about the history of the region. According to Kashmiri scholar and academic Sheikh Showkat, the Afghans were just as any other rulers who arrived in Kashmir and attempted to establish their nominal control in collusion with locals.[23] And it is especially important to highlight that this occurred when Mughal power was waning, British power was growing, and there were several other regional leaders emerging—such as the Sikhs in Punjab. Hence, the Afghans plausibly not only prevented civil war but protected Kashmir from other would-be invaders.

During Afghan rule, administrative and social control was largely, but not exclusively, commandeered by the Pandit community, in continuation of a policy adopted by the Mughals, who relied on them as go-betweens.[24] In fact, the first Afghan ruler of Kashmir, Ahmad Shah Durrani, appointed Raja Sukh Jiwan Mal—a non-Muslim and non-Kashmiri—as his governor.[25] This reasonably demonstrates that the Afghans followed a pattern of governing inherited from the Mughals. Still, it is highly unlikely that the Afghans, who were described by the Pandit historiographers as unsophisticated, racist, and despotic, would entrust the highest office in the land to one despised on account of religious belief.[26] Because of this, it leads one to suspect the ways in which the historiography in Kashmir plays into strategies of narrative construction that undermine the primary religious-ethnic demographic—the Kashmiri Muslim. Again, this is not incidental; in fact, to label others as prejudicial is also a strategy of misdirection, employed to delegitimize the communal, racist nature of the Dogra and Kashmiri Pandit narratives themselves. It follows a pattern of well-constructed misinformation, intricately connected to the ways the Kashmiri Pandit and post-colonial Indian apologists have continuously twisted history to suit their particular vested interests, seeking to possess Kashmir and deny Kashmiri Muslim agency.

Lastly, Kashmir has several monuments that attest to the positive contributions that the Afghan rulers made. For instance, the fort referred to as Koh-i-Maran by Kashmiri Muslims or as Qila Hari Parbat by Kashmiri Pandits was originally constructed by the Afghan governor Atta Mohammad Khan. Another popular fort, Shergarhi, was built by Afghan Amir Khan, who also built the famous Amira Kadal bridge.[27] In addition, Afghans built Safa Kadal bridge and Nawa Kadal bridge.[28] Another important and distinguishing feature of Afghan rule are the scores of Kashmiri families who trace their lineage to the Afghans. Afghan rule did not upset the socio-cultural religious sensitivities of society, and many Afghans chose to make Kashmir their home. Jahangir, Kasi, and Alam (2017) have scratched the surface with their research on the cultural impact of Afghan rule on Kashmir.[29]

By 1819, Kashmir had slipped away from Afghan Durrani rule. At that point, competing Kashmiri nobles were individually jostling with larger foreign entities to negotiate Kashmir's future and their own privileges—whether with the Afghan, British, or the dying and short-lived empire of Ranjit Singh. There was both collusion and collision between the various competitors along with the British on managing Kashmir.[30] Essentially, no one truly controlled Kashmir for the next 20 years, and this situation worsened with Ranjit Singh's death in 1839.[31] During the ensuing chaos, the British East India Company, a front for British imperial interests, began expanding its territories by fighting both the Afghans and Sikhs, relying on mercenaries for support.[32] The Chief of the Hindu Dogra family, Raja Gulab Singh, who had formerly been allied to Ranjit Singh but switched loyalties to the British, saw an opportunity.[33] He allied with the British and promised his British overlords the cannon fodder their imperialistic endeavor required, and ultimately the Treaty of Amritsar. For a paltry sum of 75 lakhs—7.5 million rupees—an entire nation was enslaved.[34]

DOGRA RULE AND THE TREATY OF AMRITSAR

Today, the overwhelming majority of Kashmiri Muslims trace the origins of their occupation, and the beginning of their resistance, to the 1846 Treaty of Amritsar, signed between the British East India Company and Raja Gulab Singh. This illegitimate treaty is described by Kashmiris as the "sale deed of Kashmir," in which the entirety of Kashmir—its people, land, and livestock—were sold without their consent.[35] The poet and Islamic thinker Muhammad Iqbal wrote, "Their fields, their crops, their streams. Even the peasants in the Valley. They sold, they sold all, alas! How cheap was the sale."[36] Robert Thorp writes that in no part of the treaty that the British made with Gulab Singh was the "slightest provision made for the just and humane government of the people of Cashmere."[37] Such judgments condemn the sinister *modus operandi* employed by the British imperialists, who had allied with Hindu chauvinists such as Raja Gulab Singh against the Kashmiri people. Mridu Rai succinctly summarizes the formation of alien Dogra rule over Kashmir as essentially establishing an aggressive Hindu state over an overwhelming Muslim majority.[38] She writes that it is important to consider "the question of legitimacy of a state in which a Hindu ruler who was explicitly rather than incidentally Hindu governed a numerically preponderant subject population which was explicitly and not implicitly Muslim."[39] This is what distinguishes Dogra rule from the Mughal and Afghan rulers who preceded it.

Specifically, the Dogra rulers understood their rule was precarious because their culture, religion, and ideology differed from the overwhelmingly Muslim population. According to Lawrence, the British settlement officer who was deputed to Kashmir in 1889, the Hindus comprised about 5 to 6 per cent of the population of the Valley, the Sikhs were 0.5 per cent and the Muslims about 93 per cent.[40]

Also, the 1941 Census of India indicated that the Valley of Kashmir was 93.6 per cent Muslim.[41] Today, the number is even higher at 96.4 percent of the Valley.[42] Facing these demographic realities, the following sections will describe how Dogra strategy was to systematically do the following: 1) confiscate all land and make attempts to *Hindunize* Kashmir by changing the names of localities;[43] 2) adopt extortionist attitudes on agricultural produce to impoverish society;[44] 3) enforce the practice of forced labor—known as *begǎr*;[45] 4) invent traditions to rationalize their historic presence, such as Amarnath Yatra;[46] 5) exacerbate ethnic/religious tensions to divide and conquer, such as the first major Sunni–Shia riot;[47] and 6) use brute force, ethnic cleansing, and genocide to establish authority.[48] Together, an ugly picture emerges of how the Dogra Raj set upon owning Kashmir.

LAND POSSESSION AND FORCED LABOR

After claiming to have purchased Kashmir from the British, the Dogras considered all the land, people, and resources as belonging to them. In this way, Gulab Singh "divested the peasants of their proprietary rights," which they had enjoyed even during the previous foreign rulers.[49] Under Dogra tyranny, the land "was held by his subjects in the capacity of tenants for which they were required to pay land revenue to the state as Haq-i-Malikan. If they ceased to pay the Haq-i-Malikan, they were deprived of the occupancy of the land."[50] From this, all property rights had now been transferred to Dogra regime, and the people of Kashmir essentially became renters. This had a profoundly impoverishing impact on Kashmiri Muslims especially.

After confiscating all property and land rights, the Dogra rulers enacted cruel laws impacting the agricultural produce of Kashmir. Kashmir is, and remains, a largely agrarian society. At that time, Naik writes that 75 percent of "the population of Kashmir 'was engaged in this sector (agrarian) and it constituted the main source of income of the state. Thus, the agrarian economy has been a matter of interest affecting all sections of Kashmiri society in a variety of ways."[51] Moreover, the main purpose of Dogra agrarian policies was to financially squeeze people, fill their coffers, and perpetuate their illegitimate rule. They did so by demanding regressive taxation on cultivable land—which required the cultivator to compensate cash or kind to the colonial Dogra ruler in order to meet set quotas. The net result of this policy was to indenture the people of Kashmir and take their agricultural produce as a type of unacknowledged payment. This meant that the cultivator, even after having paid the state quota, remained in debt. It resulted in the economic devastation of Kashmiri Muslims, while Hindus, Sikhs, and Peers—a tiny segment of the religious classes of Muslims—were exempt from this type of exploitative taxation.[52] These privileged classes were also exempt from *begăr*, a system of forced labor instrumentalized by the Dogra with the support of their British allies.[53] As Rai writes, the "begar system provided great opportunities for graft to Pandit revenue officials through whom demands were channeled."[54] Henceforth, as Rai continues, if a demand for forced labor was made in Srinagar, the Pandit intermediaries working on behalf of the Dogra state would double the number asked for and reap immense financial benefits.[55]

For the Muslim majority, *begăr* represented a deliberate attack on both their economic security and their liberty. Horrid tales of abuse, persecution, and murder have been shared by many Kashmiri households when recalling the tragic impact of this abhorrent practice. While the concept of forced labor existed prior to the advent of Dogra rule, the systematic application of *begăr* as a rule, rather than as an exception, occurred under their tyranny.[56] In fact, it was the Dogra rulers who sent thousands of Kashmiri Muslim villagers to their untimely deaths during the infamous *Gilgit-begăr*.[57]

The threat of Russian expansion had motivated the British and their Dogra clients to fortify the Gilgit region. To accomplish that, the Dogras forced Kashmiri Muslim villagers to carry loads through treacherous terrain, with barely enough sustenance to survive and while wearing straw shoes.[58] Rashid writes that the *begăr to Gilgit* "was not only unpaid labour but also brought risk to the life of a peasant as there were least [sic] chances for his return because of the thirst, hunger and the harsh weather conditions."[59] Long absences away from their land caused further economic loss, shortage of food, and eventually starvation. This system of abuse went on until some respite was given by British intervention in 1885. They were unhappy with the mismanagement of Kashmir, but not for moral purposes; the British feared the relentless oppression was radicalizing Kashmiri Muslims against the British and their Dogra client state.[60] Actually, this was central to British imperial strategy in the region: oppression should be strong enough to prevent resistance, but not so harsh as to provoke outright rebellion.

AMARNATH YATRA

Aside from stealing the land, life, and liberty of Kashmiri Muslims, the Dogra began justifying their presence by rewriting history. In order to protect their authority, they indulged in imagining a perennial Hindu community in Kashmir that had been forcibly converted by Muslims by previous regimes. Admittedly, the process of imagining their communities to build social cohesion and develop camaraderie is a normal part of all nation-building, as Anderson articulates.[61] Yet, the imagination of Kashmir, by the Dogra, included inventing Hindu pilgrimages and claiming ownership of Buddhist monasteries by misrepresenting them as Hindu. Also, it involved obliterating Muslim dominance in the socio-cultural life of Kashmir. In essence, they were trying to insert their own presence in the history of Kashmir to justify their rule. Consider the infamous Amarnath Yatra—a purported Hindu pilgrimage in Kashmir, the origins of which is shrouded in mystery. Researching it leads to dozens of unreferenced articles, opinion pieces, and websites run by non-Kashmiris that quote one another in a vicious circle of misinformation.[62] The majority of the web links or articles found online are all connected to Indian sites that contain imaginative innuendo or outright fabrications. This has been part of India's strategy to own Kashmir: to use social media, proliferate literature, and use film for dubious assertions. Actually, there is no evidence that the Hindu pilgrimage known as the Amarnath Yatra ever existed until the imposition of the foreign Hindu Dogra rule. For Kashmiri Muslims, the entire Hindu pilgrimage was invented for the sole purpose of the appropriation of Kashmiri Muslim land. As such, many Kashmiri Muslims are adamant that this so-called Hindu pilgrimage was invented by Hindu Dogra rulers in order to rationalize and justify their presence.[63] As if to say, as Kashmiri historian and scholar Sheikh Showkat has stated, "you see we have always been here and you (Muslims) have been forcibly converted from us."[64] What is even more revealing is that Kashmiri Pandits do not participate in this pilgrimage and it holds no historical importance for them. This imaginary ties into the ways and means through which the Dogra rulers began a systematic process of taking the land, economics, and very history of Kashmir.

Nowadays, upwards of 600,000 Hindu devotees from all over India travel to the disputed territory of Kashmir to pray at Amarnath, which is basically a cave shrine housing an ice stalagmite that is considered a symbol of Shiva—a deity in the Hindu pantheon. Unquestionably, facilitating Hindu devotees to visit the Amarnath cave, perched 3,880 meters (12,730 feet) above sea level, is a complex affair. It involves tremendous coordination, which is overseen by the Indian military. Interestingly, tracing the history of the supposed pilgrimage is challenging since there is no recorded history of Kashmir that acknowledges it. Several claims are made by Hindu socio-political and religious organizations about the Yatra being an ancient pilgrimage, but they offer no unbiased evidence. "What emerges then is that everyone is quoting everyone else and the resultant legend gets built around such hearsay."[65] This leads one to suspect the motivations behind the purported pilgrimage. Why has it suddenly become more important? And, what are the clear implications for its promotion by the Indian state and management by the Indian military?

Today, Kashmiri Pandits, and post-colonial Indian writers, argue that the Amarnath Yatra is mentioned in two primary sources, which they use to claim it as an ancient pilgrimage. Those two sources are the *Rajatarangini* and the *Nilamata Purana*. Interestingly, neither text uses the word Amarnath nor mentions a pilgrimage.

Instead, both texts do mention a temple called either Amaresvara or Amaresa, which Stein argues cannot be confused for today's Amarnath Yatra.[66] In other words, what we have here is another instance of many Kashmiri Pandits and post-colonial Indian writers deliberately misrepresenting historical names and places in order to substantiate the myth of an ancient Hindu pilgrimage in Kashmir.[67]

According to Kashmiri Muslim oral tradition, the origins of the so-called Amarnath Yatra began during the Dogra period. In 1850, a Kashmiri Muslim shepherd named Buta Malik from Batkote, a village near Pahalgam, strayed into a cave while grazing his sheep near the mountains.[68] While there, he saw the ice stalagmite and described it when he came back to his village. A group of Hindus who heard about it concluded that it must be a Shiva lingam. What is interesting about this incident is that it reveals how Hindutva appropriations may simply claim any type of natural occurring phenomenon as representation of a deity, then weaponize that claim to justify ownership. There is no evidence to suggest that the Amarnath pilgrimage has historical relevance or acceptance prior to Dogra rule; its invention is part of the process of dispossession, violence, and cultural appropriation that all happened soon after the Dogra established their rule with British military might.

Today, the Amarnath Yatra is politicized as a means to justify the large presence of Indian soldiers to protect devotees. In reality, the large military presence is associated with the hyper-anxiety felt by Hindutva propagandists following the global backlash after abrogating Articles 370 and 35A on August 5, 2019. Which has made the Indian state even more desperate to project Kashmir as Hindu, accelerate its policy of dispossession, and utilize the Amarnath Yatra for its ideological purposes. This can be seen in the manner in which the Indian state encourages an influx of hundreds of thousands of Hindu devotees to Kashmir, as compared to two decades ago when hardly a few thousand pilgrims would travel. As Swathi Seshadri writes, "In conflict areas, religious tourism in particular has been used as a political tool by the State to claim a historical right over the land. In Kashmir, the Amarnath Yatra has been a weapon to claim the land and ensure a steady stream of devotees from India into Kashmir."[69]

Swathi Seshadri considers the instrumentalization of the Amarnath Yatra in Kashmir as the first experiment by the Indian state "to use religious tourism to push a political agenda." She argues that this Hindu pilgrimage and others are used "to deify land and stake claim to it."[70] Furthermore, she insists that Amarnath Yatra has been politicized since the 1990s, coinciding with the renewed struggle for freedom in the Valley. She then goes on to mention other pilgrimages that are becoming institutionalized, such as the similarly named Buddha Amarnath and the Kousar Nag Yatra, the latter a more recent pilgrimage that was initiated in 2009. Recently, in 2021, the Indian government began the unconscionable act of facilitating upwards of 600,000 Hindu devotees to take part in the Amarnath Yatra, despite the coronavirus ravaging India. Disregarding the lives of Kashmiris, the Indian government stated that the pilgrimage would take place, though reluctantly withdrew following global condemnation. Clearly, the consequences of such actions would have led to grave breaches of the Third and Fourth Geneva Conventions, including willfully causing great suffering or serious injury to body or health.[71] The willingness of Modi's India to facilitate a super-spreader event of a deadly virus demonstrates the importance of the Amarnath Yatra to the state's ideological claim to Kashmir.

SUNNI–SHIA RIOTS[72]

Another tactic the Dogra rulers used was to exacerbate ethnic, religious, and even district/locality differences between the peoples in Kashmir. This was done in order to weaponize diversity and utilize it as a "divide and rule" ploy.[73] By pitting ethnic/religious communities against one another, as Bhan suggests, the Dogra rulers hoped to distract from their illegitimate and harsh rule.[74] This is a tactic used by settler-colonialists and colonial powers throughout the world. Bethke writes that the "concept of divide-and-rule describes a strategy for rulers to sustain power by breaking up rival concentrations of power into pieces that individually have less power than the ruler implementing the strategy."[75] Christopher examines this policy in the British Raj.[76] This further corroborates Mridu Rai's belief that the Dogra regime skillfully encouraged the Sunni–Shia riots that rocked Kashmir in 1872.[77]

In 1872, a massive riot broke out between the Sunni and Shia communities over allegations that the latter were colluding with the foreign Dogra forces. These allegations did not suddenly appear. Dogra patronage of certain segments of the Pandits, Peer families, and Shia minority was undeniable. In fact, consider the manner in which the Dogra family enticed the grandfather of Kashmiri poet Agha Shahid Ali, a Kizilbash Shia who traveled from Kandahar to Kashmir at the personal request of the Dogra ruler.[78] The Dogra rulers actively sought to give power and patronage to the Shia population and select Peer families in Kashmir, even going as far as choosing, as their personal doctor and confidante, Agha Muhammad Bakir Qizilbash, who was the grandfather of Agha Shahid Ali.[79]

In this context, the 1872 Sunni–Shia riots were carefully constructed. To explore this violence, it's important to look at how the Dogra rulers organized the shawl and woodworking industries—two of the most important exports in Kashmir. In both industries, Shia families were given control over manufacturing and trading, while the Sunni majority were the weavers and artisans. By empowering the Shia community, and giving them control over manufacture and trade, the weavers/artisans were placed at a great disadvantage, especially when extortionist taxes were placed on the industry. This compelled the manufacturers to lower the amount they paid the weavers and artisans, leading to a revolt when the shawl industry declined. Lawrence attributes the cause of the Sunni–Shia riots to this economic discontent but does not acknowledge or recognize the role the Dogra state had in deliberately creating these structural conditions.[80] During an interview, Showkat informed me that there seems to be a "concerted policy by the Indian government today, as the Dogras before," to heighten tensions between the communities.[81] Corroborating this, Bhan suggests that foreign Dogra rulers distributed power and patronage to antagonize class, ethnic and religious differences.[82] Therefore, the eruption of Shia–Sunni violence was no different.

While the Sunni–Shia riots in 1872 were serious, Kashmiri society is not sectarian and the differences were not insurmountable. The historical accommodation between Kashmiri Sunni and Shia communities persisted, despite the Dogra policy that attempted to divide the peoples of Kashmir along religious, cultural, and ethnic lines. Such a policy was particularly urgent for the Dogra as an occupying power: as Mona Bhan writes,

> The politics of identity in Kashmir, much like elsewhere, is deeply imbricated with the everyday operations of statecraft. Such operations take on more urgency in occupied zones as governments create new or intensify existing divisions to build their legitimacy, one identity at a time. Consequently, they had to resort to more brutal strategies and tactics in order to maintain their unholy rule.[83]

Interestingly enough, as will be discussed in later chapters, this policy of heightening racial, ethnic, and sectarian tensions is continuing. The Indian government under Prime Minister Modi has allowed Shia processions to continue throughout Kashmir but has banned the Sunni majority from attending Friday prayers.[84] A well-known Kashmiri Shia personality, Ruhollah Mehdi, stated that this seems to be a clear design to turn the majority Sunni community against the Shia. In a live interview with the *Kashmiriyat* paper, he stated that due to the "Eid Disaster Management Act ... Kashmiris were told to celebrate Eid at their homes invoking Covid protocols. The Friday prayers at Jama Masjid have not been allowed for last [sic] more than 100 Fridays and continue to be banned."[85] Then, he added, "given the fact that all major religious gatherings (with no exception to any particular religion) continue to be banned, this sudden isolated decision about the 10th Muharram procession ... after a gap of 30 years, raises more questions than it answers."[86] This reflects how the Indian government pursues policies designed to splinter social cohesion.

MARTYRS' DAY

After several decades of brutal rule, the Dogra regime had subjugated a Muslim-dominated socio-political landscape—not only as foreigners but aggressive Hindu radicals. As time went on, the Dogra regime became increasingly wary of Kashmiri Muslim aspirations to end their foreign occupation.[87] Several Kashmiri Muslim organizations arose demanding agency, even petitioning the Dogra rulers and the British for their inalienable rights. At this time, a sophisticated political reawakening was emerging in Kashmir, which made the Dogra rulers uneasy. Responding to growing threats to their grip on power, the Dogra resorted to heightened levels of suppression, leading to objections from within: a Bengali officer named Sir Albion Banerjee, who served the Dogras as prime minister, resigned in protest at the barbaric treatment of Kashmiri Muslims.[88] Even the British well understood the horrible conditions that the Kashmiri Muslims lived under, describing Hari Singh as "the greatest rascal in Asia" and a "cruel tyrant."[89] Still, that never stopped the British from not only supporting him but strengthening the Dogra rule. Such was the nature of British power that focused purely on self-interest without the burden of morality.

This brings us to another example of the oppressive Dogra regime, memorialized by Kashmiri Muslims as Martyrs' Day, July 13, 1931.[90] On this ominous day, 22 Kashmiri Muslims were murdered while making the Islamic call to prayer.[91] The brutality of this act led to protests forming a serious challenge to Dogra authority, and remains a great symbol of resistance for Kashmiri Muslims.[92]

The increasing politicization of the Kashmiri Muslim community against the foreign Dogra rulers was unnerving. Social bonding and camaraderie take time as it coalesces to confront colonization.[93] As that process intensifies, there is a direct correlation, as Fanon articulates, between that unity, across ethnic, religious, and class lines, and resistance to foreign colonization.[94] The emergent unity is resisted by the hegemon, who attempts to hinder its growth. In a panic, colonizers instill fear in the people, but also do not wish to own the violence that would invite retaliation.[95] Over time, the fear of violence dissipates, and the less people fear, the more resistance emerges. It was such an escalation of violence that led to the massacre of 22 unarmed Kashmiris on July 13, 1931, and it should be seen in the broader context of increased Kashmiri Muslim organization and elevated resistance at their subjugation in their own land.

Collectively, four developments took place leading to the Martyrs' Day massacre on July 13, 1931. First, as Snedden mentions, Kashmiri Muslims by the early 1900s were politically organizing themselves to "improve the pitiful lot of Jammu & Kashmir Muslims" and this "culminated in 1924 when some leading Kashmiris presented a memorandum to the Viceroy."[96] This is always the first requisite in any resistance movement: the maturation of a national consciousness that develops grassroots networks and builds partnerships. The presentation of a list of grievances by Kashmiris to the British viceroy angered the Dogra regime, who punished all involved by fines and imprisonment. Second, another catalyst for Kashmiri Muslim uprising was the continued insult and mockery of Islam by the Dogras. This was unbearable for Kashmiri Muslims. The Dogras had even attempted to ban Friday prayers, and, in one specific instance in early 1931, a Hindu policeman was charged with desecrating the Holy Qur'an.[97] This led to protests throughout downtown Srinagar as it had infuriated the religious sensitivities of the majority population.[98] Third, on April 19, 1931, the Dogras banned the Eid sermon, causing widespread outrage and protests.[99] Lastly, amid this highly charged environment, an infamous meeting was held in the Jamia Masjid, in Srinagar, attended by several well-known Kashmiri Muslims, including Sheikh Abdullah, Ghulam Abbas, and Mirwais Maulvi Yousuf Shah.[100] Among them was a young, passionate Abdul Qadir Khan—a Pushtoon/Pathan Muslim visitor to Kashmir—who pointed to the Dogra Palace and shouted "raze it to the ground."[101]

Abdul Qadir Khan's impassioned plea for Kashmiris to unite against their oppressor was just the catalyst needed to push Kashmiri Muslims over the edge. He was witness to their horrendous conditions and motivated them to revolt against foreign occupation.[102] He was arrested under the charge of sedition and instigating Kashmiris to defy Dogra rule. During his trial proceedings, a massive turnout of people had shown up for support. Tens of thousands of Kashmiri Muslims were carefully watching, when, as Ather Zia writes,

> As the time for obligatory prayers approached, one Kashmiri protester rose to give the azan (call to prayer). When he stood up, the Dogra governor Raizada Triloki Chand ordered police to fire upon him. As the wounded man fell in a heap, another Kashmiri stood up to complete the azan and was shot down as well. This went on till twenty-two men were executed in public trying to finish the call to prayer as part of their protest.[103]

This legendary moment of Kashmiri unity, courage, and resistance has been etched into Kashmir's collective consciousness as July 13, 1931, "Martyrs Day."[104]

The murder of 22 Kashmiris in such a heroic manner galvanized the entire Kashmiri Muslim population. Snedden writes that Hari Singh panicked at the uprising and responded with heavy-handed arrests, imprisonments, floggings and, in some instances, further shootings. There was significant popular unrest and violence throughout Kashmir Province, particularly in Srinagar, Anantnag (sometimes called Islamabad), Shopian, Baramulla (now Baramulla) and Sopore. The agitation spread to Jammu Province, where pro-Muslim groups also protested. As a result, the British sent three companies of armed troops (about 500 soldiers) to support the J&K [Jammu and Kashmir] ruler and to restore law and order.[105]

Here, there is explicit acknowledgment of the role the British imperial authorities had in the occupation of Kashmir by Dogra foreigners. Still, their intervention was not enough. The uprising had entered a critical phase. Indeed, Hari Singh reluctantly instituted a constitutionally based democracy in hopes of quelling the protests. "This followed some serious British intervention by J&K's Resident Officer, some official prompting from New Delhi, and an investigation by a British official, Sir Bertrand J. Glancy, from the Government of India."[106] Yet, despite these actions, the brazen massacre of Kashmiri Muslims had proven the death knell for the foreign Dogra regime. Following the loss of this control, the Maharaja committed one of the worst atrocities in the history of the entire region—the Jammu genocide of Muslims that, as discussed in the following chapter, altered the demographic balance in the plains outside the Kashmir Valley.

CONCLUSION

This chapter briefly explored the history of foreign rule in Kashmir from the Mughals and Afghans. It then focused on the colonization of Kashmir during the Dogra period, a period of rule that was propped up by the British. Rai has strongly argued that the Dogra rule over Kashmir was a form of Hindu colonization over an overwhelmingly Muslim population. This is what distinguishes the different epochs of foreign rule over Kashmir. By examining this history, the chapter explored the intersections of resistance to foreign rule in Kashmir's past and highlighted differences between them. Most importantly, it revealed how, through the 1846 Treaty of Amritsar, the explicitly Hindu Dogra state went about usurping Kashmir—a Muslim-majority area. A systematic strategy was followed by the Dogras, with British military and political collusion, in hopes of transforming Kashmir from a Muslim-majority to a Hindu-majority state. Certainly, the Dogras and the British both had their own individual reasonings. For the Dogra, it was their aspiration to establish an empire. On the other hand, the British, due to their ongoing wars with the Afghans and Sikhs, were determined to prevent Kashmir from also posing a thorn in their side, especially considering the wider geopolitical realities emerging from Russia and China. For that reason, the British supported the Dogras, even while loathing them. What followed was the enaction of a series of discriminatory and racist policies, imparting false education and disempowering the Kashmiri Muslim community. Then the Dogras even had the audacity to blame the people for their own misery.

To reiterate, to accomplish the goal of owning Kashmir, the Dogra state did the following: 1) confiscated all land and attempted to *Hindunize* Kashmir by changing names of localities; 2) used extortionist taxes on agricultural produce to impoverish Kashmiri Muslim society; 3) enforced the horrid practice of forced labor—known as *begăr*; 4) invented traditions to justify their presence, such as Amarnath Yatra; 5) exacerbated socio-cultural and religious tensions to divide and conquer, such as the first major Sunni–Shia riot; 6) used brute force, ethnic cleansing, and genocide to instill authority, such as the murder of 22 Muslims on July 13, 1931. Altogether, an ugly picture emerges of how the Dogra Raj set upon ravaging the land, the people, and its resources. However, once the Dogras had realized that their rule would come to an end, they conducted one of the most grotesque murder sprees in the history of the region—the Jammu genocide.

Lastly, interestingly enough, the brutality of Dogra rule awakened a sense of camaraderie among Kashmiri Muslims. Although Kashmiri society had historically tolerated difference, successive periods of foreign rule had led to some tensions exploited by the Dogras. That internal dissension made it possible for the foreign Dogras, with British military might, to take over. Yet, the monstrous rulership of the Dogras compelled the Kashmiri Muslims to make common cause. Once that happens, no colonial power on earth can sustain its rule. In fact, with every successive generation, the spirit of Kashmiri resistance has only become more emboldened.[107] This should be unsurprising, since the hegemon may delay but cannot suppress freedom in perpetuity. The long life cycle of oppression and resistance in Kashmir is directly tied to the infamous day in 1846 when the British bequeathed Kashmir to foreigners. Yet, despite the death and destruction, Kashmiri people resisted, and continue to resist.[108]

4

Jammu Genocide

Among the cruelest and most heartbreaking memories in the history of the disputed territory of Jammu and Kashmir is what has come to be known as the Jammu genocide, which began in August 1947 and continued until November of that year.[1] And, as will be evidenced in the following sections, the genocide was planned long before the British withdrawal. It involved complicity from the Indian state and was driven by the Dogras' sense that they had special ownership of Jammu and that their dominance demanded ethnic cleansing of the Muslim majority. Consequently, the Dogra rulers conceptualized a harrowing plan for the ethnic cleansing of the Muslims of Jammu.[2] It is important to note that, in 1947, according to the Census of India 1941, the approximate population of the entire princely state was 3.7 million, with Muslims comprising between 76 to 80 percent of the people.[3] Specifically, the Valley of Kashmir was an overwhelmingly Muslim-majority (93 percent) province. In the Jammu region, including the areas now in Azad Kashmir, Muslims formed approximately 65 percent of the population.

What followed was a grotesque frenzy of genocidal violence that directly impacted my maternal and paternal families. Several members of both sides of my family were murdered. Many others were arrested, only to escape from jail later. The genocide holds particular importance for my family since it was the reason we were violently uprooted and forced to flee Kashmir. My paternal grandfather Muhammad Din Chak, a scion of the royal Chak family, was born in Kupwara. His father, Hakim Din Chak, was a wealthy landlord who had homes in downtown Srinagar in a locality named Chachbal, as well as a palatial house in Jammu City, adjacent to the home of late Air Marshal Asghar Khan. Moreover, he had several other properties in Kupwara and Trehgam—the ancestral home of our branch of the Chak tribe. My grandfather Muhammad Din Chak was married to my paternal grandmother Zubeida Dar who was born in Baderwah to the well-established Dar family who still reside there. Both her parents, Abdul Ghani Dar and Feroza Dar, and two siblings, twelve-year-old Abida Dar and eight-year-old Danish Dar, were all mercilessly killed.

Later, most of the surviving members of my family—both maternal and paternal sides—resettled in Sialkot, Pakistan. Still, the family was scattered. My paternal grandfather chose to relocate to Muzaffarabad, Azad Kashmir, while my maternal grandfather, Ghulam Hussain Butt, chose Quetta, Baluchistan, after settling his wife, my maternal grandmother, Sughra Butt, in Mirpur Khas, Sindh. Interestingly, those forcibly displaced are never easily settled. They wander. Constantly moving from town to town, city to city, searching and hoping to find the peace they lost. And, once they stop moving, the vicious memories emerge. From Muzaffarabad, Peshawar, Quetta to Sialkot, without realizing that only when they stop and confront their pain does the process of healing begin.

However, some never stop moving. This was the case for my maternal grandfather's cousin, Abdul Rashid Butt—whose parents, wife, and three children were all massacred in Jammu. He was a childhood friend of my paternal grandfather's younger brother, Muhammad Sharif Chak. And it was he who recalled this painful memory to me in his home in Peshawar, Khyber-Pakhtunkhwa. Ever since Abdul Rashid Butt survived the carnage and arrived in Sialkot, he would just wander, murmuring to himself, with a cold, empty stare that one could only describe as shock. Up and down the narrow streets of Kashmiri Mohalla. For the next 20 years of his despondent life, he continued walking, until one day he was never seen again. He vanished. Some say he walked until his death. Others, that he fell into a ravine or began walking back to Jammu and was killed along the border. No one knows for certain, but his story is well known among the first Kashmiri refugees who settled in Sialkot.

Growing up as a child, I would sit and listen in anguish to the horrifying stories that were being shared. Typical Kashmiri families, products of the forced exodus of Jammu, would sit together, huddle, and share their painful memories. It was those memories that shaped me. That is one way that Kashmir has been kept alive all these years—by sharing the stories of resistance, courage, and even pain. All this becomes a part of the social imaginary of the Kashmiri Muslim community and leads to the coalescing of a unified identity. It must also be remembered that tyrants will do everything in their power to prevent those stories from emerging.[4] In other words, genocide denial is a major factor in understanding the politics of extermination and the psychology of the perpetrators of gross violence.[5] This is precisely the type of erasure that happened with the Jammu genocide, which is also closely related to Islamophobia.[6]

In the context of how the illegal, foreign Dogra regime was losing its hold on power, they initiated a methodical campaign of ethnic cleansing and outright murder of any Kashmiri Muslim with even the slightest suspicion of anti-Dogra sentiment, especially in Poonch.[7] Through guile, the Dogra forces led by Maharaja Hari Singh tried to entice the Muslim army officers to give up their weapons. Seeing that as evidence of a nefarious plot, many flatly refused. This made matters worse in the sense that Dogra oppression increased, leading to open revolt. Realizing his time was up, Maharaja Hari Singh began a vicious smear campaign, including Islamophobic carica- tures of Muslims. Stanton refers to this as the preparatory stage of genocide.[8] Then, the unthinkable crime of extermination happened, followed by a deliberate attempt to cover up the genocide, even to deny any atrocity took place.

To explore these issues, this chapter investigates the conditions in the state of Jammu and Kashmir prior to the massacre, laying the foundation for how violence was operationalized. Second, it analyses the systematic and state-sponsored nature of the genocide. Relatedly, it studies what happened to the leadership of the Muslim community and critiques how it responded to the violence. Third, it scrutinizes the controversy surrounding the numbers of those killed and discusses how it continues to impact the memory of Kashmiri Muslims—not just in Indian-Occupied Kashmir but just as sharply for the millions of Kashmiris forced to migrate to Pakistan and elsewhere throughout the world. Lastly, it inquires as to why the Jammu genocide became among the least understood massacres in the twentieth century.

AN ARTIFICIAL STATE

When it became clear that the British Raj was coming to an end, there was the issue of the so-called princely states. These were self-governing, autonomous regions, numbering 565 in the British Raj.[9] Among them was the state of Jammu and Kashmir, ruled, as previously mentioned, by a foreign tyrant, Maharaja Hari Singh, with British collusion. During a conversation between Jawaharlal Nehru and Karan Singh—the Maharaja Hari Singh's son—both acknowledged the borders of the state of Jammu and Kashmir as artificial.[10] In fact, Karan Singh unreservedly claimed that the five separate regions of Jammu, Kashmir, Ladakh, Gilgit, and Baltistan had been forcibly joined together and had nothing in common with each other.[11] While true, this ethnic diversity is weaponized by the Indian successor state with *mala fide* intent to disregard Kashmiri aspirations of self-determination and complicate Kashmiri political rights.[12]

In addition to the state itself being an artificial creation, the Dogra rulers established their writ with British military assistance and based their authority upon a treaty with no popular consent. In other words, the Dogras had no legitimacy among Kashmiri Muslims. To corroborate this, Kulkarni writes that it "must be remembered that the Dogra rulers of Jammu were unpopular in every other part of the princely state," and even among Kashmiri Pandits.[13] As Kashmiri Pandit writer Prem Nath Bazaz wrote, "The Dogras have always considered Jammu as their home and Kashmir as their conquered country ... they established a sort of Dogra imperialism in the State in which all non-Dogra communities and classes were given the humble place of inferiors ...."[14]

Granted, while the artificial state of Jammu and Kashmir has five distinct areas, the demographic composition of each is more blurred. Prior to the Jammu genocide, the entire Jammu region had a Muslim majority with upwards of 70 percent of the population.[15] This included Gujjar, Pahari, Rajput, and ethnic Kashmiri Muslims. The Valley, for the past several centuries, has had an overwhelming Muslim majority with several ethnicities, and the official statistics attest to this being almost 96.4 percent Muslim.[16] Yet, it must be understood that ethnic Kashmiri Muslims were not just confined to the Valley of Kashmir, neither is the Valley home only to ethnic Kashmiris—other ethnicities relocated there as well. Nonetheless, an overwhelming majority of scholarly accounts reflects an almost unanimous animosity towards the Dogra rulers; as Kulkarni asks, "If such was the inimical sentiment of Kashmiris (both Muslim and Hindu) towards the alien Dogra rule, is there any reason to believe that the people of Gilgit, Baltistan and Ladakh were happy under it?"[17] Similarly, the late Jammu Hindu journalist and writer Ved Bhasin corroborated this animosity during my conversations with him.[18]

What made the region of Jammu important for the Dogras is that it constituted the home of the Hindu non-Kashmiri Dogra family, gifted to them by the British. As such, as Bhasin explained, "they (Dogra rulers) considered Jammu their property, even though, as Punjabi Hindus, they were not indigenous to it."[19] Moreover, they understood the precarious nature of their rule and were resigned to eventually losing control of Gilgit, Baltistan, the Valley, and even Ladakh. But they had hopes for Jammu. They harbored a desire to wrest control of Jammu and carry on their family legacy from there.[20] This provides the background and reasoning for the Dogra regime's focus on the Jammu region and their sudden acknowledgment of it being an artificial state. It was the only place where they even had a chance to establish their writ. However, if an independent Jammu region was to be ever established under Dogra rule, Muslims would need to be ethnically cleansed.

STATE-SPONSORED SYSTEMATIC EXTERMINATION

The genocide in the Jammu province was pre-planned, well organized, and merciless. As previously mentioned, the killings began in August 1947 and continued until November of that year. The Jammu genocide has in large part slipped through the history books, while there are even some that attempt to lessen the severity of the violence or question its magnitude. Notwithstanding that, there is widespread consensus by many historians and academics that a grave crime against humanity occurred and that attempts were made to cover it up. And, as will be described, there is even evidence to support the assertion that the killings were orchestrated by the highest levels of the Dogra state.

First, the evidence concerning the Jammu mass killings reveals a clear, systematic policy of ensuring the Muslim community was either pushed into the areas that became Pakistan or wiped out entirely.[21] Kanth claims, "the Muslim subjects from different parts of Jammu province were forcibly displaced by the Dogra Army in a programme of expulsion and murder ...."[22] Ahmad concurs, suggesting that there was a clear Dogra policy to ethnically cleanse the Muslims of Jammu.[23] Other scholars such as Rashid,[24] Naqvi,[25] and Choudhary[26] all write that there was a systematic policy of genocide of Muslims. Snedden is somewhat ambivalent and both attempts to diminish the severity of the crime by questioning official state-sanctioned support for it and acknowledge the killings were "alarming."[27] Then Snedden cites two Quakers who documented the killings of Muslims in Jammu, which were reported by the *Civil & Military Gazette* on December 18, 1947. In that report, seven massacres of Muslims were documented that occurred in Kathua, Akhnoor Bridge, Sambad, Maogaon, Jammu, and Suchetgarh, claiming as many as 70,000 Muslims were butchered.[28]

Lamb asserts that the Dogra regime had openly supported an "anti-Muslim policy" and on a "number of occasions Jammu & Kashmir State Forces [belonging to the Dogra Chieftain] actually crossed over into Pakistan and destroyed villages there ...."[29] Furthermore, in early October 1947, "British observers saw in one such village on the Pakistan side of the border no fewer than 1,700 corpses of slaughtered Muslim men, women and children."[30] Concurring, Khalid Bashir Ahmad writes, "What sets Jammu massacres—for there were many across the region—apart from those in Punjab is the official connivance. From the Prime Minister to Governor to Hindu component of the Dogra Army, everybody in the administration had his hands soaked in blood."[31] Ahmad traces the genocide planning to before the British had even finalized their departure and documents how "arms were being distributed among Hindu communalist groups even as Muslims were ordered to deposit with the government all weapons they possessed. Muslim soldiers in the Maharaja's army too were disarmed."[32] In addition, there were indications of the establishment of weapons and arms training camps for Hindus and Sikhs in Jammu City. For any honest observer, these are clear indications that preparations were in "full swing for organizing bloodbaths" in Jammu.[33]

Poignantly, Rashid asks,

How far then was the violence connected to the idea of bringing about a demographic change in Kashmir? How did the Government of India negotiate between the Muslim and Hindu and Sikh communities during the crisis? The Dogra regime, at the behest of the Indian government, began making arrangements to evacuate Muslims from Jammu in November on the pretext that they were unable to provide protection to them.[34]

These are powerful questions that lead to damning accusations against both the Indian government and Dogra regime. Both as the occupying power in the state of Jammu and Kashmir and the successor power to the British Raj, the Dogra regime had the moral, ethical obligation to protect civilians. Not only did that not happen but the Muslim community were disarmed. And, it seems that was the moment that the Indian government, in collusion with the Maharaja and his Dogra regime, operationalized their plan to remove the Muslims from Jammu. As Rashid goes on to state, "In many ways, this episode of communal violence punctures the narrative of the state as a benign source of order and a rational arbitrator in the atmosphere of 'communal frenzy' during the Partition of 1947."[35] In other words, the Indian state and the Dogra regime colluded in the strategic orchestration of sectarian violence.

Secondly, the "role of Maharaja Hari Singh in fueling communal riots cannot be overlooked. He was responsible for fueling
attacks on Muslims. The Maharaja visited many places and instead
of dousing communal flames he encouraged rioters."[36] Ahmed
mentions eyewitness accounts that claim Maharaja Hari Singh was
personally involved in some killings, having shot three Muslim
Gujjars at Mishriwala.[37] Shahab corroborates the involvement of the
Maharaja in the killings when he "let loose like hounds the contingents of Dogra army, police and Rashtriya Swayamsewak Sangh on
Muslim subjects."[38] As the chief executive of the state, the Maharaja had the power to stop much of the violence. After all, this was
not just a handful of isolated attacks. Hundreds of thousands of
people were killed, and several hundred thousand people were ethnically cleansed and pushed into Pakistan. Violence of this scale
was neither spontaneous nor the product of reprisal attacks organized by disgruntled communities. For that reason, Naqvi squarely
places blame on Maharaja Hari Singh. He says, "Maharaja Hari
Singh's involvement, with the support of the RSS, is evident from a
letter Jawaharlal Nehru wrote to Vallabhbhai Patel on 17 April 1949
(quoted in *Frontline* magazine)."[39] In that damning letter, Jawaharlal Nehru acknowledges that the Maharaja was directly funding
Hindutva fanatic organizations in Jammu responsible for the mass
killings. In other words, radical Hindu fanatics were under the
command of the Maharaja.[40]

Third, the role of Hindutva fascists from the RSS also needs to
be closely scrutinized. Evidence reveals large contingents of radi-
calized RSS Hindu youths were brought into Kashmir. This was
coordinated through the relationship of Maharaja Hari Singh's
wife Tara Devi and Rajguru Swami Sant Dev.[41] Ahmed describes
them both as rabidly Islamophobic, even suggesting Tara Devi was
enamored by the Swami.[42] Initially, the Maharaja disapproved of
his wife's relationship with this yogi charlatan, but eventually he
conceded. In fact, he went so far as to provide him with residency
as an official state guest.[43] Balraj Puri corroborates this and writes
that the RSS leader had close relations with the Maharaja.[44] It does
seem curious as to why and how the Maharaja had a sudden change

of heart. But the answer seems to be in the relationship the Swami had with hordes of RSS extremists, who came from all over India to train alongside Dogra soldiers. Chattha mentions this relationship in several instances, drawing connections between the mass killings and the RSS fanatics.[45] This indicates that the RSS fanatics had a major role in the orchestrated violence and had been groomed for that exact purpose. This would seem to offer some clues as to why the Maharaja had a sudden change of heart concerning an unscrupulous person uncomfortably close to his wife. The Swami provided the Maharaja with the fanatical hordes specifically trained for mass killing, which would enable him to hold Jammu.

Fourth, the involvement of the Indian government in the genocide cannot be ignored. Lamb writes that one of the most conspicuous bits of evidence is the "presence in Kashmir, well before the tribal invasion [from Pakistan], of a battalion of infantry of mountain artillery loaned to the Maharaja Hari Singh by the Sikh Maharaja of Patiala ....".[46] In fact, the Patiala armed forces participated in the Jammu massacres and may well have been present in Kashmir by August 1947. Furthermore, Lamb writes that in theory these Patiala troops were "subordinate to the Commander-in-Chief of the Indian army."[47] This implies that by interfering in Kashmir's internal matters, India violated international law, partition terms, and the rights of Kashmiris. This also means that the presence of the Pakistani tribesmen was a direct response to the killings in Jammu and the arrival of foreign Patiala troops, not the other way around.[48]

Finally, Ahmad squarely puts the blame on an unfortunate combination of factors that includes the radicalism driven by the "RSS ideology, the Hindu and Sikh refugees from Pakistan and the Maharaja's troops [that] had set the stage for the kill."[49] He concludes that Tara Devi, Swami Sant Dev, Prime Minister Mehr Chand Mahajan, Deputy Prime Minister Ram Lal Batra, Governor Chet Ram Chopra, and Hari Singh "inspired and abetted the violence."[50] Concurring, Rashid writes that there is overwhelming evidence to suggest that the RSS were being facilitated by the Maharaja's armed forces.[51]

THE LIVING DEAD

The exact number of people slaughtered in the Jammu genocide is inconclusive, but there is consensus on a range between 237,000 and 500,000 people.[52] When we evaluate the available data, newspaper reports and corroborated eyewitness accounts, a horrifying massacre emerges. Despite that, there is sparse academic work on these mass killings, which requires careful deliberation. Snedden argues that the Jammu massacres "slipped through the cracks of subcontinental history" due to the violence that was happening throughout the British Raj.[53] But that argument is unsatisfactory. Do upwards of 500,000 people simply slip through the cracks? It is important to ask how this genocide was permitted to remain hidden for so long.

To begin, the methodical violence against Muslims primarily began in the regions of Kathua, Reasi, Udhampur, and eastern areas of Jammu. Ahmad acknowledges that there are different versions on the number of Muslims killed in the planned massacres, but insists the number is at least 237,000.[54] Rashid concurs that there is a broad consensus that a crime against humanity took place and that the numbers are staggering—at minimum 237,000 people.[55] Ian Stephens puts the figure at 500,000, writing, "within a period of about eleven weeks starting in August, *systematic savageries*, similar to those already launched in East Panjab and in Patiala and Kapurthala, particularly eliminated the entire Muslim element in the population, amounting to 500,000 people."[56] Chattha writes, "One million Kashmiri Muslim refugees were uprooted and an estimated 250,000–300,000 were massacred in the Jammu region alone in August–October 1947."[57] In addition, *The Times* (London) in its publication dated August 10, 1948, gave the number of exterminated Muslims as 237,000.[58] The newspaper further stated that "by all the forces of the Dogra State, headed by the Maharaja in person ... this elimination of two-thirds of the Muslims last autumn has entirely changed the present composition of eastern Jammu Province."[59] The "extermination of 237,000 Muslims" in Jammu was raised by Pakistan's representative to the UN, Sir Zafrullah Khan, in the UNSC during its 468th meeting held on February 28, 1950.[60] Sadly, even though the scale of the atrocity was raised at the highest international forum in the world, no action resulted.

Overall, the data reliably suggests that a genocide took place and at least 237,000 Muslims were killed. When including the several hundred thousand Muslims that were pushed out of Jammu, it becomes the single largest displacement in the entire British Raj, clearly intended to alter the geography of the Jammu province. How was it possible to cover this up for so long? Rashid asks, "But why did the 'Jammu massacre' not become inscribed into the collective official memory of the state of Jammu and Kashmir as the 'tribal invasion' was?"[61] Here, two issues are important to isolate. First, the erasure of the mass killings in Jammu was deliberate. This was done by downgrading the seriousness of the violence or positioning it in the frame of "violence and counter-violence," a framing intended to somehow rationalize the violence and reduce its brutality. Second, the image of India as a secular, non-communal, and pluralistic society made it deflect accusations of ethnic cleansing.

To characterize the mass killings in Jammu as retributive violence betrays the organized nature of the genocide and political/ideological motivations of the Dogras. Mahajan justifies the violence as reprisals by displaced Sikhs and Hindus, who arrived in droves to Jammu City. Undoubtedly, crimes were committed by all sides, but to whitewash the seriousness of the Jammu massacres in the framing of retributive violence is illogical and unfounded.[62] To do so leaves many questions unanswered, especially since exact figures are not known on how many non-Muslims moved to Jammu and participated in the atrocities. In fact, no one has put forward any evidence to corroborate tales of persecution of non-Muslim minorities in the areas liberated from the Dogra regime. Moreover, as the areas of the state of Jammu and Kashmir that were liberated from the Dogra regime, namely Gilgit-Baltistan and Azad Kashmir, were almost entirely Muslim, the number of non-Muslims uprooted in these areas was negligible according to the Census of India of 1941.[63]

Ahmad and Chattha acknowledge the role of Hindu and Sikh migrants in contributing to anti-Muslim sentiment but argue that this does not explain the magnitude, scope, or methodical level of the violence.[64] Rashid differs and suggests there is no hard evidence that displaced Hindus or Sikhs perpetrated organized violence against Muslims.[65] Rashid specifically critiques this line of reasoning by stating that it defies logic to frame the murder of so many people in such a coordinated way as "action and reaction." Rashid argues that the intentional disappearance of the Jammu massacres is "disturbing" and fits the propagation of a false narrative in which India was seen to represent a secular, non-communal, and multi-ethnic entity unable to commit this kind of violence.[66] The policy of ethnic cleansing and wiping out the Muslim population directly contradicted the promotion of a secular, universalist Indian narrative. It conflicted with the ways Indians were caricaturing the Pakistan movement as religious bigotry. Here, it is important to emphasize the role of Islamophobic tropes that are utilized in the demonization process that make such mass murder possible. Butalia argues that prior to the Jammu massacres there was a longstanding process of demonization that considered Muslims to be filthier than dogs.[67] Even Mahajan, while loosely acknowledging that crimes took place against Muslims, frames them as reprisals for what allegedly happened in Pakistan, including threatening statements against the Maharaja broadcast on Radio Pakistan. "Every time one of these leaders issued a sharp statement from Pakistan radio, firing on Muslim neighborhoods intensified."[68] However, to explain the mass ethnic cleansing and murder of so many in this way is not supported by the demographic evidence. Especially since it ignores the role that Islamophobia played in justifying the killings. Bhasin courageously acknowledges this factor when he vividly describes how "the Rashtriya Swayamsevak Sangh (RSS) played a key role in the killings" and that most of the gruesome pogroms were "planned and executed by the RSS."[69]

Individuals responsible for this crime against humanity would do everything in their power to prevent those stories from emerging.[70] Without question, those responsible certainly did not want to be held accountable, to allow such stories to emerge, or to provoke defiance in the oppressed populace. For that reason, they wished to stop the stories, erase memories, and obfuscate reality. And it seems that the entire Indian government at the time was complicit in hiding the massacre or lessening its seriousness.

DEMOGRAPHIC CHANGE

Those who planned and executed the genocide and forced migration of Muslims from Jammu had succeeded in their design. The demography of post-1947 Jammu province was significantly changed. As Ahmad writes, "in areas where Muslims were in the majority they were reduced to negligible minority and there were villages which remained uninhabited for years. The fall in the proportion of Muslim population was phenomenal in urban areas compared to rural areas."[71] In the urban Udhampur district we see a fall of 1757 per 10,000 (17.57%) from 2252 in 1941 to only 495 in 1961 ... In urban Jammu district, the fall was recorded by 1781 per 10,000 (17.81%) from 3213 in 1941 to 1432 in 1961. The urban Kathua district represented a worse scenario with Muslim population ratio decreasing by 2887 per 10,000 (28.87%) from 3114 in 1941 to only 227 in 1961. The rural Jammu district was the worst hit. The proportion of Muslim population here fell by 2972 per 10,000 (29.72%) between 1941 and 1961.[72]

Concurring, Chattha states that, according to the available evidence, "the Hindu Dogra state authorities' aim was to change the demographic composition of the region by expelling the Muslim population."[73] Chattha cites the 1961 Census of India, comparing it to the 1941 Census of India, to ascertain the extent of the depopulation of the Muslim population in the Jammu province. For instance, in the Jammu province about 123 villages were "completely depopulated," while the decrease in the number of Muslims in Jammu district alone was over 100,000. Here Muslims numbered 158,630 and comprised 37 percent of the total population of 428,719 in the year 1941, and in the year 1961, they numbered only 51,690 and comprised only 10 percent of the total population of 516,932.[74]

Furthermore, the district of Kathua "lost" nearly half of its Muslim population.[75] Following the massacre, the Jammu province had now become a Hindu-majority province. For that reason, the 1947 Jammu violence may be reasonably characterized as a genocide led by Islamophobia and engineered to ensure the dominance of Dogra rule.

CONCLUSION

The magnitude of the Jammu genocide cannot be denied. Menon has described such gruesome violence during the last days of the British Raj.[76] Nearly a quarter of a million dead—at a minimum—and at least half a million pushed into Pakistan, with countless millions more scarred across generations, completely altering the ethnic composition of the Jammu province. The genocide transformed a Muslim-majority area into a Muslim-minority area. With all that happened, it is inconceivable how this tragedy of such monumental proportions was never officially recorded by authorities in Kashmir or in India. The framing of a "good" secular, cosmopolitan India, and a "bad" Muslim Pakistan, as well as the violence/counter-violence narrative and genocide denial by the perpetrators of the violence and their enablers, has contributed to its erasure. Here, the role of Islamophobia is also important to acknowledge. Would it have been possible to erase this level of mass killings if the victims were not Muslim? Certainly, Islamophobia played a major role in erasing the killings of Muslims, and more scholarly work needs to be done on this.

Secondly, what this chapter aimed to establish was that the Jammu massacres were systematic, organized, and merciless. They were overseen by the Dogra army led by the Maharaja, who colluded with racist and fanatical Hindutva RSS elements. Also, there is considerable evidence to conclude that the Indian state supported, even if it did not participate in directly, the demographic change. As Rashid mentions, both the Dogra regime and the Indian state had responsibilities to protect people and that did not happen.[77] Third, the Jammu massacres were a crime against humanity in which at least

237,000 Muslims were killed. Much more rigorous academic work needs to be done to uncover this genocide in its full ugliness.

While Muslims were a majority in the region, they were disempowered, divided, and terrified. They were simply unable to conceive of and prepare for the massacres that were being planned for them, and they had "no answer to state sponsored violence. The elite among them were migrating to Pakistan and their leadership was in jail."[78] Ghulam Abbas, the president of the Muslim Conference, was imprisoned by Maharaja Hari Singh in October 1946, and the Muslims of Jammu had no other leaders to take his place.[79] Ahmad suggests that had "Abbas been there perhaps it might have generated confidence among Muslims to stay put. The rest of the Muslim Conference leadership simply disappeared from the scene and left the panicky Muslim population in the lurch."[80] Snedden concurs that with "Abbas [Ghulam Abbas—Head of Muslim Conference] prevented from influencing or leading Jammu Muslims, anti-Muslim elements, including the RSS and disgruntled Hindu and Sikh refugees, were able to harry Muslims in eastern Jammu Province virtually unhindered and with little publicity."[81] The ongoing ramifications of this decapitation of the Muslim leadership were the devastation of the Muslim community.

5

The Myth of Partition

Language, rather than being abstract, is tangible, perceptible, and concrete—particularly in its impact. Its influence leads to the construction of discourses, framing of narratives, and shaping of minds. Words, after all, are a form of ownership, which contain rooted, unspoken ideas and concepts. Or, as Fairclough describes the relationship of power *behind* a particular discourse.[1] Similarly, language and its accompanying frameworks help us to understand an important moment in the historiography of the British Raj; the "1947 partition," which led to the emergence of the two new nation-states—Pakistan and India.[2]

With widespread recognition, the term partition has become commonplace in everyday language, borne of thousands of bits of information in the form of films, books, journals, magazines, articles—even comedy shows.[3] To this day, several decades after the British Raj, the partition is spoken of in irresponsible and even surreal ways. The term is often used to explain away acts of violence. Such framing arguably facilitates violence and stalls peace efforts. In fact, many Indian intellectuals have argued that partition has had a monumental impact on the Indian mentality—imperiling relations with Muslims in India, Pakistan, and Kashmir.[4] The late Indian journalist Kuldip Nayar directly said as much to me when he said, "India will never accept another partition."[5] Interestingly, partition is not understood in this way in Pakistan, that is, the cutting up of the country, even though the majority of those who migrated, and those killed, were traveling from India to Pakistan.[6] And, this should not be surprising since the areas that became Pakistan always had a very small non-Muslim minority. Hence, to uncover this pathology of partition and how it relates to denying Kashmiri agency, I explore and question how the concept of the partition was weaponized. Moreover, how does the weaponization of the term partition suppress indigenous Kashmiri agency? Relatedly, I explore if the conceptualization of the partition was manufactured to suit vested ideological interests, pursue hegemonic designs, and justify the dispossession of Kashmir.

Consequently, this chapter takes a new approach to scrutinizing the Kashmir conflict by deconstructing the idea of the partition and its related concept of "one India." This is important because there is compelling evidence for a deliberate attempt by modern Indian historiography, nudged by Hindutva ideologues, to appropriate Kashmiri history—and other alternative identities such as Pakistan—in order to make it fit into a carefully crafted idea of what India is. This is done to delegitimize and undermine attempts to develop alternative identities—whether nationalist Kashmiri, Sikh, or faith-based nationalism such as in Pakistan. Hence, resistance to this monolithic and appropriating Indian imaginary is the catalyst for the acrimony. Neither Pakistan nor individual ethnicities, such as Kashmiris, Khalistanis, Nepali, Balochi, or Pukhtoon, identify as Indians, which irks the Hindutva ideologues and their supporters. The imaginary idea of a monolithic India was gaining traction in the last years of the British Raj but was not accepted by several ethnic groups. Hence, behind the erasing of Kashmiri identity—or any alternative identity—is a fear of exposure of the artificial construction of the hegemonic Indian imaginary.

Lastly, by deconstructing the conceptualization of partition and unraveling those embedded ideas, this chapter demonstrates how demonizing narratives justify the dispossession of Kashmir. Yet, this is not gratuitous. There is a sophisticated process involved in the perpetuation of what I describe as the partition industry. This encompasses three intersecting variables: 1) myth; 2) demonization; and 3) dispossession. Altogether, each variable of the partition industry interconnects to deny Kashmir agency, to demonize it, and then erase this identity in order to possess it. So, in order to uncover the workings of the partition industry, this chapter begins by examining the last days of the British Raj, during which questions of partition became overwhelming. What was being partitioned? What is a nation? Was India a country? Looking closely, this brings forth a contentious assertion: There was no partition of India in 1947. Instead, the British Raj was divided, creating two political entities—India and Pakistan—led by dominant and competing identities/ideological trajectories.[7]

Thereafter, this chapter describes how those contesting narratives came to the forefront but focuses on the Hindutva social imaginary and its key defining characteristic—namely, myth. This includes writing false history, claiming a monolithic ancient India, and appropriating the Indus civilization and ancient Kashmir. Second, the partition industry indulges in demonization of Islam and Muslims and, consequently, erases competing historiography. That demonization is furthered by painting a perennial battle between Hindu and Muslim communities, which condemns the latter as violent marauders who invaded India and tore it apart, and want to split it again, that is, through control of Kashmir. For that reason, Muslims must be annihilated unless they return to Hinduism, which Hindutva fascists insist are the original roots of everyone in the British Raj. Third, the partition industry works to justify the dispossession of Kashmir by disregarding/erasing the primary ethnic religious demographic—the Kashmiri Muslim. Together, this chapter deconstructs those unspoken ideas, concepts, and discourses that form the ideological foundation from which the word partition becomes imaginable, and explains how it is weaponized into the partition industry to deny Kashmiri agency.

DECONSTRUCTING PARTITION

To begin, all the ostensible familiarity with the term partition, and the breadth of its use, masks bewilderment. Many have uncritically accepted the term, along with its accompanying frames, without scrutiny. Consequently, that has given credence to many presumptuous ideas, such as how the term partition may be used to reflect the idea of a monolithic India torn asunder by foreign invaders, or the Hindutva-propagated myth of a single Indian nation divided by Muslims. This myth goes on to denigrate those who refuse to accept one India as separatists, anti-nationals, or, worse, terrorists. Essentially, all those who wish to choose an alternative identity are accused of aspiring to carve up an imaginary Mother India. The imagery of a sacrosanct Mother India, which was violated by partition, is central to understand how the term is weaponized to mock, exclude, demonize, or even dispossess others, especially in Kashmir. Importantly, this weaponization of dissent has occurred in other contexts, such as with Sikhs, Dalits, and Nagas.[8]

Granted, part of contestation surrounding the term partition is because privileged individuals—especially writers and academics—who were uprooted during the splintering of the British Raj, use this term to express personal loss. Many of these elites, whether Hindu, Muslim, or Sikh, were among those migrating to either India or Pakistan, and came to occupy critical positions in politics, education, culture, and music.[9] And, it was this small elite minority—on both sides—for whom partition undeniably meant suffering or loss. Mistakenly, perhaps inadvertently, many of those writers wrote as if their own specific experiences of loss reflect the majority indigenous sentiment. Does the Kashmiri feel this way? Or, how about the Sindhi, Baloch, Pushtoon, or Brahui? What about the Hazara, Gilgitis, and Baltis? Pandey acknowledges that shortcoming but does not go into detail.[10] That is because the idea that India was divided has almost always gone unchallenged. In that vein, Kashmir, too, has often been referred to as the "unfinished business of partition"—another misnomer.[11]

Surprisingly, even though the word partition carries so little clarifying weight, it has become the explanatory variable. The word of all words, so to speak, meant to explain all the complex antagonisms between India, Pakistan, and Kashmir. A guilt-infested narrative blaming Muslims for leaving and, worse, dividing India. Now Kashmiris are accused of wishing to enact further partition. This accusation is constantly weaponized. For that reason, Indian Home Minister Amit Shah used the memory of partition to rationalize the doing away of Article 370.[12] Absurdly, many Indian Muslims often use the partition to evoke hostility to Pakistan, and its people and genesis—even blaming their suffering in India on it.[13] Recently, Prime Minister Modi inaugurated a new national day in India known as Partition Horrors Remembrance Day,[14] which coincides with Pakistan's Independence Day on August 14, 1947. To reiterate, in 2011, at the annual Kashmiri Conference in Washington, DC, organized by World Kashmir Awareness Forum, a respected Indian journalist, Kuldip Nayar, told me that "India will never accept another partition."[15] This meant there can be no shifting of borders to resolve the Kashmir dispute. I responded by telling him there was no partition and we "Kashmiris are not Indian."

Prime Minister Modi, when questioned on rising chaos throughout India as a result of the discriminatory Citizenship Amendment Act (CAA)—which denaturalized millions of Indian Muslim citizens—shifted focus by asking people to instead protest against Pakistan and its crimes during the partition.[16] Looking closely, there is a pathology fueling this vitriol, leading to the almost constant reference to Pakistan no matter what is happening inside India—and then, directly or by implication, partition is brought up. In this way, India deflects the issue of Kashmir, by sandwiching it between India–Pakistan relations. Examination of the partition industry allows us to begin to unravel this pattern that continues today.

THE LAST DAYS OF THE BRITISH RAJ
AND CONTESTED IDENTITIES

When calls for the British to leave its South Asian dominion were reverberating everywhere, a pointed question was raised: "Independence for whom?"[17] In other words, what does independence mean and who qualifies for it? At that time, several politically organized nationalist communities emerged, advocating for their own constituencies. This included movements such as Pukhtoon, Baloch, Sindhi, Tamil, Marathi, Punjabi, and Bengali nationalists. Also, there were religious fundamentalist organizations, such as the Hindu fundamentalist RSS.[18] At the forefront were two political/ideological organizations that canvassed for a multi-ethnic identity. Namely, the All Indian National Congress (AINC) (soon after to become the

Indian National Congress) and the Muslim League—a multi-ethnic, multi-denominational religiously inspired movement.

Similarly, as mentioned previously, there was the issue of the 565 semi-independent princely states—Kashmir being the largest—as the British power in South Asia was ending. Each of those princely states, for all intents and purposes, had their own unique culture, language, and history.[19] It is clear that during the last days of the British Raj there was a contest surrounding identity. There was vibrant debate, and little agreement, on what India, Pakistan, and even Hindu or Muslim meant. It is this ideological contestation where the roots of acrimony in the region emerge. Especially since the emergence of the Hindutva Indian social imaginary with Savarkar in the late nineteenth century, which developed as a sweeping, all-encompassing narrative denying other identities.[20] Perceptibly, the British colonizers recognized the artificiality of imposing this narrative on all. Accepting it amounted to painting diverse communities and identities with a so-called Indian brush. Yet, post-colonial Indian writers and intellectuals—whether Congress or Hindutva—persisted to the point of outright dishonesty to claim a Greater India all the way to Indonesia.[21] That was necessary for them, since only by creating a false imaginary of India could the Indian intelligentsia claim to demand its establishment as an independent state or, later, lament its partition. That post-colonial Indian identity would deny variations in Muslim identity and the diversity of communities in the region.[22]

The rise of a monolithic Hindutva social imaginary becomes understandable during the end of the British Raj. Adamant on inheriting the British Raj, the Hindutva movement decried the multiplicity of ethnic identities that wished to carve out their own territories. In fact, post-colonial Indian political leaders of all hues were adamant on subsuming everything under their own expansive social imaginary. In particular, the demand for a separate Muslim homeland in the Muslim-majority provinces was resented since this offered a direct assault on their monopoly of power, privilege, and identity. "How can there be a Pakistan, when India is one country?" they would argue. But was it ever? How do millions of people without a mutually intelligible language communicate? The customs, culture, and day-to-day living were so vastly different. Still, the Hindutva social imaginary carefully constructed an ideal of India and what it means to be Indian—and by implication, Hindu. In other words, in order to substantiate their claims of sovereignty and later to bewail the division of Mother India, she must be created. And that creation emerges through the prism of Hindutva teaching. Thereafter, once the ideal of Mother India was created, its supposed denigration through partition had to be perceived as an outrage. That denigration was done by the partition—which it is alleged was initiated by Muslims. Then this narrative goes on to embellish Hindu–Muslim antagonism as perennial. In the context of this narrative, the presentation of Kashmiris as now desiring to violate Mother India again by asking for another separation is framed as a similar outrage. This perspective required the "othering" of the Muslim communities and various historical Muslim empires that came to inhabit the vast expanse of land today known as India.[23] It is in this background that the weaponization of the term partition occurs.

To further understand this, consider the formation of the AINC in 1885. There, the seeds of India's quest for independence were planted. The founder of the AINC was not an ethnic Indian per se, but a decorated British civil servant named Allan Hume.[24] He, and a small group of wealthy, elitist Parsi, Brahmans, and Englishmen, among others, created the AINC to negotiate better salaries, positions, and privileges.[25] Eventually, that organization transformed into the Indian National Congress that we have today. Nevertheless, at its inception, the AINC was not opposed to British overlordship. On the contrary, it was intricately connected to British imperial authority. Essentially, it was formed only to negotiate and distribute the perks of colonialism among loyal patrons of the British Raj.

During the last decades of the British Raj, the AINC changed. It transformed to ostensibly resist British supremacy. When it became clear that the British were quitting their South Asian territories, power was up for grabs. Realizing that, the AINC reinvented itself as a vehicle for India's emancipation. This effort was largely led by Mohandas Gandhi and Jawaharlal Nehru. Eventually, both of them joined the AINC party and altered it to appear more representative of the Hindu community. That led to serious disapproval from several minority communities, especially Muslims, as it seemed discriminatory and a signal towards rising majoritarian impulses. Unsurprisingly, Muhammad Ali Jinnah—the eventual leader of the Muslim League—left the AINC party, presciently realizing that Hindu majoritarianism would ultimately have its way in India.[26] Such concern was not unfounded, as there was always a deep suspicion by several major minority organizations, including Muslim, Christian, Sikh, Jain, Dalit, or Buddhists, that the country's new direction was problematic. At issue was whether those representing the majority ethnic/religious demographic in the British Raj—the Hindu—had a genuine commitment to the rule of law, democracy, human rights, and protection for minority rights. Hansen argues that democracy in India has never really taken root.[27] In caste-ridden India, not only Muslims but Dalits, Buddhists, and other minorities feared inequality, and therefore understandably sought assurances. Those were not forthcoming, which led to the emergence of the demand for Pakistan for Muslims.[28]

There were several valid accusations against the AINC: that it was subservient to British power; that it was elitist; and that it was Brahman or high-caste dominated and aloof.[29] The AINC was criticized most vociferously as being out of touch with the common people.[30] Of course, the entire idea of championing the common people and equality is something alien to caste-ridden Hinduism wherein inequality is normalized. So, while there were legitimate criticisms against the AINC for being elitist, the AINC used the rhetoric of the common people to attract the masses. It worked, and their membership skyrocketed. At the same time, the AINC party began to target British authority and launched the "Quit India" movement. The British colonial power responded with calculated ferocity and began to openly question the very existence of India, even going so far as to mock those who called for it: Winston Churchill was quoted to have said India is "no more a country than the equator."[31]

James Rennel wrote, in his memoirs of the Mughal Empire, "There is no known history of Hindoostan (that rests on the foundation of Hindu materials or records) extant, before the period of the Mahomedan conquests."[32] Concurring, Mill, in his magisterial six-volume work entitled *The History of British India*, wrote, "it is acknowledged on all hands that no historical composition whatever appears to have existed in the literature of the Hindus."[33] Mosley, too, acknowledges this ambiguity when considering the Indian movement for self-determination by asking, "independence for whom? And in what circumstances? India at the end of the war was a country divided ...."[34] Yet, more accurately, it was not a country at all. As Ambedkar said, "to know India was to forget that there is such a thing as India."[35] Mosley goes on to describe the different languages, religions, and customs of the people of India, yet states politically it was run by two opposing camps—the Congress and the Muslim League, with the British at top.[36] What is important to highlight is that the question "what is India?" grew more pressing as a reaction to British mockery of demands for Indian independence.

The debate from all sides as to what India is leads to the questions of how and why one could lament the partition of something that did not exist. As described, many competing intellectual/ideological trajectories, both ethno-nationalist and religious, surfaced during the last days of the British Raj—each advocating for their own imagined community. Among them, the Hindutva imaginary deserves closer examination. It advocated for a monolithic united India that manufactured a new ethno-nationalist Hindu hegemony that worked with the British, while publicly denigrating them. Similarly, the AINC party subscribed to this Hindutva ethos though operated under a veneer of democracy and pluralism.[37] Essentially, Indian Congress leaders subscribed to Hindutva ideas in lukewarm fashion and did nothing to counter the supremacist ideas embedded within them. Instinctively, the rise of a monolithic Indian imaginary, with its corresponding history, was seen by the Muslim League and the Muslim Conference in Kashmir as a power move that could lead to their annihilation.[38]

HINDUTVA SOCIAL IMAGINARY

Taylor describes a social imaginary as "the ways people imagine their social existence, how they fit together with others, how things go on between them and their fellows, the expectations that are normally met, and the deeper normative notions and images that underlie these expectations."[39] It is, for all intents and purposes, a binding creed that makes existence intelligible for social actors. With this concept in mind, this section explores the nature of the Hindutva social imaginary. To do that, it scrutinizes three inter-related variables: 1) the meaning of social imaginaries; 2) the origins, growth, development, and eventual widespread usage of Hindutva imagery, symbols, and ideology to manufacture post-colonial India; and 3) the weaponization of that narrative to demonize and dispossess, especially relevant to Kashmir, but also to other competing identities. To reiterate, this process of Hindutva mythmaking began in the mid-1920s as a reaction to British dismissal of any such thing as single country called India. From there onwards, this imaginary played a critical part in the invention of identity in India.

Taylor describes a social imaginary—as distinct from social theory—on the basis of three conditions. First, the emphasis is on ordinary people and manner in which they "imagine" their surroundings—especially by way of images, stories, and legends. Second, social imaginaries are shared by large groups of people, if not the whole society. Third, the social imaginary leads to shared practices and a widely shared sense of legitimacy. Of course, a social imaginary is complex. It is the collective expression of norms—the way things should be done—that are often unspoken but have great resonance. In this way, Taylor describes it as "the very nature of what contemporary philosophers have described as the background."[40] It is in fact that largely unstructured and inarticulate understanding of our whole situation, within which particular features of our world show up for us in the sense they have. Importantly, it need not be rational, logical, or even sensible. It just is.

All social imaginaries consist of a repertory—or the collective actions at the disposal of a given group of society. Essentially, a repertory is defined as the behavioral and attitudinal norms understood by participants in a given social setting. It is the

> common actions that they know how to undertake, all the way from a general election, involving the whole of society, to knowing how to strike up a polite but uninvolved conversation with a casual group in a reception hall.[41]

Importantly, the relationship between actions, their conceptualization, and the background is not unidirectional. Intelligible action embeds an imaginary for those who experience it. This is how imaginaries become so widespread and embedded into the consciousness.

The Hindutva social imaginary clearly works to determine the way ordinary people imagine their surroundings—the past, present, and future.[42] It uses symbols, stories, and legends to embed specific ideas and invoke certain emotions. By doing so, it attempts to concretize a specific reading of world—of India and Kashmir. The word Hindutva was first coined by Chandranath Basu in his 1892 Bengali work entitled *Hindutva—Hindur Prakrita Itihas* ("Hindutva—An Authentic History").[43] Yet, it was not until the imprisoned Vinayak Damodar Savarkar wrote "The Essentials of Hindutva," in 1923, that the term was popularized in ideological/political ways.[44] Savarkar was in prison in the Andaman Islands, and had written several mercy petitions to the British Crown.[45] He even wrote that he would renounce all his former beliefs and work solely for the British as a loyal servant. Because of that, many of his detractors call him out as a charlatan, while his supporters point out his pleas were merely a tactic employed to escape the hardships of prison life.[46] Nonetheless, it was Savarkar who politicized the meaning and definition of Hindutva.

Importantly, Savarkar's projection of a Hindutva social imaginary was reactionary, focused on "othering," and against perceived slights against the Hindu community.[47] As mentioned previously, the British colonialists were actively working to undermine resistance to their imperial authority. One of the British arguments made was that India as a single, unified socio-cultural unit did not exist. While there was much truth to that statement, it did not justify their colonial presence or negate the idea of self-determination. Nevertheless, Savarkar was insulted at the accusation that there was no India and no such thing as a Hindu.[48] This provides the backdrop from which the term Hindutva originates. It explains why it was conceived and how it was used to create a sense of what it means to be Indian—one that was directly linked to a living land. This is how the process of nation-building in India took an ugly turn. It became spiteful and exclusionary, and demonized those who insisted on alternative identities, such as Sikhs, Kashmiris, Bengalis, or even alternative transnational confessional identities such as the Pakistan movement. Hindutva would target them all. This would play a very important psychological role in deepening antagonism against the idea of partition. In many ways, the Hindutva movement was among the first ways of conceptualizing a local, exclusionary, indigenous Hindu identity, as opposed to a secular, liberal, Westernized one.

Commenting on Savarkar's treatise on Hindutva, Bakhle describes the

> four rhetorical strategies Savarkar employs: the politics of naming, the poetics of the list, the enchantment of territory, and the management and evocation of affect. Through these strategies he names into being a mythic Hindu community, identifies the magical territory it inhabits, and invokes through his enchantment of territory a militant affect of love. Savarkar uses a number of registers in Hindutva, from the theoretical and declamatory to the polemical, but the one he deploys most often is the poetic.[49]

Essentially, Savarkar's militant and fantastical conceptualization of the Hindu *Rashtra* ("nation") denies all other identities. This is how the Hindutva imaginary contributes to animus between the myriad of communities in India, and with Kashmir. As Ratan points out, Hindutva is "a cultural community bound together by a common religion (Hinduism) and veneration for a piece of territory that was both the *Pitrubhumi* (fatherland) and the *Punyabhumi* (holy land). Muslims and Christians were suspect in this view because of their 'foreign origin.'"[50] Most Indian intelligentsia, whether Congress or Hindutva, accepted this rationalization. For that reason, this inaccurate idea has become mainstream in India. As Ambedkar acknowledges, this explanation was needed to counter those who denied India existed and, therefore, did not have a right to self-determination.[51] The irony of this is that what British colonialism did to the peoples in the British Raj, present-day India does to Kashmir: deny their identity, appropriate it, and demonize it at the same time.

THE MYTHS OF HINDUTVA:
FALSE HISTORY AND DEMONIZATION

The myths associated with Hindutva ideology are closely related to Pakistan—hence the partition—and directly linked to denying Kashmiri agency and identity. Hindutva conceptualizes the land of their imagined India as holy and portrays Muslims as wishing to take sacred Hindu land.[52] A part of this is a misleading belief that Muslims tore India apart by creating Pakistan, and now Kashmiri Muslims wish to do it again. Therefore, understanding Hindutva is to investigate its social imaginary or, as Kuruvachira puts it, the "myths of Hindutva."[53] Those myths can be broadly categorized into three thematic areas: firstly, the myth of a Vedic Golden Age; secondly, the myth of eternal Hinduness; thirdly, the myth of Aryans as the original Indians. All three are intricately linked to denigrating the creation of Pakistan and skillfully weaponized to deny Kashmiri Muslim agency, and all have had an undeniable impact on the Indian psyche.

First, Hindutva proponents eulogize an imaginary Vedic Golden Age. As Sampath suggests Savarkar appealed to a fictionalized Hindu past—"one that was imagined and defined by a monolithic Hindu identity, linked geo-culturally to a mythical and ageless Hindu nation."[54] For Savarkar, the Hindu *Rashtra*, or nation, existed beyond the fluctuations, changes, and transformations of antiquity and political power. For that reason, his treatise on Hindutva begins, "when the first Aryans 'settled down' in different parts on the banks of the Indus river ...."[55] Describing this, Thapar says Hindutva ideologues project this concept of a Vedic Golden Age theory as one of the corner stones of their ideology, occurring during the period 1200–600 BC.[56] A "golden age," Thapar further articulates, is designed to be at once "distant and mythical—enough that no one could question the historicity of the era or the values the historian wished to propagate."[57] Arguably, that explains why Savarkar chose to speak of this "magnificent" Hindu past that was violently disrupted by marauding Muslim warriors—even though in the seventh century the majority of the inhabitants of "Sindh," in present-day Pakistan, were Buddhist, not Hindu.[58] Yet, Hindutva ideology rejects historical nuance for superficial, easy-to-believe theories that play on popular stereotypes of Muslim authority. By twisting the historical record of Muslim rulership throughout the region for several hundred years, Hindutva ideologues are nurturing at once a sense of admiration and resentment for Muslims. That is precisely why extreme Hindutva propagandists denigrate Pakistan and then promote absurd assertions of its forcible rejoining with India.[59] This perplexing imaginary is carefully constructed to mix fact with fiction, in ways that are not readily disprovable. By superficial explanations, rejecting historical/archaeological evidence, and ignoring competing historiography and cultural and ethnic heterogeneity, Hindutva propagandists propagate a mythical Vedic Golden Age. Through this, they suppress the right of any community to have their own historiography. This is how it directly impacts Kashmiris.

Using a mythical past to reinvigorate community, as Harris documents, is a time-tested stratagem that fundamentalist trajectories use to facilitate identity construction.[60] This has immense emotive power, especially in a society ridden with class, ethnic, and religious differences. Imagining communities and manufacturing history is a method that is not altogether different from other populist or nativist movements that do so to inspire their communities.[61] This process is not the point of contention. After all, societies should develop some type of camaraderie, as is well understood in the scholarly work on nation-building and state-building. Admittedly, cultural appropriation and usurpation almost inevitably form a part of any nation-building process. However, foregrounding the extremity and particularity of Hindutva ideology is important in the ways it manifests as a post-colonial process. It is in the cultural appropriation of others, denial of another's right to participate in their own exercise of identity construction, and/or by demonizing them for choosing an alternative identity that is problematic. In that denial, erasure, and demonization, cultural violence originates. This is precisely what the Hindutva ideology explicitly demands.[62]

Furthermore, Kuruvachira describes how Vedic culture was an amalgamation of many influences, especially those from the Indus Valley civilization and the Indo-European immigrants, who some say originated from Central Asia and migrated to parts of Northern India.[63] Interestingly enough, the earliest of the Vedic texts, the Rig Veda does not resonate with what is contemporaneously projected as Hindu culture. Instead, it reflects a pastoral and cattle-keeping people. Moreover, the Vedic gods, like Varuna and Indra, are largely absent in the unlimited pantheon of the Hindu deities. Actually, major festivals of the Hindu calendar are based on the grand exploits of Rama and Krishna.[64] Secondly, as Thapar notes, this assertion, that links Vedic culture to Hindu culture, was consciously appropriated to provide what was "thought to be an unbroken, linear history for caste (Brahmin) Hindus,"[65] even though the discovery of the

Indus civilization and its city culture in the 1920s contradicted this theory of linear descent. The cities of the Indus civilization are of an earlier date than the composition of the Vedic corpus— the literature of the Indo-Aryan speaking people—and do not reflect an identity with this later culture. The insistence on a linear history for the Hindus is now the reason for some attempts to take the Vedic culture back in time and identify it with the Indus civilization.[66]

Thus, to believe in a Vedic Age is to take refuge in a myth that has no historical foundation.[67]

Secondly, another belief that Hindutva ideologues promote is the "Myth of Eternal Hinduness." As Ratan writes, the "notion of a unified Hindu identity is troubling in so far as it ignores the fact that Indian archaeologists and historians have for years challenged the idea of Hinduism as a monolithic, Brahmin-dominated religion with a distinct philosophy, iconology and rituals."[68] Initial Western researchers into Hinduism documented this peculiarity. Unlike the Abrahamic faiths of Islam, Christianity, or Judaism, what was called Hinduism "did not profess to have a prophet, church, revealed book, and did not recognize the practice of conversion, but they made little attempt to understand the different sects and religious communities which co-existed within this 'Hindu' fold."[69] And this, in particular, is what is most important to uncover—without any core beliefs, structure, messenger, or book, what does it mean to be a Hindu? This concern is what compelled Hindutva mythmaking and identity construction. Unfortunately, that process of identity construction led, simultaneously, to deliberate cultural appropriation. With the power of the state, it led to hegemony. Also, Hindutva ideologues felt that the cultural assertiveness of other communities was a threat to their imagined India.[70]

Relatedly, the belief in eternal Hinduness is associated with demonization and "othering"—particularly against Muslims, Christians, and Dalits.[71] It demonizes those who are unwilling to subscribe to the belief of eternal Hinduness. By having an alternate view of history, identity, and culture, Muslims in particular are on a direct collision course with Hindutva. Yet, the Hindutva narrative has a particular vehemence directed towards Muslims. This is because many Muslims, understandably, conceptualize their origins and history as outside India proper and this irks the idea of eternal Hinduness. As a result, Hindutva ideologues accuse them of being disloyal, no matter whether indigenous or otherwise. And that disloyalty is rationalized with evidence of partition and the cutting of India into two pieces. Now, these same Muslims, albeit in Kashmir, are demanding their right to self-determination and their own homeland. Herein lay the strange contradiction so powerful in the popular Indian imagination that Muslims are demonized as foreigners, whose presence is a reminder of their cruel historical rule and an affront to the Hindutva fantasy of eternal Hinduness. Simultaneously, the working of the partition industry propagates the "we are all Indian" myth and encourages an undoing of partition to include the very people despised. However, even that is only possible if they should return/reconvert to their ancestral Hindu religion.[72] It is a political process with massive institutional and financial support that coerces Muslims and Christians to return to their allegedly Hindu roots based on the belief of eternal Hinduness.

At the heart of the matter is Hindutva uneasiness with diversity. Their propagandists describe Indian culture as Hindu culture, which is an assertion that utterly belies the massive diversity and plurality of Indian society. Recently, the Indian Consul General in New York outrageously described "Kashmiri culture as Hindu culture," even though 96.4 percent of the Kashmiri Valley heartland is Muslim.[73] Even today, an official Indian government website laughably described the Kashmir Valley as "predominantly Hindu."[74] Eminent academic Audrey Truschke has it right when she writes, "Hindutva has a fact problem ...."[75] Still, they promote the absurd position promoting Hindu culture in Kashmir. Thapar describes this as a form of nationalist historiography that is political rather than scholarly.[76] She says the "who was here first'" argument put forth by those

> claiming to speak on behalf of Aryans, or Dravidians or Austro-Asiatics, or whatever, is historically not viable. Not only are the claims to these identities as being historical and having an immense antiquity untenable, but the paucity of the required evidence to prove this makes it impossible to give answers with any certainty.[77]

Adding to this, Thorat writes that it "will not be an exaggeration to say that the BJP tried to appropriate Dr. B. R. Ambedkar, knowing completely that Ambedkar's views on many issues deviated considerably from the party's ideological position."[78] This was evident when Prime Minister Modi claimed to be "indebted" to Ambedkar for inspiring him to support marginalized segments of Indian society.[79] This appropriation of Buddhist culture, the depressed classes, and all other communities—especially the Muslims—has been done to attempt to concretize the theory of eternal Hinduness, redirect grievances towards an imagined enemy, and present a misleading caricature of supporting the poor, marginalized people. All the while, Hindutva propagandists are entirely in cahoots with the affluent and elites.[80]

Thirdly, another myth associated with the Hindutva social imaginary is that the origins of India begin with the Aryan migration. Or, in other words, the Aryans were the first Indians. Romila Thapar maintains that "Indo-Aryan is in fact a language label, indicating a speech-group of the Indo-European family, and is not a racial term. To refer to the Aryans as a race is therefore inaccurate."[81] Again, Hindutva ideology uses the Aryan migration theory in a political manner. Claiming the original Indians are the descendants of the Aryans directly contradicts their own animosity against Christians and Muslims, whom they denigrate as foreigners. In a way, the Hindutva belief in the Aryan migration theory points to the Aryan Brahmans as foreign, too. This ridicules their own claims of being authentic, indigenous Indians. For that reason, noted Dalit specialist Jyotiba Phule argues that the Sanskrit-speaking Aryan Brahmans are alien to India. Upon arriving, they claimed authority and essentially relegated the indigenous peoples to lower castes—those who were, actually, the rightful inheritors of the land.[82] This is Phule's explanation for the origins of caste hierarchy in India.

For Sampath, Savarkar locates Hindutva as an all-embracing "ideological phantasm of a Hindu identity," which was used "to create a common rallying point."[83] It must be mentioned that contentious debates are still under way on the subject of the Aryan invasion theory. Many scholars have refuted the Hindutva Aryan theory, both through scientific and genetic studies, as well as scriptural studies of the Rig Veda. However, Savarkar seems to believe in the Aryan migration theory which articulates that the migrating Aryan immediately felt a deep sense of belonging when entering Sindh and witnessing the Indus River. At that point, the invading Aryans began to call this land Sapta Sindhu and another part of the land as Bharat-Varsha.[84] Yet again, looking closely we realize another major inconsistency. The lands of Bharat-Varsha and Sapta Sindhu were not the same, nor were the peoples inhabiting the regions. In fact, neither were their language, ethnic stock, food, livelihood, or culture. Even to this day, these regions largely speak different languages, have different cultures, and follow different religions. Linking Sindh with Hind is pure fiction.

The entire edifice of Hindutva propaganda rests on the assumption that the lands of the British Raj, that today consist of several countries and peoples, are a single, unitary socio-cultural unit of *Akhand Bharat*—or, "one India," as they call it.[85] In fact, upon entering the BJP headquarters in Delhi, a massive expansionist map of "Greater India" can clearly be seen that includes Afghanistan, Pakistan, Kashmir, Maldives, Nepal, Bhutan, and Bangladesh.[86] Consequently, the partition of this imagined country is seen as the most grotesque affront to it. As Tanika Sarkar writes, this is all being done to showcase and emphasize Muslims as "alien," and to promote this eternal Hindu–Muslim feud.[87] Naturally, if history is taught and viewed as such, then the partition of their holy land would invite fury. Here, it's important to reiterate how Phule asserts that Indo-Aryan speaking peoples imposed the caste system on society to sanction their power and privilege against the indigenous people of India—the Dalits.[88]

COUNTERING THE HINDUTVA FALLACY

In the seventh century AD, a young Arabian general by the name of Muhammad bin Qasim al Thaqafi, representing the Caliph in Damascus, arrived in the land of Sindh with 6000 soldiers.[89] At that time, the land of Sindh was approximately half of present-day Pakistan, including the important present-day city of Multan. The land of Sindh was ruled by the Chach Dynasty, which had a Brahman king named Raja Dahir, but the majority of inhabitants of the land were Buddhists, not Hindus.[90] Also, it is important to reiterate that the religion described as Brahmanism should not be confused with the later development of Hinduism.[91] And, as Phule argues, the high-caste Brahman relegated other communities to diminutive status in order to establish their own authority.[92] Nevertheless, the majority of the inhabitants of the land of Sindh were Buddhists, who largely welcomed the arrival of the Muslims. Kazi explains this because the Buddhist community were promised relief from the oppression of Raja Dahir.[93]

The descendants of the conquering Umayyad general Muhammad bin Qasim wrote a fascinating Arabic treatise entitled *Tarikh Hind wa Balad Sindh* ("A History of the Lands of Hind and Sindh).[94] Clearly, the author's description of two lands, Hind and Sindh, as not one country, is indicative—why write a treatise describing two lands if it were one and the same? This treatise was later translated into Persian and described as the *Chach-nama* or *Fateh-nama Sindh*. It provides invaluable evidence that directly contradicts the Hindutva and post-colonial Indian narrative of the region. It describes the ancient rulers of Sindh, including the Buddhist Rai Dynasty that preceded the Chach Dynasty. Also, the treatise describes the social mannerisms and customs of the peoples in Sindh during the time of the Muslim conquest. Ultimately, it describes the presence of three communities: first, the Buddhist majority; second, the defeated elite Brahman upper-class; third, the new Muslim sovereigns and their accompanying soldiers. Considering this, how could someone refer to Sindh as a part of India, when they never used such a term to describe themselves? In fact, Sindh is not and has never been a part of India. What is even more strange is that despite these historical facts the Indian national anthem mentions the land of Sindh as its territory even though no part of Sindh is in India. This is deeply telling of the pathology of dispossession and appropriation in the post-colonial Indian psyche.

Similarly, not a single historical document or verifiable text attests to Kashmir being part of historic India. Actually, post-colonial Indian historiographers when rewriting their history imposed the words India, Sanskrit, and Hindu, arguably with cultural hegemonic intent. Deliberately, they mistranslated the word Sindh as India, with its associated connotations, when the evidence to claim this is tenuous.[95] Truschke comments on how Hindutva scholars brazenly invent evidence and then are later called out for the fictitious seal meant to show linkages between the Indus and Vedic civilizations.[96] Moreover, the terms Hind and Hindu are not original Indian words. Actually, even the word India is the British way of saying Hind, which is a distortion of the Persian word *Hind*. This word was adopted by Arabs to describe a land south of the Indus River—certainly not everything around it. Accordingly, the question arises, what did "Indians" call themselves? Actually, there are several answers to that question. And this clearly points to our assertion that there never was one nation called India—until the British arrived.[97] Even the Mughals never referred to their empire as a single country. In a way, believing in one India lumps together disparate ethnic, religious, cultural pantheistic communities into a singularity of sorts as part of a dispossession strategy that Indian intellectuals, with Hindutva proclivities, utilize in post-colonial India's nation-building strategy.

RESISTING DISPOSSESSION: MULTI-NATION THEORY

At the forefront of the ideological contestation in the British Raj were two major rival imaginaries: one that advocated for a two-nation theory—promoted by the Muslim League; the other, a one India/one-nation theory as upheld by the Indian National Congress. Behind both theories are deep assumptions on the region, and intimately different conceptions of freedom. Those advocating for the two-nation theory wanted to carve out their own pluralistic nation-state while being predominantly Muslim. Alternatively, those championing the one-nation or one India theory also claimed plurality but with a Hindu majority. This is the intricate rationale for and against dividing the British Raj and creating two new nation-states—Pakistan and India. And this contestation between these two major intellectual trajectories conjures up the most aggressive posturing. The truth of the matter is that neither is an entirely accurate portrayal of the cultural and social reality in the British Raj. Particularly worrisomely, a great disservice has been done to Muhammad Ali Jinnah—the relentless pioneer who led the Muslim League and articulated the misunderstood/misrepresented two-nation theory.[98] Simply put, he did not subscribe to the one-nation or "we are all Indian" theory, or the imposition of it. Here, Talbot persuasively argues that nations are not self-evident but rather made, and attempts at compelling identity will largely fail.[99]

First, the one-nation theory is propagated by both Hindutva fanatics and even many post-colonial Indian intellectuals who may not be directly associated with Hindutva.[100] It is pervasive, and the field of South Asian studies largely supports this inaccurate assumption, feeding the partition industry. Today, in India, there is widespread agreement that a monolithic India exists, and it was torn asunder by Muslims during the partition—whether as "separatists" or "foreigners."[101] The logic goes that since it was one country then those who wanted Pakistan divided India. Now, these same Muslims in Kashmir want to carve India again. This is how the one-nation/one India argument has embedded a false utopian idea of oneness that demonizes those who struggled for their own identity rights and self-determination, which continues to be promoted by post-colonial Indian historiographers.[102] In this theory, all the people of the British Raj were Indians or one people, which is obviously incorrect by any stretch of the imagination. Unless, of course, people by their own free will and volition accept such a label as Indian, to spread such disinformation is grossly hegemonic and simplistic, and has underhandedly worked to undermine Kashmiri aspirations for self-representation. The entire one-nation theory is nothing more than wishful thinking based on a persuasive ideal of a pluralist India. Of course, there is much to admire about that pluralistic sentiment that ought to be respected, and there certainly were many Indians who genuinely subscribed to that ideal. Today, those voices of inclusion have steadily diminished or have been violently confronted.[103]

The infamous two-nation theory is also a misnomer. Part of the problem with this labeling is that it misconstrues what we are really talking about. The so-called two-nation theory should instead be described as the multi-nation theory as distinct from the one-nation/one India theory. Or, even as faith-based identity rather than cultural identity, as heterogenous Muslim polities conceptualize identity with values, not race. And these distinctions are important.[104] Regardless, the champions of this ideology did not subscribe to the idea that India was a single country. Nor did they identify as political Indians. Indeed, some might have described themselves as cultural Indians, yet that identity did not supersede their faith. In other words, the majority of Muslims in the British Raj chose to give primacy to their faith identity rather than ethnic or sectarian identity. Also, they did not trust the Hindu leadership to honor its commitments to minorities. Consequently, the Muslim League asserted that all who choose to define their primary identity as "Muslims—followers of Islam" should put aside their ethnic sectarian or cultural differences and unite as a single political unit in order to protect their rights. Moreover, the areas that the Muslim League were demanding should become part of their new nation-state called Pakistan were overwhelmingly Muslim. As for those who chose to forsake their own linguistic, ethnic, and religious identity to join a broad-based Indian identity were also within their own rights. Undoubtedly, both occurred. Many Muslims chose an Indian identity, whereas a majority chose an Islamic identity that superseded ethnic, cultural differences.

Interestingly, those subscribing to the two-nation theory have been caricatured as communalists, separatists, and religious chauvinists. Such mislabeling of the two-nation theory contributes to the demonization of Islam, Muslims, and Kashmir. In reality, the British Raj was divided, not India. And there is no legal or moral justification for denying any people the right of self-determination. Alternatively, the one-nation theory has been presented as egalitarian, liberal, secular, and freedom-loving. Both caricatures belie the reality of the situation.

At the heart of the multi-nation theory is a recognition that the British Raj had many nations, and, among them, the Muslims represented a nation, a people, with clearly defined values, principles, ideas, and a corresponding worldview.[105] Why is this important? Because Muslim nationalism was not premised on demonizing any other socio-cultural or religious group—nor should it be. It did not require a monolithic "other," rather it was based on recognizing and foregrounding certain doctrinal, political, cultural, and religious choices.[106] Simply put, it was not a movement that was against India or Hindus. It is not guilty of carving an imaginary Mother India. Nor is it responsible for caste or religious violence in India today. It was motivated by Muslim intelligentsia residing in the British Raj who had a deep sense of pride in their own civilizational ethos.

Yet, those invested in the ideal of one India found the prioritization of a faith-based identity antithetical to their particular secular vision. Immediately, they reacted harshly towards any attempt by minority communities to fashion their own identity. The Pakistan movement advocated a faith-based identity in which ethnic and cultural differences were supposedly meant to be subsumed by a shared religion and worldview, which competed with the well-entrenched post-colonial Hindutva narrative—prodded along by Congress—of "one" India.[107] Yet, post-colonial Indian nationalists and Hindutva ideologues took alternative identities as an existential threat and began to speak of India in mythic ways. The nation was living and, unfortunately, Kashmir was its head, or *mundu*, so obviously then any attempt at violating its sacred boundaries was tantamount to high treason.[108] This is the deep pathology of loss and conflictual identity that the idea of partition elicits to impact the relations between Indian and Kashmiris. For post-colonial India, recognizing distinct identities, such as Kashmir's right to self-determination, poses an existential challenge to the way their identity has been formed.

CONCLUSION

The Hindutva narrative that was propagated during the last days of the British Raj enacts dispossession as an inevitable part of its project. It weaponizes a sense of separation—that never occurred. It imagines a community—the "monolithic and perennial Hindu" community—that did not exist. Then it punishes those that challenge that figment of their imagination. It creates a fictitious narrative of a perennial battle between good and evil that demonizes Islam and Muslims. Worse, many mainstream post-colonial Indian historiographers borrow these racist Hindutva myths. This has led to the alarming demonization of Muslims as those who forcibly converted people, conquered the land, and destroyed Hindu shrines.[109] These poisonous ideas are embedded in the minds of hundreds of millions of people through film, media, and literature. Admittedly, this dishonest narrative is deeply evocative. It builds upon a psychological resentment at thousands of years of perceived subjugation.[110] Even if untrue, there is a tremendous painful, emotive reality at work when dealing with loaded, designations of myth, identity, and self-image. That pain is weaponized to justify both a delegitimating process and dispossession of the Kashmiri Muslim. This narrative becomes further enflamed when intertwined with hyper-nationalism and militarism. That is how the contemporary Hindutva social imaginary functions through the partition industry.

It is from this backdrop that the term partition—and its associated ideas, concepts, and framing—has turned into an industry that continues to manufacture and propagate a false historical reality—one of unity torn asunder through sectarianism—blamed on Muslims. It positions Muslim-led demands for self-determination in Kashmir as repeats of this violence against the sanctity of Indian land. In the face of this perception, the hegemonic imposition of a singular cultural ethos for South Asia can be tackled by recognizing the ethnic and cultural heterogeneity and alternative identities that exist within both India and Kashmir. It is vital to challenge this demonizing narrative, which not only prevents resolution of the ongoing quest for self-determination in the disputed territory of Kashmir—or even acknowledgment that a problem exists—but makes rapprochement between India, Pakistan, and Kashmir near inconceivable.

Subsequently, if one holds any hopes of changing the current unfortunate tense relations between India, Pakistan, and Kashmir, then it would first require a radical new thinking. A realization that partition did not take place in the sense presented by the dominant narrative, and that the ubiquitous Hindutva social imaginary with its falsehoods and half-truths is facilitating war. For that reason, this chapter unequivocally asserts there was no partition of India in 1947. Instead, the British Raj was divided, creating two political entities—India and Pakistan, led by dominant and competing identities/ideological trajectories.[111] And the reality of the British Raj is that it was home to not one nation, or two nations, but many nations. Acceptance of that reality is not meant to be insulting, but enlightening. It would remove animus from the discussion and stop demonizing those who chose an identity other than India.

Instead, many Indian analysts and political commentators rationalize the dispossession of Kashmir, or mock the creation of Pakistan, around metaphors of a recalcitrant child who needs to be disciplined by a father, that is, the Hindu. The father–son metaphor is constantly invoked, in order to impress the power dynamic of Hindu over Muslim as father over son. Yet, in a contradictory twist, another pervasive Hindutva trope describes Muslims as foreign invaders who settled in the lands of Mother India, forcibly converted locals, and, eventually, split the country—and that will not be allowed for Kashmir.[112] Even now, massive state-sponsored pogroms against minorities—Muslims, Christians, and Dalits—are ongoing throughout India. For Indian Muslims, in particular, they are accused of secretly supporting the creation of Pakistan and being disloyal to India. Then, at the same time, Prime Minister Modi refuses to involve third-party mediation in his conflict with Kashmiris or Pakistan on the basis that "we were all one so understand each other well." Pakistanis say they are not Indian, and Hindutva ideologues disagree. Indian Muslims insist they are Indians, and Hindutva ideologues again disagree. Such contradictory, inconsistent viewpoints that are constantly shifting reveal the pathology of hate and the ways the concept of the partition has been weaponized by the Hindutva social imaginary.

Actually, neither India nor Pakistan, culturally or politically, existed as a unity prior to 1947—though Kashmir did.[113] Still, the way the partition industry has been written, spoken of, and used has led to rationalizing dispossession and all kinds of cultural, structural, and direct violence.[114] Defamatory, insulting labels were used not only against dissenting voices such as those leading the Pakistan movement, but for Kashmiris, Sikhs, Christians, and other minorities too. Why should one be penalized for imagining themselves in distinct ways? Actually, this goes to the heart of the matter—the crux of the psychological challenges that make relations between India and Pakistan so fraught with difficulty, and anti-Kashmir antagonism in India so intense. Why do many seemingly reasonable, decent people turn away when Kashmiri identity and rights are mentioned? Hansen attests to this, when writing "most political forces in the country (India), including the mainstream left, have tacitly supported this policy of large-scale, perpetual human rights violation [in Kashmir] in the name of national sovereignty and fending off 'anti-national' forces within the country."[115] In fact, this is what makes Hindutva India so preoccupied with Kashmir—its history, language, race, and people. The deep realization, and lament, that it is not India. And, in response, it foregrounds the inconsistencies/illogic embedded within the Hindutva nation-building ideology to rationalize its policies.[116]

When the British Raj abandoned the jewel in their crown, the world comity of nations witnessed the bloody emergence of two independent political realities in 1947: Pakistan and India.[117] Now, more than 75 years later, much in their antagonistic relationship deserves scrutiny, not least the refusal of Indian historiography to acknowledge alternative identities and Kashmiri identity and self-determination.[118] To start, the demonizing narratives that facilitate violence must be countered. Corroborating this, the great Indian jurist, humanitarian, and thinker Ambedkar wrote a striking analysis of the Pakistan movement, arguing that the regions that would amount to Pakistan are not Indian since wave after wave of invader has forever transformed their genealogy.[119] Again, a careful reading of history, language, and identity and Ambedkar's writings on Jinnah and the Pakistan movement are important to make sense of contested identities and nation-building in the British Raj.[120]

Of course, denying all that, and insisting on characterizing Muslims as home-wreckers feeds the false imaginary that prohibits the maturation of healthy, good neighborliness. The relationship is described as a divorce—with all the bitterness and acrimony that conjures. But, in truth, there was no divorce, no fleeting encounter, and barely a tryst. Out of the several indigenous languages in

Pakistan, only Punjabi is spoken in India, and that, too, a widely divergent dialect vis-à-vis its Indian counterpart. Neither Balochi, Seraiki, Pushto, Sindhi, Brahui, Hindko, Balti, or Gilgiti is native to India.[121] In the same breadth, Gujarati, Marathi, Telegu, Kannada, Tamil, and a host of other Indian languages are not spoken in Pakistan.[122] In the same vein, highlighting the significant diversity between the two nations is not meant to embellish difference. There is much that both India and Pakistan find in common, especially in Punjab. Yet, there are glaring differences—historical, cultural, and religious—that cannot be overlooked. Denying that, and presenting a false imaginary, has done the single greatest harm to addressing the core pathological point of contention between them, and could very well lead to another war over Kashmir.

6

India, Islamophobia, and the Hindutva Playbook

With the emergence of two new, independent nation-states arising from the British Raj in 1947—Pakistan and India—arose profound possibilities for freedom and equality. However, the withdrawal of British paramountcy, while leading to independence for millions, did not improve the situation for Kashmiris. Alongside that conflicted liberty were the corpses of at least 237,000 Muslims killed in Jammu, and several hundred thousand killed elsewhere in the British Raj.[1] Specifically speaking, Kashmiris never had a taste of freedom. Instead, they were thrown into a tussle between the emergent states. As Wirsing writes, "within the complex jurisdictional framework of the British Empire, Kashmir had retained quasi-autonomous status in a feudal arrangement that placed a Hindu Maharaja in control over an overwhelmingly Muslim principality. British paramountcy over Kashmir ... lapsed at their departure."[2] When British supremacy lapsed, who would be the adjudicator between the rights of the people, the Maharaja, and other stakeholders? At that time, the Maharaja toyed with the idea of creating his own independent country, or at least a little fiefdom in Jammu. Yet he was hated by the people. And neither India nor Pakistan accepted such an outcome. In the meanwhile, gruesome violence was occurring throughout Jammu, the stories of which spread far and wide. This infuriated tens of thousands of people inside the disputed state, and especially from the neighboring tribal areas of Pakistan who collectively raised a ragtag group of volunteer fighters. Eventually, this would lead to what has infamously, and misleadingly, been called the "tribal invasion."[3] Importantly, however, had there been no

Jammu massacre—aided and abetted by the Indian government—there would not have been a so-called tribal invasion.

Admittedly, for purposes of brevity, this chapter largely avoids rehashing the considerable scholarly work done on the Kashmir dispute since India sent troops there in 1947. This by no means suggests that the time period from late 1947 until the armed uprising in 1989 was inconsequential. Crucially, the events that transpired during those post-British Raj years are the primary reason the region is on the brink of nuclear war today. Wani (2018) summarizes that epoch as a time when crucial decisions on the "future of Kashmir were taken by Indian and local leadership to the exclusion of the will of the people … by sheer deception."[4] In fact, Sheikh Abdullah was instrumental in disenfranchising the will of the Kashmiri people in hopes to secure his own power over an autonomous state, but soon after regretted his decision.[5] Similarly, Para (2019) mirrors that sentiment by describing how Sheikh Abdullah somewhat duplicitously helped engineer a client–patron relationship between India and the disputed territory of Jammu and Kashmir, only to be thrown in prison.[6] This was after he vigorously defended India's position on Kashmir at the UN. While in prison, Sheikh Abdullah attempted to continue his politics with the formation of the Plebiscite Front—a movement demanding a plebiscite to ascertain the sentiments of the people of Kashmir.[7] Yet, the post-colonial Indian state worked tirelessly to undermine his appeal with Kashmiris by elevating his former deputy head, Ghulam Muhammad Bakshi, who turned on his former friend, initiated treason proceedings against him, and readily obliged India to establish what Wani (2018) describes as a "patronage" state.[8] Similarly, both Kanjwal (2018) and Hussain (2021) corroborate how Bakshi's rule, emboldened with Indian financial support, helped establish the post-colonial Indian state's dominance over Kashmiri lives and property.[9]

In fact, that crucial phase is explained by Zia and Bhat (2019) as turbulent years that initiated a process of disenfranchising Kashmiris.[10] Bose, while not disagreeing, focuses on the Indian state's aversion to allow democracy to flourish in Kashmir, which he claims pushed Kashmiris away from the Indian state.[11] Tariq Ali et al. (2011)[12] and a host of other scholars have written extensively on these critical years between 1947 and 2000, and summarized it as the inability of the post-colonial Indian state to trust Kashmiris. Eventually, the lack of trust and withdrawal of rights would lead Kashmiris to revolt, leading to the short-lived armed uprising during the 1990s.[13] Yet this book shifts focus to concentrate on those foundational events central to the narrative of the post-colonial Indian state, that is, the so-called tribal invasion and accession, then moves on to more recent events with the BJP election victory. By doing so, it uncovers the way the post-colonial Indian state has carefully constructed a narrative based on half-truths and falsehood in order to deny the people of the disputed territory of Jammu and Kashmir their history, identity, rights, and agency.

This chapter begins by scrutinizing the so-called tribal invasion along with the validity of the treaty of accession of Jammu and Kashmir to the Indian Union. Importantly, it clarifies how Islamophobic tropes heightened the believability of a biased narrative that framed Muslim resistance to their occupation as terror. Second, it then introduces the way that the issue of Kashmir was brought to the UN and explains Indian attempts to obfuscate its responsibility of respecting the will of the people. Third, it moves forward to study the most pivotal moment for Islamophobia in India—the BJP electoral victory in 2014 and the weaponization of Hindutva myths.[14] Following that, the BJP ruling elite were unhindered by respect for international law, the Indian constitution, procedural regulations, or ethics of any sort. Consequently, an unbridled and aggressive Islamophobia emerged that continues to terrify the people of Kashmir. Specifically, now, all pretenses to respect the sentiments of the people of Kashmir and win their hearts and minds have been thrown away.[15] India has embarked on a dangerous majoritarian path that will lead nowhere but war. This has reignited the tinderbox of Kashmir in dangerous and, as of yet, unknown ways. Lastly, the final sections look at how Islamophobia is weaponized in India and what Hindutva strategies are being operationalized in Kashmir.

MYTHS: TRIBAL INVASION AND ACCESSION

The tribal invasion refers to the crossing of Kashmir's boundary in October 1947 by Pakistani irregular forces, Pukhtoon tribesmen, and Kashmiri volunteers, who joined hands to fight the Dogra forces, RSS volunteers, and other Indian soldiers. These so-called tribals overwhelmed the combined Indian forces and liberated what is known as Azad Kashmir and Gilgit-Baltistan.[16] Since then, Indian accounts have been replete with condemnations of the "tribal invasion," without recognition of the Jammu massacres or arrival of Indian armed forces into Kashmir before the so-called tribal invasion.[17] As Ahmed writes, "preposterous allegations were made in a feeble attempt to divert attentions away from the Maharaja's ruthless methods of subjugation inflicted on the Kashmiri masses."[18]

Frightened and alarmed at the rapid collapse of the Dogra state as a result of local uprisings and the so-called tribal invasion, Maharaja Hari Singh appealed to India for additional military support. Then, as the Indian narrative goes, they agreed on the condition that he yield the Muslim-majority state of Jammu and Kashmir to India. After reaching this agreement, a "decision to intervene was quickly taken, and with Mountbatten now Governor-General taking official charge of military operations, combat forces were soon on their way."[19] On October 27, the first airborne troops landed at Srinagar just in time to mount a successful defense against the tribal/irregular forces. "Stipulated by the Indian government, as a condition of the military aid granted, was the state's accession to India. That, too, was very rapidly consummated. On the same day that the troops landed in Srinagar, Mountbatten officially accepted the state's accession to India."[20]

Taking a step back, there are several problems with the Indian version of events. On what authority did the Maharaja, without the consent of the majority of people, decide to accede to India's condition? He did not have authority or legitimacy because he was an imposed ruler placed over Kashmir by British mandate, not the indigenous people. And why did Mountbatten accept this accession without consulting the indigenous people of Kashmir? Of course, ethics is of no concern in realpolitik and these moral omissions are reflective of the pattern of British complicity in the abuse of the region. The Indian government's entire narrative rests on their armed intervention being a consequence of the tribal invasion. Yet this narrative relies on the omission of facts: the Indian and Patiala troops already stationed inside Kashmir, and the horrors of the Jammu genocide. Disregarding that, the Indian narrative holds that when the so-called tribal raiders entered into the disputed state, it warranted a response. In explaining its position and actions, the Indian government produced a document called the White Paper on Jammu and Kashmir, which stated, "India's military intervention in Kashmir was undertaken entirely as a reaction to the tribal invasion of the state on 22 of October."[21] Yet there are glaring inconsistencies regarding the tribal invasion and accession.

The manner in which the partition plan was operationalized meant that the "transfer of power ... left ample grounds for suspecting the impartial application of pre-independence rules for integrating the princely states into successor dominions."[22] Wirsing clearly outlines that the Pakistanis were well within their rights to suspect the way the states were being integrated into the new Indian union, and the suppression of the rights of Kashmiris. Second, Lamb highlights the "rapid changeover in the political coloration of key officials in the Maharaja's government that occurred in the preceding months prior to accession."[23] This included the removal of Prime Minister Kak—a Kashmiri Hindu, who was vocally opposed to Kashmir's accession to India—on August 11, 1947.[24] Later, he would even be imprisoned. His replacement was none other than Mehr Chand Mahajan, ally of the Maharaja, who was a known Congress party sympathizer and, in his autobiography, openly spoke of "the urgency of Kashmir's accession to India."[25] Third, there exists damning correspondence between Sardar Patel and Jawaharlal Nehru, replete with concerns of Kashmir's political direction to Pakistan and ways/means to prevent that eventuality. In a letter addressed to Patel on September 27, 1947, Nehru writes, "take some action in this matter to force the pace and to turn events in the right direction ... so as to bring the accession of Kashmir to the Indian Union as rapidly as possible with the cooperation of Shaikh Abdullah."[26] This is clear evidence of official connivance to wrest control of Kashmir away from its primary religious/ethnic demographic.

Still, there is another glaring piece of evidence that undermines the entirety of the Indian narrative on Kashmir—the presence of foreign troops in Kashmir prior to the so-called tribal invasion. Lamb writes of the "presence in Kashmir, well before the tribal invasion, of a battalion of infantry of mountain artillery loaned to the Maharaja Hari Singh by the Sikh Maharaja of Patiala."[27] In fact, the Patiala armed forces had participated in the Jammu genocide and were present in Kashmir by August 1947. Furthermore, Lamb notes that in theory these Patiala troops were "subordinate to the Commander-in-Chief of the Indian army,"[28] which implies that by interfering in Kashmir's internal matters, India violated international law, partition terms, and the rights of Kashmiris. This also means that the presence of the tribesmen was a direct response to the killings in Jammu and arrival of foreign Patiala troops, not the other way around.[29] As Wirsing states, "the contention that India's intervention in Kashmir at the end of October was entirely reactive, unpremeditated and entailed no territorial ambitions whatsoever ... is not worth a moment's consideration."[30]

Therefore, if there was no violation of the sovereignty of the disputed territory by the tribal raiders, then the accession is deemed fraudulent. For that reason, the issue of accession prompts heated debate on whether it was legal and who was the initiator of the violence. Clearly, the presence of foreign troops in Kashmir, prior to the arrival of the so-called tribal invasion, upends the dominant narrative that squarely puts the blame on Pakistan and the tribals. With this often-overlooked evidence the entire narrative changes. Similarly, ignoring the mass killings in Jammu, the imprisonment of anti-Indian Kashmiris—both Muslim and Hindu—in the Maharaja's government, and the focus on "tribal raiders" as "Islamic terrorists," all serves the underlying Islamophobia in India used to deny Kashmir its rights.[31] All of this needs to be overlooked if one is to accept the Indian narrative concerning the tribal raiders and accession. If it is not, then both the Indian leadership and the

British colonialists, who accepted accession without the consent of the people, contributed to this bleeding wound that has caused prolonged misery for the whole region.

Lamb describes Mountbatten as "thoroughly Indian" in outlook and someone who saw "Pakistan as an enemy."[32] Yet this important evidence of bias, prejudice, and whitewashing murder have not been scrutinized by historians documenting the process of accession. Importantly, Sayyid writes persuasively about the knowledge production, systems, and space that Islamophobia and "othering" have snatched away.[33] It is important to consider "how the British Empire administered its rule through 'varying constitutional and political arrangements' across a range of territories, and which were 'connected by a diverse set of strategic, cultural or historical links, rather than by allegiance to Crown or mother country.'"[34] This indicates the level of control and subordination running throughout the British imperial project and which prejudiced the newly formed Pakistan and Kashmiri Muslims, while favoring India.

Lone has written extensively about the illegitimacy of the so-called treaty of accession and considers India's position in Kashmir as one of "unlawful occupation."[35] This, she explains, is particularly true from a perspective of international law.[36] Given this illegitimacy, most Indian discourse surrounding the accession and the tribal invasion is false and misleading. The legal efficacy of the treaty of accession is a serious matter; acceptance of it by the British may be considered morally and legally invalid considering there was no "ratification of accession ... by the Kashmiri populace."[37] Considering this, Ahmed writes that had "Pakistan been any less suspicious of New Delhi's motives, the eventual outcome in Kashmir might have been even less in Pakistan's interest than what actually occurred."[38] Given the British decision to accept the accession, predicated on highhandedness and innate Islamophobia, war was almost inevitable.

WAR, RESISTANCE, AND THE UNITED NATIONS

In late November 1947, fighting was raging in the disputed territory of Jammu and Kashmir between a volunteer force comprised of

Pushtoon tribesman, Kashmiris, and other ethnic Muslims, facing off against the Dogra army, Indian army officers, and RSS fanatics. Ahmad argues that the numbers of Muslim fighters have always been exaggerated. Suhrawardy writes that the irregular soldiers, tribals, and volunteer fighters were nothing more than "a few thousand undisciplined tribesmen, rapidly outnumbered and wholly out-gunned by the Indians with logistical problems, and very poorly led."[39] Despite this imbalance, India panicked. It may have accepted the accession of Kashmir, but the Kashmiri people did not. Bangash documents how news spread to Gilgit that Hari Singh had agreed to accede to India, prompting immediate revolt. Understandably, the Gilgit Scouts raised the Pakistan flag and swiftly defeated the Maha-raja's forces.[40] The rapid advance of Muslim forces was driven by stories of the genocide inflicted on the Muslims of Jammu. India, sensing it would lose control over the entire area, decided to take the matter to the UNSC, taking the initial step in internationalizing the conflict. This step also implied that Kashmir was not a part of India, and that the matter would be decided by a free and fair plebiscite under international oversight. Akbar criticizes Nehru's decision by suggesting that "by referring to the United Nations, Nehru allowed what was legally a domestic Indian problem to become an inter-national issue."[41] Yet, this criticism is bewildering considering it ignores Kashmiris' right to self-determination under international law. The largest democracy in the world refuses to allow Kashmiris to exercise their democratic rights.

Notwithstanding resistance, Nehru took the matter of Kashmir's accession to the UN. This was tactical on his part, since he was not interested in respecting the wishes of the people, but in buying time. On several occasions the Indian government repeated that acces-sion was temporary. Nehru stated, "we have declared that the fate of Kashmir is ultimately to be decided by the people ... we will not, we cannot back out of this pledge. We are prepared when peace, law and order have been established to have a referendum under international auspices like the United Nations."[42] Hollow words were used to cool passions, win over international detractors, and continue to usurp the rights of Kashmiris by promising a freedom that would never come. In fact, ever since Nehru's promise, he has done everything in his power to resist holding a plebiscite in the disputed territory. Bose argues that "India's initial espousal of the conditional accession was far from unqualified. It had been clothed in virtually impenetrable ambiguity from the very outset."[43] The continued dispossession of Kashmiris is an ongoing legacy of this ambiguity.

On January 1, 1948, India called upon the UN to intervene in the disputed territory of Jammu and Kashmir on the grounds the conflict was a threat to international peace and security.[44] India brought the dispute to the Council under Chapter VI, Articles 34 and 35 of the UN Charter. In its complaint, India promised to settle the question of accession of Kashmir in accordance with the wishes of the people, yet only after Pakistan had its armed forces vacate the state and normal conditions returned. In response, Pakistan pointed to the Indian armed forces inside the state and asked them to vacate, arguing that the "presence of Indian armed troops in Kashmir would vitiate the conditions necessary for the people to express their will."[45] At that point, on January 17, 1948, Security Council Resolution 38 was passed, which encouraged both countries to mitigate the atmosphere of hostility.

A few days later, on January 20, 1948, the UNSC passed Resolution 39, which provided for the establishment of a three-member mediatory commission. This commission was designated as the United Nations Commission for India and Pakistan (UNCIP) and expected to investigate the facts pursuant to Article 34 of the Charter.[46] Then, on April 21, 1948, Security Council Resolution 47 recognized that concerns over the accession of Kashmir should be decided through the democratic method of a free and impartial plebiscite.[47] Moreover, it called on Pakistan to withdraw its forces in the disputed territory, and asked India to reduce its own to a minimal level for the maintenance of law and order. India rejected a simultaneous withdrawal proposal and insisted that all of Pakistan's troops should leave first, which Pakistan was unwilling to do. For Pakistan, as Lamb writes, "the territory was a subject of dispute between two nation-states and the issue of its legitimate accession could only be determined on the

basis of an impartial administration of the state and internation-
ally supervised plebiscite."[48] Moreover, while the UNCIP managed
to arrange a ceasefire agreement between both India and Pakistan,
which was signed on January 1, 1949, it was unable to encourage a
mutually agreeable troop withdrawal. As Miller writes, "both countries accepted UNCIP's resolution but with such qualifications as to
vitiate their adherence."[49] In total, 18 UNSC resolutions have been
passed from 1948 until now. The overall gist of the resolutions, and
their mandate, make it clear that the will of the people is paramount.
However, implementation of these resolutions has continually been
hindered, primarily by Indian resistance.

BHARATIYA JANATA PARTY, ISLAMOPHOBIA,
AND HINDUTVA

In the meanwhile, delays to agree on a timetable for withdrawal
of soldiers worked to India's advantage. Zia and Bhat write that
"India concertedly began a policy of legitimizing its government
through holding elections …. The United Nations Security Council
… warned India that the assembly might conflict with its recom-
mendations still *sub judice* and deemed the course of action out
of order."[50] However, this did not prevent India from using elections as public relations stunts to legitimize its rule and project
normalcy. Rhetoric aside, Indians were well aware that Kashmiris
were fuming.[51] Concurring, Schofield writes that a "400,000-strong
crowd, marched to the UN office in Srinagar to handover memo-
randa demanding plebiscite."[52] With all their attempts to hoodwink
the world, India's propaganda came to naught. For that reason, Zia
describes the "fraught era between 1947 and 1989" as "characterized
by undying political aspirations for azadi (independence), a section
seeking alliance with Pakistan, aborted movements for liberation
from India, and Indo-Pak wars."[53] On the other hand, post-colonial
Indian policymakers project this period as normal, only because
they ignore the "suppressed political desires of the Kashmiri people
and how since 1947, political intrigue, arrests and electoral mach-

inations had become the central motif of India's relationship with Kashmiris, until 1989—the year when it came fully undone."[54]

In 1989, Kashmir erupted. People launched a full-scale armed uprising against the Indian state. For India, this was among the most difficult periods in its history. India has no doubts that any referendum would reveal that Kashmiris want India out, so they will never allow a plebiscite to occur. In fact, graffiti of "get out" is spray-painted all over walls in Kashmir. Bose explains Kashmiri disenchantment with India from 1951 onwards as a result of it rigging elections and denying genuine democratic space. By doing so, India has created the oppressive situation in Kashmir in which democracy is denied.[55] However, Bose fails to adequately acknowledge the extent of oppression and brutality, such as the hanging of Kashmiri leader Maqbul Butt in 1984.[56] That was a watershed moment. And India has been desperately trying to rein Kashmir in as a subdued region ever since.

Behind this is the complex, deeply entrenched obstacle towards peace: enforced identity. This is the irrationality of India's infatuation with Kashmir. Imagine someone insisting that you must love them, carry *their* flag, sing *their* songs, and chant *their* anthem. Why? Because they claim to love you. And, if you refuse, at first they will curse you. Then, if you continue to be immune to their charms, they threaten your life. Love me, or else.

THE WEAPONIZATION OF HINDUTVA

Ever since the BJP electoral victory in 2014, India has pursued a policy of distraction through demonization, popularity through victimizing, and power through disenfranchising the powerless. Jaffrelot attributes this to India being an ethnic democracy that has different rules and regulations for the majority community and for minorities.[57] India is fast becoming an apartheid state; nowhere in the world is Islamophobia as dangerously manifest as in India today.[58] This is not just because of the frequency of Islamophobic attacks (a daily occurrence now), the demonizing language, or exclusionary practices that even refuse medical services to ailing

Muslims. Beyond that, the danger of Islamophobia in India is three-fold: 1) institutional support for Islamophobia at the highest political office in the country; 2) no recourse for Indian Muslims to appeal to the police or other legal authorities for meaningful protection; and 3) the scale of its genocidal intent in the disputed territory of Jammu and Kashmir—which increases the likelihood of war with Pakistan and China. Today, it's open season on Muslims in India and Kashmir. It is an unadulterated hatemongering that is demonstrated in the most shocking of ways. This includes well-documented, blatant prejudice and discrimination against Muslims and other minorities that has stripped citizenship from millions of people,[59] demagoguery that threatens to rape dead Muslim women,[60] and lynching of Muslims in broad daylight—with police watching in India.[61] And, in Kashmir, an altogether different kind of settler-colonialism and apartheid system of control has emerged.

This section advances from previous chapters to explore precisely how the Islamophobic Hindutva social imaginary is weaponized to create a sense of victimization among the majority community, which leads to retaliation.[62] Furthermore, it is important to recognize that the reactionary self-projection of the Hindutva social imaginary not only focuses on "othering," but against perceived slights that taunt their historic irrelevancy.[63] At its heart, it is insecure and ashamed, as Truschke explains, being that Hindu victimization by Muslims is a key trajectory in their world.[64] And, it is that shame that has propelled the use of fiction to encourage bravado. Bringing this all together, how has the BJP weaponized Hindutva imaginary to deepen Islamophobia in India? Christophe Jaffrelot clarifies that in India "the strategy of stigmatization and emulation of 'threatening Others' is based on a feeling of vulnerability born of a largely imaginary threat posed by 'aliens,' principally Muslims and Christians."[65] However, "within Hindu nationalist discourse, the 'threatening Other' has historically been the Muslim community ... [and] protecting the 'Hindu nation' against conversion to Islam has, in turn, been of central concern to leading Hindu nationalist organizations."[66] Specifically, the act of protecting the Hindu majority results in criminal acts that have been well documented, and take a grotesque Islamophobic turn. Those criminal acts have political support and include the following: 1) cow vigilantism, also known as *gau rakshak*; 2) *ghar vāpasī*—forced conversion for Muslims and Christians to Hinduism; 3) love jihad—hatred against Muslim males wedding Hindu females; and 4) *Bahu lao, Beti Bachao*—bring a Muslim daughter-in-law and protect your Hindu daughter from rapacious Muslim males. All in all, there is a carefully orchestrated strategy, supported at the highest levels of government, to demonize Islam and Muslims in order to rationalize crimes against them.

First, since the political victory of the BJP in 2014, India has witnessed a new type of brutality by cow vigilante squads.[67] In Hindi, these cow vigilante squads are called *gau rakshaks* or, literally translated, "cow protectors." Hordes of saffron-clad men roam the countryside searching for those who they claim are unlawfully slaughtering cows. Bazian et al. write that

> cow related violence at the hands of vigilantes (gau rakshaks) who take the law into their own hands in the name of "cow protection" is among the leading recorded source of violence against Muslims in India. It has increased annually since Prime Minister Modi took office.[68]

Gangs of Hindutva criminals, after accusing Muslims of disrespecting the cow, unlawful slaughter, or stealing Hindu livestock, lynch them. Human Rights Watch[69] and Amnesty International[70] have all well documented these atrocities, of which there have been hundreds of cases. Pehlu Khan and Junaid Khan are two such cases that received considerable media attention, as their lynching was uploaded onto social media for the world to see.[71] Sadly, the perpetrators of the violence roam free, and the victims' families remain terrified.

In 2017, a Special Investigative report by Reuters uncovered the murky world of Hindutva fanaticism, with special attention to the economics behind cow vigilantism. The report revealed how the cow-theft racket, under the guise of protecting cows, was a huge financial boon for the BJP.[72] The report meticulously detailed how almost every single instance of cow theft was from Muslims, which amounted to 190,000 cattle stolen since 2014.[73] Altogether, the report presented a factual account of the damning reality behind the cow-protection racket, which is intricately tied to further economic disempowerment of the Muslim community in India.

Second, Hindutva propagandists have also launched a sinister campaign that insists Muslims should return/reconvert to their ancestral Hindu religion. The reconversions are a large-scale spectacle, with massive political and grassroots support. Often attended by tens of thousands of people, the forced conversions of Muslims, Christians, and Adivasis to their allegedly Hindu roots and religion is cheered on. With theatricality and pomp, these reconversions are happening with fanfare bordering the absurd. A Hindu priest performs a ceremony that is meant to signify the return of the lost souls to their original Hindu roots, while onlookers chant religious hymns. All this is happening in an atmosphere of fear and coercion, as Arundhati Roy alleges.[74]

As Gupta writes, "Ghar vāpasī has been touted as the return to authentic origins, the starting point, the abode of birth. It produces and enforces notions of a primordial religious identity, whereby all and everyone are declared Hindus. Thus, states Praveen Togadia of the Vishnu Hindu Parishad (VHP): "At one point of time, the entire world was Hindu. There were 700 crore (seven billion) Hindus, and now there are just 100 crores (1 billion)." The shift from the whole world to the Hindu nation is swift, as *ghar vāpasī* denationalizes Islam and Christianity, facilitating their "othering."[75] However, this movement is not just encouraging Muslims, Christians, and Adivasis to become Hindu. It is also passing strict laws to prevent Hindus from becoming Muslim or Christian. This is happening through a bizarre series of anti-conversion laws that penalize through imprisonment or fines someone seeking to convert to either Christianity or Islam. These laws have been passed by six legislatures in Chhattisgarh, Himachal Pradesh, Gujarat, Rajasthan, Madhya Pradesh, Arunachal Pradesh, and Odisha.[76] And the irony of these laws is that government officials are required to personally assess whether or not these conversions are valid or have been made by "force."[77]

It is in that ambiguity that Hindutva ideologues operate to prevent conversion away from Hinduism.

Third, among the most sinister narratives that Hindutva ideologues have launched in India is love jihad. Even the name is embedded with deep Islamophobic tropes of Muslims waging war, here implied to be doing so through romantic liaisons with Hindu women. The love-jihad campaign is almost so absurd as to be unbelievable, but it is precisely the type of demonizing and Islamophobic narrative that Hindutva spreads throughout India.[78] Posters, film, social media, and music all push these messages of a threatening, wily Muslim out to dupe Hindu women unawares. The gullible Hindu girl is attracted to the virile, masculine Muslim, who has a ploy to snare her. Tropes such as this are used then to promote hyper-nationalism and Hindu machismo to save their girls from the cunning Muslims. As Gupta writes, "In actual practice, 'love jihad' was an emotive mythical campaign, a 'delicious' political fantasy, a lethal mobilization strategy, and a vicious crusade—a jihad against love —for political gains in elections" for the BJP.[79]

Gupta writes, "'Love jihad' rests on a series of lies, whereby reckless and venomous generalizations have been made, without concrete proof, of abductions and conversions of Hindu women. Outrageous claims have been made that 30,000 to 300,000 thousand [sic] women have been converted till now."[80] Of course, there is absolutely no truth to these statements. But, as Audrey Truschke writes,

> Hindutva has a fact problem ... the vast majority of their claims about premodern India are incorrect. But their falsehoods about history—many of which center around an imagined Hindu golden age of scientific progress interrupted by Muslim invaders who sought to crush Hindu culture and peoples—serve clear political goals of projecting a modern Hindutva identity as an ancient bulwark of Indian culture and maligning Muslims as the ultimate Other.[81]

Fourth, Hindutva ideologues have also launched the *Bahu Lao, Beti Bachao* campaign, which translates as, "save your daughter and

bring a (Muslim) daughter-in-law." The campaign has the backing
of the state and is openly propagated on news and social media.
While this campaign is closely linked to the concept of love jihad, it
is reversed. It encourages Hindu males to adopt the warlike, martial
traditions of how Muslims have been historically described and
not only save naïve Hindu girls from Muslim paramours but also
wed Muslim girls to bring them into the Indian fold.[82] The ways
and means of its propagation are bordering on encouraging rape
and abduction of Muslim women. This is occurring in the so-called
largest democracy in the world. There is a global veil of silence over
atrocities that are committed on a daily basis.

THE HINDUTVA PLAYBOOK FOR KASHMIR

Within the disputed territory of Jammu and Kashmir, especially
the Valley, the aforementioned Hindutva campaigns do not have
the same effect, due to the Kashmiri Muslim demographic. Therefore, in Kashmir, India's Hindutva fascist movement must pursue
a different strategy. This section describes the Hindutva policy in
Kashmir, which pursues three contradictory, irreconcilable tactics.
And the current Modi-led BJP government plays an integral role in
the unfolding of this three-part process: 1) weaponizing pluralism to
enforce homogenization; 2) utilizing a rhetoric of upholding the law
to apply various punitive measures including mass arrest, cordon
and search operations, and murder. In this way, law is instrumentalized project stability, while increasing militarization and heightening
fear; and 3) claiming to champion freedom of speech, assembly, and
dissent while labeling Kashmiri Muslims who express their voice as
guilty of terror. Further, each of these deceitful stratagems contain
internal dissonances that only add to the Hindutva enigma, which
can only be understood with reference to historical power dynamics
within Kashmir, or to what Simon refers to as "predatory aggression" or "narcissistic bullying."[83] This is precisely what Hindutva
and the RSS fanatics exhibit, designed to further their broader political objectives of disempowerment and pacification of Kashmir. The
connection between Islamophobia and deeper psychological under-

pinnings of inadequacy, covetousness, and desire deserves further exploration.[84]

First, the monolithic Hindutva project is desperate to propagate the seemingly righteous but insincere claim that "we are all the same" or equal. Earlier, we described the Hindutva concept of eternal Hinduness. Yet, in the context of Kashmir, this slightly changes. Under the veneer of universality and equality, BJP playbooks use a type of moralizing to insist that non-Kashmiris should have the same rights in Kashmir as Kashmiris since "are we not all equal?" Such duplicitous ideas are propagated by the BJP to champion universalism but, at the same time, deny Kashmiri agency or smother it under an overbearing, contrived Indian identity. In Shepherd's analysis he cites this as a key component of the BJP narrative.[85] Yet, the manner in which the BJP weaponize a rhetoric of celebrating universal identity that encompasses diversity to deny Kashmiri identity is unique. Recall that in the previous chapter we have explored the practical manifestation of post-colonial Indian intelligentsia's "one-nation" policy. Even if high minded, that idea was unsustainable at the time of independence, and the consequences of its deception are most clearly seen in Kashmir. The insistence of cultural and racial homogeneity—ludicrous in the vast expanse of South Asia, home to several dozen languages, cultures, and ethnicities—is sugarcoated with universalism to secure the moral high ground. This sweet-tongued universalism is really meant to erase Kashmiri Muslim identity, to remind Kashmiris not to be so narrow, myopic, and insular concerning the loss of their language and culture. Then, as they become marginalized in their own communities, Kashmiris are told to celebrate India.

Essentially, Hindutva shrewdly uses a weaponized version of inclusion to stigmatize dissenting voices as bigoted. In this ideological trap, plurality submits to their hegemony, and therein lies the internal duplicity. The Hindutva *modus operandi* in India comprises razing mosques, lynching Muslim traders, and threatening to abduct Muslim women. Simultaneously, it invokes Mohandas Gandhi, calls for peace, and supports enforcing conversion because we are all "one." Or, coercively made into one. In Kashmir, it rationalizes the absence of Muslims in political power and demographic changes by arguing "are we not all Indian?" For instance, take the examples of the primary bank in Jammu and Kashmir, JK Bank, in which one person in the entire board of governors is Kashmiri.[86] Or, take how the entire political leadership is in the hands of non-Kashmiris.[87] Kashmiris who complain of this are mocked as ethnophiles or Islamic bigots. Imagine someone stealing your house and calling you the thief when you protest. This is how Islamophobia in Kashmir undermines Muslims from defending themselves from occupation, humiliation, and cultural theft. This, too, deserves close scrutiny as there is considerable theory on the tendency to enforce homogeneity while ostensibly celebrating inclusion and diversity, such as in the promotion of Catholic nationalism in independent Ireland.[88]

Second, Hindutva propagandists weaponize a narrative of upholding the law to heighten militarization and create a police state in Kashmir. Specifically, the Indian states utilize laws to rationalize their settler-colonial policies in Kashmir and, basically, justify the military occupation. Those five laws are the Public Safety Act (PSA)—which Amnesty International refers to as a "lawless law"[89]— Disturbed Area Act (DAA), Unlawful Activities Prevention Act (UAPA), National Security Act (NSA), and Armed Forces Special Powers Act (AFSPA).[90] Consider the appellation "lawless law," Amnesty International has coined. It does so due to the manner that these security laws are weaponized to remove any laws that would curtail abuse of authority, meant to remove all law. These laws, according to the Indian narrative, create stability. They are necessary to prevent terrorists, often claimed to be from Pakistan, from destabilizing the disputed territory. Henceforth, due to the nature of the terrorists, laws must prioritize security. However, according to Indian sources there are no more than 158 "terrorists" in the entirety of Kashmir.[91] And yet this small number is used to justify wide-scale militarization. Ghosh and Duschinski explore how the Indian occupational state indulges the systematic abuse of law, arguing that

the everyday legality of the preventive detention regime in Kashmir as (is) a means of waging war against political dissidents. We (They) follow the circulation of detainees and their files across multiple legal venues and regimes to show how the counterinsurgency state reinscribes spectacular and terrifying forms of violence through modalities of banal paperwork and iterative performances of the rule of law.[92]

The BJP's Harvard-educated Subramanian Swamy has point-blank declared Muslims as "not equal" in India.[93] This is in clear violation of Article 14 of the Indian Constitution. However, in the BJP's India, the law is not worth the paper it's written on. Its only utility lies in the party's ability to manipulate it. This is evidenced by the Indian government's unilateral, illegal, and unconstitutional abrogation of Articles 370 and 35A,[94] and alteration of the occupied state's domicile law (the Jammu and Kashmir Reorganization [Adaptation of State Laws] Order, 2020) to allow demographic flooding.[95] Hindutva policy flouts Indian laws and uses political skulduggery to justify doing so.

Third, the Hindutva strategy also pays lip service to India's legacy—real or imagined—of secularism, cultural tolerance, and freedom of expression. But, in reality, it seeks to prevent any type of authentic Kashmiri Muslim political participation. In other words, a rhetoric of freedom of speech, expression, and assembly, that is, a democratic ethos, is the macro-level policy that is manipulated to undermine authentic representations of Kashmiri Muslims. This encourages the existence of non-practicing, outwardly non-distinguishable "Muslims" who are propped up as the "ideal" Kashmiri. In other words, Kashmiris cannot chant any Islamically inspired slogans on the grounds that doing so may lead to feelings of exclusivity. But in a Muslim socio-cultural context, God is often invoked in sacred or secular affairs. An authentic reading of the Islamic tradition recognizes the intertwining of sacredness and secularity based on intent. However, the ability of Kashmiri Muslims to express their faith in healthy, productive ways is gone. A case in point is how India has banned Friday prayers in Kashmir due to fear of so-called threats, but what this really reveals is the ways the settler-colonial Indian state wishes to prevent the practice of normative Islam in

Kashmir. Overall, any Kashmiri Muslim who proudly uses Islamic culture or religious vocabulary is seen as "communal," "anti-national," or as supporting "terror."[96] Even pointing out that Kashmir's newly formed local administration is unrepresentative—it includes no Kashmiris![97]—is tantamount to "provocation."[98] Today, calling out such an obviously sectarian policy by the Indian occupation forces now gets one labeled as a "sectarian." Thereafter, Kashmiris may be reprimanded, fired, or imprisoned.[99] Such is the absurd state of affairs in India's occupation of Kashmir.

CONCLUSION

This chapter aimed to deconstruct the certainties that have been peddled by the post-colonial Indian state, dealing with the so-called tribal invasion, the treaty of accession, and the UN's involvement in Kashmir. Moreover, it looked at the ways in which Islamophobia in India is accelerating at an unprecedented pace, especially after the BJP election victory in 2014. It traced the roots of Islamophobia to the Hindutva social imaginary and certain myths that it promotes in its rewriting of history. Actually, the Hindutva social imaginary creates a repertory of meaning that then is propagated throughout society. That repertory includes writing a misleading, false image of historic India and then positioning Muslims as its nemesis, which creates a sense of victimization among the majority community.[100] It is there, in the discourse where the roots of Islamophobia are located, which then contribute to an overall demonizing narrative against Islam and Muslims. This began during the last days of the British Raj but has been steadily intensifying over the years. Naturally, if Muslims are described as licentious home-wreckers who have violated the sanctity of Mother India by "partitioning" her, then it is understandable how people fed this nonsense would develop a hatred—revealing that this hatred is played out (in part) in the manufacture of conflict about women and marriage. But in actuality, as Gupta writes, the Hindutva fanatics escape genuine questions on male chauvinism, ethnic, religious, cultural, and caste differences in India by scapegoating Muslims.[101]

Next, this chapter explained how Hindutva myths are weaponized to justify acts of criminality. Well-organized, Islamophobic campaigns of cow vigilantism (also known as *gau rakshak*), *ghar vāpasī* (forced conversion), 'love jihad' (hatred against Muslim males wedding Hindu females), and the *Bahu Lao, Beti Bachao* movement ("save your daughter and bring a (Muslim) daughter-in-law") are all instances of how the Hindutva social imaginary is weaponized. All in all, there is a carefully orchestrated strategy to vilify Islam and Muslims in order to rationalize crimes against them. However, in Kashmir, the Hindutva strategists follow a different policy for the similar aim of oppressing Kashmiri Muslims through the manipulation of discourse. Ultimately, these Hindutva strategies are three-fold: 1) weaponizing universalism to erase Kashmiri identity; 2) creating "lawless laws" to stifle dissent and subjugate the people; and 3) claiming to champion the democratic ethos but disempowering the life force of Kashmiri Muslim camaraderie. First, this pluralism is instrumentalized to weaken societal solidarity and create a sense of shame in privileging Kashmiri identity. Second, the government will break every rule in the constitution related to minority rights in occupied Kashmir, and doing so by claiming to follow the law. Disgruntled segments of society will be directed to the courts, where their cases will drag on for years in the hope of pacifying the passions that spark revolt and limit blowback. Third, Hindutva Islamophobia wishes to demonize as "fundamentalist" all Muslim social bonding practices or gatherings that provide the necessary cultural capital needed to resist oppression. Essentially, they want to erase what it means to be Kashmiri.

Lastly, there is much insight and merit to Truschke,[102] Gupta,[103] and Chatterji's[104] claims that in the heart of Hindutva is a deep shame, insecurity, and aspiration for manliness. This includes a resentment that areas that were part of the Hindutva imagined idea of India are in Pakistan or Kashmir. There is a resentment that the places and monuments that the world knows of India were a product of Muslim rule and civilization, that is, Kashmiri handicrafts/shawls, the Taj Mahal, and the Red Fort. Rather than take a sense of shared pride in this shared heritage, it is seen as humiliating due to the demonizing narratives Hindutva ideologues have pushed for so long. After all, how can you admire the legacy of those you loath? As mentioned, much of the Islamophobic animus behind the criminality in India is a way for Hindutva fanatics to regain their sense of manhood. A sense of manhood that involves both punishing, lynching, and intimidating minorities in their country and in dominating Kashmir. It is a pity they do not know, or care enough to understand, that real strength does not target the weak, impoverished, and disenfranchised, nor target unarmed, defenseless people. Therefore, at the heart of Hindutva fanatics is not just insecurity, and shame, but cowardice masked by ideological posturing.

7

The "Final Solution":[1]
Abrogation of Articles 370 and 35A

On November 23, 2019, the Indian Consul General in New York, Sandeep Chakraborty, attended a private gathering of Kashmiri Pandits and Indians.[2] During that event, a video was uploaded onto the internet in which the Indian Consul General is seen saying, "I don't know why we don't follow it," as the camera shifts to the abrupt sounds of thunderous approval. "It has happened in the Middle East. If the Israeli people can do it, we can also do it."[3] The appalling comments made by the former Indian Consul General went viral.[4] In it, he was brazenly advocating for ethnically cleansing Kashmiri Muslims from Kashmir, citing how the Israelis drove out Palestinians from their homes and forcibly reclaimed their land. It should be remembered that this private event was held after the abrogation of Articles 370 and 35A where fears of forced demographic change, settler-colonialism, and threats of genocide were already intense. Moreover, in the video, the Indian Consul General explicitly stated that his goal was to rid the disputed territory of Jammu and Kashmir of its indigenous inhabitants and majority community—the Kashmiri Muslims—then repopulate it with Hindus, since Kashmir is Hindu.[5] Looking closely, his description of Kashmir as Hindu was mirroring the official BJP stance which advocated for a "final solution" in Kashmir, a term meant to invoke panic and fear. Even stunned Indian Congress party leaders have asked BJP Indian Home Minister Amit Shah to explain what he meant when he said, "final solution."[6] But he responded only with silence.

Considering the Indian Consul General's rhetoric, this chapter explores the unilateral and undemocratic abrogation of Articles 370 and 35A of the Indian constitution on August 5, 2019. This monumental decision has permanently transformed the geopolitical dynamics of the disputed territory of Jammu and Kashmir, amounting to its annexation by the Indian state. This is in total disregard to UN resolutions and the primary religious/ethnic demographic—Kashmiri Muslims.[7] Now, the Indian state justifies the occupation of the disputed territory by pointing to its own laws—the laws of the occupier. Imagine the absurdity of a colonizing power enforcing its writ on the colonized, then characterizing it as legal and morally sound. In her latest book, Anuradha Bhasin (2022) writes that with the abrogation of Articles 370 and 35A a "democratic architecture for Jammu and Kashmir, built on the foundation of military might and without representation of the people of J&K, was being envisioned"[8]

To explore the significance of the abrogation, this chapter dissects the issue four-fold. First, it provides the background of Articles 370 and 35A, explaining how it was written and under what circumstances it came about. Second, it explains the immediate impact of its abrogation on the Simla Agreement—a treaty between India and Pakistan. Third, it details how the abrogation has led to a flurry of Indian settler-colonial policies in Kashmir operationalized through multiple strategies. Fourth, due to the extreme steps being taken by the extremist Hindutva Indian government, the reputable NGO Genocide Watch, led by Dr. Gregory Stanton, has issued two genocide alerts for Kashmir.[9] The final section scrutinizes the implications of these policies for heightening instability in the region and the ever-increasing likelihood for war. Collectively, India's policies aim to pursue a settler-colonial path in the disputed territory, and its machinations have led to a serious rekindling of regional instability.

ORIGINS OF ARTICLE 370

As previously discussed, the foreign Dogra rule, supported militarily by the British colonial power, was not the legitimate ruler of the disputed territory of Kashmir. And its last presumptive ruler at the time of so-called partition, Maharaja Hari Singh, flouted the agreed rules of partition as he attempted to navigate a way to maintain his fiefdom.[10] India, too, had its own expansionist claims on the territory. In that scenario, India decided to rein in the Maharaja and utilize a handful of Kashmiri opportunists to speak on behalf of the majority community. This was a cynical attempt to give a veneer of legitimacy to India's settler-colonial project in Kashmir. On the one hand, Prime Minister Jawaharlal Nehru of India took the Kashmir matter to the UN and promised to uphold the will of the people. On the other hand, he concurrently began sabotaging his own words by organizing a group of Indians and a tiny, carefully selected group of Kashmiris—handpicked associates of Sheikh Abdullah—to void the plebiscite.[11]

As Noorani writes, "Article 370 was discussed for five months by the Prime Minister of India Jawaharlal Nehru, and his colleagues, with the Prime Minister of Jammu and Kashmir, Sheikh Mohammad Abdullah, and his colleagues; from May to October 1949 (Chapter 2, Doc. Nos 1–9)."[12] Importantly, these negotiations took place between two sovereign entities: India and the state of Jammu and Kashmir.[13] The lengthy deliberations were prickly, but both Articles 370 and 35A laid the foundation for a highly autonomous relationship between both states and gave clear protections to Kashmiris in regards to their culture, language, and property rights. However, soon problems began to surface. As early as June 1949, serious disagreements between Sheikh Abdullah and Indian members of the negotiating team emerged. At the heart of the problem was how Sheikh Abdullah viewed Kashmir's relationship with India. Snedden writes, "the assertive Abdullah was trying to ensure that 'his' state had as much autonomy and administrative distance from New Delhi as he could secure. New Delhi wanted the total opposite."[14] Sheikh Abdullah eventually realized he was being duped by Indian disingenuity in their approach to the negotiations but was clueless on how to respond. Among the Indian negotiators was an individual named Gopalaswamy Ayyangar, who, as Indian scholar Noorani claims, tried to reconcile the differences. But Ayyangar was in fact colluding with Nehru. In his own words, Noorani later goes on to say that "a text, agreed on 16 October, was moved in the Constituent Assembly the next day, but was unilaterally altered by Ayyangar."[15] While

Ayyangar claimed this was a trivial change, it was that legal jargon that allowed Sheikh Abdullah's government to be sacked and jailed in 1953.[16] In this way, a small, unrepresentative group of Kashmiri Muslims were enticed by Nehru to forgo their collective rights in return for personal privilege and promises of unrivaled autonomy. In the end, they got nothing. Except, perhaps, an open-air prison for the Kashmiri people.

Meanwhile, after placating several disgruntled and influential Kashmiri people, the Indian government went on the diplomatic offensive to claim that Kashmiris would have their say about their future. However, while India was loudly proclaiming that they would respect the decision of the Kashmiri people, this was nothing more than bombast. Ultimately, after India engineered an agreement with Sheikh Abdullah, they imprisoned him for nearly 20 years.[17] Once his use was over, they discarded him.

Ever since Articles 370 and 35A were incorporated into the Indian constitution, India began sabotaging them. As Lalwani and Gayner write, "New Delhi effectively eroded this autonomy (Article 370) through constitutional orders of integration, national laws applied to the state, and continuous political micromanagement."[18] Then why abrogate? It was not enough for India to own Kashmir; they would have to erase Kashmir, recreating it in the Hindu image. Important safeguards remained in Articles 370 and 35A, meant to protect the Kashmiri culture, language, and identity, which were contrary to Hindutva ideology, so had to be removed.[19]

Specifically, according to a strict reading of the text, both Articles 370 and 35A were inviolable. "A solemn compact,"[20] as Noorani argues, that "neither side can amend or abrogate unilaterally, except in accordance with the terms of that provision."[21] Many Indians argue that the BJP-appointed governor of Kashmir has the authority to override the constituent assembly and elected representatives of Kashmir. This is how through a legal backdoor, in utter contempt of the will of the people, India justifies the abrogation of the articles. By directly violating the UNSC resolutions on Kashmir regional tensions have intensified, the conflict is further internationalized, and China is now directly a part of the dispute. Moreover, it has transformed the disputed territory into occupied territories. Most importantly, by taking these actions, India has directly impacted the Simla Agreement with Pakistan. It is no wonder that senior Indian politician and Congress party member P. Chidambaram stated that this decision would have "catastrophic" consequences.[22] He went on to say to the BJP: "You may think you have scored a victory, but you are wrong and history will prove you to be wrong. Future generations will realize what a grave mistake this house is making."[23]

SIMLA AGREEMENT NULLIFIED

The Simla Agreement was signed by India and Pakistan on July 2, 1972. It was a watershed moment between the two countries, and the treaty has been hailed as a relative success.[24] According to Bhasin, there were three main features that Pakistan sought to achieve by signing the Simla Agreement. Respectively, those are: that India continue to accept Kashmir as disputed territory, and acknowledge Pakistan was a party to the dispute; that the UNSC on Kashmir resolutions were not nullified; that Kashmir remained the core issue between the two countries and there could not be permanent, lasting peace without considering the principle of self-determination for the people of Kashmir.[25] Indians spun the Simla Accords, arguing that they "defeated" Pakistan by participating in its civil war in the erstwhile East Pakistan, thereby helping create Bangladesh. Also, India claimed it forced the terms of the Simla Agreement, especially by confining Kashmir to a bilateral dispute.

Margolis states that even though India took advantage of Pakistan's civil war, which resulted in its dismemberment, it did not dictate terms during the Simla Agreement. Pakistan may have lost "its eastern half, which became the independent nation-state of Bangladesh," however, "the impasse in Kashmir remained."[26] Moreover, as Wirsing writes, the

Simla agreement did not explicitly de-establish UNMOGIP (United Nations Military Observer Group for India and Pakistan), and neither did it constitute a formal repudiation of the UN resolutions that, apart from spelling out the conditions for demilitarization and the conduct of a plebiscite, had brought UNMOGIP into being in the first place.[27]

Certainly, as Wirsing states, the Simla Agreement does not supersede the UNSC resolutions on Kashmir nor obviate the plebiscite requirement.[28]

Yet the Simla Agreement did have an important section that could arguably be read as preferring bilateralism, though not necessarily restricting it to bilateralism. The treaty stated that the resolution of all outstanding issues between India and Pakistan should be through peaceful and bilateral means. Specifically, it states that the "two countries are to resolve to settle their differences by peaceful means through bilateral negotiations or by any other peaceful means mutually agreed upon between them. Pending the final settlement of any problems between the two countries, neither side shall unilaterally alter the situation."[29] In other words, while the agreement encourages bilateral, goodwill negotiations it does not strictly limit them to that, although many read it as such. But now, by unilaterally abrogating Articles 370 and 35A, India stands in clear violation of the Simla Agreement making it defunct. India has foolishly erased their own argument put forward ever since signing the treaty. Even if there was a reasonable argument to limit engagement on Kashmir to bilateral relations, that is now terminated.

In all likelihood, the BJP Hindutva-led government of Prime Minister Modi did not entirely appreciate the significance of abrogating Articles 370 and 35A. The seriousness of the abrogation's impact on the disputed territory is monumental in that it has overwhelmingly alienated any support that India had, no matter how lukewarm, in Kashmir. Consequently, this decision has led to unifying the position of the people of Kashmir against India and, as Noorani argues, "invited the people of Jammu and Kashmir to rise in revolt."[30] In many ways, this decision reflects poorly on the Indian state. The Simla Agreement clearly states that neither side will "unilaterally alter the situation" and that is precisely what Modi's government has done. Therefore, according to Noorani, the abrogation of the said articles "renders the attempted dismemberment of J&K's special status void in international law as being violative of this bilateral agreement and the UNSC's resolutions."[31]

All being said, if "truth be told, the Simla pact is dead."[32] Actually, in 1972, many Kashmiris objected to its signing since they were not a part of the discussions. Then, after the hanging of Kashmiri icon Maqbul Butt and the people's uprising in 1989, a new dimension was added to Kashmiri resistance.[33] Now, with the abrogation of the aforementioned articles, yet another provocation has been added, which has galvanized Kashmiris against India but poses huge security risks for the region and world.

SETTLER-COLONIALISM IN KASHMIR

The rapidity of the changes in Indian-Occupied Kashmir—its legal, political, constitutional, and demographic reality, since August 5, 2019, have led to international outrage. This has thrown Indian policymakers into disarray. Yet, they have doubled down. Concertina wire, massive numbers of Indian soldiers, and military checkpoints are everywhere. If before the presence of Indian soldiers was relatively sparse, now it is flagrant. Kashmir is clearly recognizable as a military occupation. Today, Kashmir is in the throes of blatant settler-colonialism. This section outlines the precise ways the Indian state aims to accomplish control, which are as follows: 1) inventing Kashmiris through issuance of domicile/citizenship certificates; 2) land theft; 3) altering maps, changing the names of public institutions, schools, and places of interest to enforce "Indianization"; 4) misrepresenting Kashmir on official government websites to falsely show it as having a Hindu majority; 5) coercive patriotism; 6) removing all Kashmiris from top bureaucratic positions to solidify the occupation; and 7) a delimitation process to project normalcy. Altogether, these policies aim to transform Kashmir from a Muslim-majority to a Hindu-majority land.

First, India's abrogation of Articles 370 and 35A allowed for the invention of Kashmiris in preparation for settler-colonialism. Veracini describes settler-colonialism, as distinguished from colonialism, in the ways the hegemon wishes to replace, rather than simply rule over, the indigenous population.[34] As is powerfully explained, the difference between colonialism and settler-colonialism is that colonialism states, "you, work for me," while settler-colonialists will say, "you, go away."[35] And there can be no clearer evidence of the latter than the ways the Indian state issues fake citizenship certificates. In fact, the Indian government has so far issued at least 4.1 million fake domicile/citizenship certificates to non-Kashmiris.[36]

To further explain, Article 35A conferred upon Kashmir's legislative assembly the exclusive authority on how to define "permanent residents."[37] Notably, as a result of that authority, Kashmir's local government was able to restrict the purchase of land only to those rightly qualified. This meant Indians could not purchase land in Kashmir or alter its unique socio-cultural reality. By revoking Article 35A, "the Indian government unearthed a fear that Kashmiris had been wrestling with since independence: that India would recruit non-Kashmiri settlers to dilute the region's ethnic and religious makeup."[38] This is precisely what is happening. The issuance of these fake citizenship certificates is completely transforming the demography of the disputed territory. This insidious form of "demographic flooding" is in direct violation of all mutually agreed treaties signed by India and Pakistan, as well as 18 Security Council resolutions, and the Geneva Conventions.[39]

Admittedly, this policy to invent Kashmiris is unlikely to work as there are few buyers for this type of scheming. As Beg writes, the

> new domicile rules are a major departure from an established body of historical precedent, law and jurisprudence. This position was guaranteed to Kashmiris under the Delhi Agreement of 1952, the Presidential Order of 1954, Article 35A of the constitution of India and Part III Section 6 of the constitution of Jammu and Kashmir.[40]

For that reason, five UN Special Rapporteurs issued a tersely worded letter on February 10, 2021, reprimanding the Indian government for its policy of demographic engineering and disregard for

Kashmiri rights.[41] Signatories included the UN Special Rapporteur on Minority Issues, the Special Rapporteur on the Promotion and Protection of the Right to Freedom of Expression and Opinion, the Special Rapporteur on the Rights to Freedom of Peaceful Assembly and Association, the Special Rapporteur on Contemporary forms of Racism, Racial Discrimination, Xenophobia and Related Intolerance, and the Special Rapporteur on Freedom of Religion or Belief. In a first, they wrote that the new domicile/citizenship law "may cause demographic changes" and "risks undermining the linguistic and cultural rights and the freedom of religion or belief of the people of Jammu and Kashmir in the autonomous region which had been established in 1947 to guarantee their ethnic, linguistic and religious identities."[42]

Second, and closely related to India's settler-colonial project is the transference of Kashmiri land and resources to the Indian state, its armed forces, and non-indigenous Hindu boards. In this way, India is stealing Kashmir's land and resources. As Peer persuasively shows, the Indian government seizes land for hydroelectricity projects, such as the Kishanganga Hydroelectric Project, that come under the jurisdiction of the National Hydroelectric Power Corporation of India (NHPC). In this way, thousands of Kashmiris, especially in the rural areas, have been disentitled of their lands. Peer explains that in the global context there is a lively debate on mega corporations seizing land and resources of marginalized communities, but India's actions raise the issue of state-owned corporations stealing land on the pretext of national/public interest. The Kishanganga project is a clear instance of an Indian state corporation exploiting peripheral resources and leaving behind dispossessed and displaced peasantry.[43]

In addition, land grabs in Kashmir are also undertaken by the Indian army for use in so-called counter-terror measures. Nabi and Ye argue that under the guise of winning "hearts and minds" the Indian army began counter-terror operations that eventually disentitled people from their lands. They write that the Indian army's "occupation of large swathes of land in Kashmir has resulted in de-peasantization of rural areas, compounding the alienation of the people."[44] Fareed explains that this happens by the Indian government passing new laws that "authorize the Indian army to declare any area as 'strategic' for operational and training purposes against the Kashmiri rebels," areas of which it then takes possession.[45] By some estimates, the Indian army has stolen 125,000 acres of Kashmiri land.[46]

Furthermore, the occupying Indian government's theft of Kashmiri land and resources continues unabashedly with the recent grant of 25 Kanals (3.125 acres) of land at Pathan Chowk to the Amarnath Shrine Board (SASB)—a non-Kashmiri Hindu organization.[47] This is allegedly for construction of an office and accommodation for Hindu pilgrims. The land is given on a "lease basis" for a period of 40 years from the date of taking possession and, as per the new legal order, the Hindu Board has been granted the land on a nominal payment of ten Indian Rupees per Kanal (0.125 acres) per annum.[48] Note, this is without any premium charge, which is subject to the condition the land be used only for the specific purpose granted. In this way, the Indian state takes possession of land that is claimed to be related to infrastructural development for Hindu religious pilgrimages to Kashmir. This ensuing construction upon and diversion of Kashmiri land not only threatens the environment, and its fragile ecosystem, but changes the nature of the disputed territory by providing cover for Indian settlements. The Hindutva project of owning Kashmir is rapidly gaining pace.

Third, India has also initiated an aggressive campaign to change the names of roads, schools, important places, and landmarks to effectively "Indianize" Kashmir. While this has been happening since the foreign Dogra regime—for instance, in changing the name of the city of Islamabad to Anantnag—it has taken on renewed urgency with the BJP Hindutva government.[49] On August 4, 2021, an announcement was also made to change 75 roads and 75 schools to Indian names.[50] Even old castles/forts such as Koh-i-Maran are changed to Hari Parbat, and Srinagar's famous Takht-i-Sulaiman has been forcibly changed to Shankaracharya.[51] Yet, this is a long-standing policy, as Ahmed writes, on "24 October 2018, the State Government inaugurated in Srinagar a 'library building' named after the third generation Dogra ruler, Pratap Singh, whose memory in Kashmir only evokes painful feelings of oppression."[52] Not only are they changing names of cities, schools, roads, and landmarks, they are renaming them in complete hostility to the primary religious/ethnic demographic—the Kashmiri Muslims.

Fourth, Official Indian government websites on Kashmir are now showing the disputed territory as majority Hindu. The misrepresentation of Kashmir by post-colonial Indian authorities is telling at a time "when fears of a demographic invasion are running rife. In Indian administered Kashmir a government website has declared the conflict-ridden Muslim-majority region a Hindu majority."[53] Specifically, the InvestJK website, run by the Industries and Commerce Department—directly connected to the Indian government—states: "be it Kashmir or Jammu, the population is predominantly Hindu."[54] Here, we see how the "RSS [Rashtriya Swayamsevak Sangh] mindset that desires the erasure of Muslims has percolated to government institutions."[55]

Fifth, post-colonial India fetishes Kashmir and indulges in coercive patriotism with the threat of violence.[56] An example of the chimeras of India's faux nationalism is the compelled participation of Kashmiris in Indian Independence Day celebrations. On August 15, 2021, for the first time, the official state flags of Indian-Occupied Kashmir were removed from all government schools and colleges, and only the Indian flag was allowed to be unfurled.[57] Then, in my conversation with Sheikh Showkat, Kashmiris were forced to raise the Indian national flag, while Indian onlookers cheered.[58] Worst of all, the Indian army forced the father of legendary Kashmiri martyr Burhan Wani, Muhammad Muzaffar Wani, to raise the Indian flag. Muzaffar Wani, whose two sons were murdered by the Indian occupation forces, was turned into an accessory for an artificial display of nationalism. Disturbingly, not a single person or organization in the entire Indian media and/or civil society came forward to denounce this coercion. Instead, mainstream Indian media described the event: "Signs of a new dawn surfaced in Jammu and Kashmir on Sunday, with the Tricolour being unfurled at all government schools, colleges and other institutions, and father of the slain terrorist Burhan Wani doing the honors at a government school in Tral where he is the Principal."[59]

Never in the post-colonial history of the Indian state has its inequality, fragility, and cruelty been exposed as it is today. The self-doubt within Indian nationalism, and its failure at consensual nation-building, has compelled it to engage in these forms of coercion. In fact, "the J&K government on Thursday [September 16, 2021] said that every government employee is mandatorily required to maintain allegiance to the Union of India and its Constitution."[60] But the breadth of this ordinance is so wide that it includes reviewing social media accounts of employees and their family members, to assess how they "think" about India.[61] Post-colonial Hindutva India seeks to police not only actions, but thoughts.

Sixth, the Indian government has begun to pursue settler-colonial policies in Kashmir by removing all Kashmiri Muslims from positions of authority, whether in the erstwhile state's bureaucracy, judiciary, or police. When Kashmir's special status was stripped away on August 5, 2019, "local Muslim officers disappeared from key positions in the secretariat .... Today when you go into the secretariat you find non-Kashmiris and non-Muslims holding important meetings, making decisions and keeping the Muslim and Kashmiri officers away."[62] In fact, every public institution and position of authority in Kashmir is led by non-Kashmiris and non-Muslims. For instance, the Lieutenant Governor of Kashmir—the political authority—is Manoj Sinha. He is a non-Kashmiri, non-Muslim, and BJP leader from India. He has a ruling secretariat council called the Raj Bhavan, in which there is no Muslim or Kashmiri representation. Carefully consider that, "[of] sixty-six top bureaucrats in Muslim-majority Jammu and Kashmir at this time, 38 are from other states [meaning from India]. Of the twelve sitting judges at the high court, only two are Muslim. And there is not a single Muslim officer in the LG's [Lieutenant-Governor] secretariat."[63] Similarly, there are no Muslim officers among the senior staff of chief secretary B.V.R. Subrahmanyam, who is also a non-Kashmiri and non-Muslim, and all high-level positions in the police and judiciary are held by non-Kashmiris and non-Muslims.[64] This is an occupation, and the world should recognize it as such.

Seventh, the Indian government, in pursuit of its settler-colonial project in Kashmir, is gerrymandering electoral districts to disenfranchise the Kashmiri Muslim majority.[65] This serves two important purposes: 1) it allows the Indian occupation forces to project elections, no matter how low the turnout, as representative of the people accepting Indian sovereignty; and 2) it manipulates the elections in a way that would ensure a Hindu majority, especially when considering the fake citizenship certificates. As Kaiser and Amin write, "the delimitation program envisions breaking up the electoral constituencies of the erstwhile semi-autonomous state into several new voter units in a manner that's likely to give numerical heft to the southern region of Jammu, where there is a larger concentration of Hindu voters."[66] In other words, the demographic changes, "when combined with a clever reconfiguration of electoral constituencies, would allow Hindu-nationalist politicians to realize their long-standing goal of installing a Hindu chief minister in Kashmir."[67]

Ultimately, following the abrogation of Articles 370 and 35A, the Indian state is working aggressively to erase Kashmir's identity, culture, and language.

GENOCIDE: THINKING THE UNTHINKABLE

A genocide has already taken place in the disputed territory of Jammu and Kashmir, as detailed in Chapter 4. Now, several decades later, the NGO Genocide Watch, led by eminent Professor Gregory Stanton, has issued two "genocide alerts" for Kashmir.[68] After all, a leading Indian BJP leader made a direct threat recently to the Muslims in Kashmir, reminding them to not forget the massacres that took place in Jammu in 1947—alluding to the genocide of Muslims.[69] The entire world should be alarmed. As Kashmiri academic Binish Ahmed writes, there is "a reluctance to use the term genocide to describe the events that have unfolded in Kashmir over the decades. But the legal definition of genocide fits."[70] Ahmed continues: "The Kashmiri people have been targeted for a demographic transformation on their territory by an outsider group by introducing mass permanent settlements of outsiders. The outsider group is the Hindu nationalist Indian state under the leadership of the Bharatiya Janata Party ... and Prime Minister Narendra Modi."[71] This is the background for which an Indian leader at one of the highest offices in India used the term "final solution" for Kashmir. Even Indian Congress leaders were shocked at this statement because the term has "a very disturbing historic connotation."[72] When Indian Home Minister Rajnath Singh was asked to clarify what he meant, he refused to respond.[73] Disturbingly, Kashmir exhibits several stages, especially when considering India's onslaught on Kashmiri civil liberties, terrorizing of the population, cutting off all of their communication, flouting international law and norms, and conducting a litany of crimes against humanity.

To start, Stanton's first genocide phase is called "classification," which leads to the development of a binary of us versus them. In Kashmir, the Indian state translates "us" as supporters of their army/occupation forces, and "them" as Kashmiri Muslims, and others, who oppose Indian rule. Of course, preventive measures would include fostering pluralist institutions that transcend ethnic/racial divisions and actively promote inclusion. Yet, this is precisely what the BJP does not want. Rather, they spread the false threat of terror to rationalize their measures of oppression. Truschke writes that not only is their narrative "hateful and incorrect, it is notable that Hindu nationalists rarely distinguish between groups of Muslims, whether past versus present, or those with political power versus those without, and so forth."[74] Most extremist organizations peddle such sweeping generalizations in order to indoctrinate the masses.

The second phase is "symbolization," a process that leads to "othering" of the targeted populace. In other words, when symbols are forced upon unwilling members of the purported pariah group, combined with visceral hate, it may lead to genocide. Stanton cites the "blue scarf for people from the Eastern Zone in Khmer Rouge."[75] Further, not just imposing symbols but removing them can also have an identical impact, at least with regard to dehumanization, such was the rage and humiliation in Kashmir when the Indian government attempted to ban traditional Kashmiri clothing called the *pheran*.[76] Kashmir's distinctive clothing frightens the occupier, not just because it verifies the distinction between them and the oppressed but due to the irrational fear occupiers have of the occupied. The occupiers know they are not welcome and remain forever vigilant at any indication of the people collectively rising up against them. When the Indian occupation forces see the loose-fitting Kashmiri *pheran*, they claim that it may conceal a weapon.[77] Everyday norms such as dress may be positioned as posing a threat to the occupier.

Third, the genocidal project moves forward by clear "discrimination." At this third stage, the political/militarily dominant group, that is, Indian occupation forces, use their power to deny Kashmiri Muslims basic rights. It is driven by an exclusionary ideology that wishes to replace the local and inherit the land and resources. This we have already seen, considering that the entire political authority in Kashmir excludes Kashmiri Muslims.[78] More specifically, the Indian state, having placed its own representatives in critical leadership positions in the disputed territory, then utilizes at least five types of laws to rationalize marginalization and discrimination against Kashmiri Muslims, and to justify the military occupation. Those laws are the Public Safety Act (PSA)—which Amnesty International refers to as a "lawless law"[79]— Disturbed Area Act (DAA), Unlawful Activities Prevention Act (UAPA), National Security Act (NSA), and Armed Forces Special Powers Act (AFSPA).[80] Together, the Indian government uses these laws to arrest anyone and hold them for up to two years without charge.

Heightened levels of prejudice lead to the fourth "dehumanization" stage, which incapacitates the normal human revulsion against murder. At this stage, hate propaganda in print, radios, and on social media is used to vilify Kashmiri Muslims in their own homes and land, such as despising their clothing and culture.[81] This is done by spreading the hateful, false narrative that Kashmiri Muslims are "outsiders" who forcibly converted Kashmiri Hindus to Islam. It is essential to recognize the role that this type of false social imaginary has on the rationalization of dehumanization. Truschke strongly critiques this Hindutva propaganda in the ways it "Others" Muslims and blames all ills in Indian society on them.[82] Such is the type of propaganda that the Indian armed soldiers are taught when they are sent to occupy Kashmir. This hate-filled narrative has become mainstream and is even incorporated into Indian school textbooks, preparing the way for further incitement.[83]

The phenomenon of genocide is always well planned and requires "organization." Genocide requires state and institutional support. Hindutva militias, who provide deniability of state responsibility, are trained for this purpose. Recall that in Jammu 1947 many of the killings were carried out by foreign RSS/Hindutva thugs affiliated with Maharaja Hari Singh's army. Today, a similar groundwork is being prepared for radical groups to enact violence. In fact, Kashmiris traveling to the disputed territory after the abrogation would be shocked to see buses traveling to Kashmir full of saffron-clad RSS fanatics. There are credible reports that some armed personnel traveling to Kashmir are actually RSS/Hindutva fanatics who may be disguised as the additional 38,000 Indian soldiers.[84] While numbers are unclear, and Indian government officials refuse to declare how many Indian soldiers are deployed in the disputed territory, Kashmiri activist Khurram Pervez writes that there are at least 700,000 heavily armed Indian army troops, not including RSS irregular soldiers and other armed security personnel.[85] For that reason, Indian journalist Vikram Sharma placed the total Indian armed forces in Kashmir at nearly one million.[86] If that is the case, why send more troops? Simply put, in preparation for a level of violence that may justify use of the term genocide.

The Indian occupation forces in Kashmir boost "polarization," in order to fracture society and pit diverse groups against one another. Even though the Valley of Kashmir is almost entirely Muslim, these strategies are pursued based on ethnicity, locality, religious affiliation, and skin color. This is accomplished in several ways—as Sheikh Showkat shared with me in an interview—to incite the people's religious sensitivities, encourage different groups to turn on one another, and allow extremist organizations and hate groups to broadcast their polarizing propaganda. This occurs under the full protection of the Indian army and other paramilitary groups. In addition, laws are passed that forbid intermarriage and are utilized to discourage social bonding between disparate groups. As Stanton argues, "extremists target moderates"—from all religions/ backgrounds—in hopes of intimidating and silencing the center.[87] However, in the heavily militarized disputed territory of Kashmir, this targeting of moderate, everyday life takes on an even more extreme slant. Consider, the case of a Sikh girl living in Kashmir who fell in love and married a Kashmiri Muslim man.[88] Sikhs comprise a tiny minority of the population in Kashmir. A member of this minority, Manmeet Kaur, and Muslim Shahid Nazir Bhat had fallen in love and married. This incident was not notable to anyone within their community, until a particular Sikh organization aligned with Hindutva organizations traveled from India to Kashmir to protest.[89] As a result, their marriage was annulled, and the girl was forcibly wed to another despite her protestations. Meanwhile, her Muslim husband was imprisoned and remains behind bars for no reason other than the allegation of "tricking" the Sikh girl into loving him.

Stanton cautions that "moderates from the perpetrators' own group are most able to stop genocide, so are the first to be arrested and killed."[90] Because of that, it is essential that the international community intervene and seize the "assets of extremists" and deny them "visas for international travel."[91] Crimes against humanity, especially genocide, demand international involvement. Yet, even though there is clear evidence implicating Hindutva extremists of just this kind of genocidal violence, there has been little international condemnation.

Seventh, is the "preparation" stage, which is the ominous lull before the storm. It is when all the necessary groundwork for genocide to occur has taken place; the "final solution." Recently, in June 2021, the Indian government made an announcement that 200 paramilitary organizations will be deployed to Jammu and Kashmir: "A huge number of paramilitary forces—200 companies—are being deployed in Jammu and Kashmir, some of which have arrived and others are on their way."[92] There is no explanation for this escalation. As previously mentioned, there are no exact figures on how many Indian soldiers are in Kashmir, nor how many soldiers will be deployed by each of the paramilitary organizations. The Indian government refuses to disclose this information. As Kashmiri journalist Zulfikar Majid writes, "a large movement of troops in recent days has led to rumors flying thick and fast in Kashmir that 'something big' like August 2019 was going to happen again."[93] For now, Kashmiris are kept in the dark.

Eighth, as the stages of genocide advance, "persecution" is heightened. This is the moment immediately before extermination begins. The victim group's most basic human rights are systematically violated through extrajudicial killings, unlawful arrest, torture, and forced displacement. Describing this stage, Stanton writes that "victims are identified and separated out because of their ethnic or religious identity. Death lists are drawn up …. Their property is often expropriated."[94] Most worryingly, all of this is happening in Kashmir now, as this book goes to press. At this very moment, Kashmiri Muslims are under a prolonged lockdown and are subject to arbitrary arrest, torture, and murder: "Since Aug. 4, India has eliminated all access to and communication with Kashmir."[95] This has actually resulted in the longest communication blockade in history. Even now, internet, mobiles, and landlines are regularly disconnected, with sporadic connectivity. As Binish writes, "14.7 million people have no access to essentials like food and medical support while India advances to take full control of their land using military power."[96] The entire Jammu and Kashmir region is essentially imprisoned under house arrest.

The persecution of Kashmiri Muslims has been heightened ever since the abrogation of Articles 370 and 35A. More specifically, Kashmir had its own "legislative assembly, constitution, flag, and independence in all matters except communications, foreign affairs and defence. Revoking this status is the latest attempt to annihilate the Kashmiri people, extinguish their rights and eliminate their linguistic, social, cultural, economic and political existence as Indigenous people."[97] Journalists who decry the crimes that are occurring are beaten, thrashed, or imprisoned for no discernable crime, such as Aasif Sultan, who has spent more than one thousand days in an Indian prison.[98]

From January 2021 to September 30, 2021, there have been at least 113 Kashmiris killed.[99] Most are Kashmiri civilians, and many are those the Indian army captures and kills in what has been ominously referred to as "fake encounters."[100] These are instances of the Indian army randomly murdering Kashmiri youth and presenting them as resistance fighters in order to collect hefty payouts by the Indian government.[101]

Hundreds of cordon and search operations (CASO) are also taking place in which Indian occupation forces claim to "search" and capture/neutralize young Kashmiris. As with other examples of information suppression, no one knows for sure how many of these CASO operations were conducted in the last year, since the Indian government does not disclose these figures. However, just by looking at a report published by the Jammu and Kashmir Coalition of Civil Society Organizations headed by the eminent Parvez Imroze, then in the first six months of 2020 there were 229 killings, 107 CASOs, 55 internet shutdowns, and 48 properties destroyed.[102] Taking that report into consideration and the fact that persecution has intensified over the past year, we can comfortably say that these are dark days for the people of Indian-Occupied Kashmir.

Lastly, Stanton explains there are two final stages of genocide—"extermination" and "denial"—that are yet to occur in the disputed territory of Jammu and Kashmir.[103] The ninth phase, "extermination", quickly devolves into the mass killing legally called "genocide." Should that terrifying moment arrive, the Indian armed forces, RSS militias and Hindutva paramilitaries would work together to eradicate Kashmiri Muslims, as done during the Jammu genocide. Following the mass killings, the final stage is "denial." This lasts throughout the entire violent process and is counted among the surest indicators of the likelihood of genocidal massacres.[104] The perpetrators of genocide dig the mass graves,[105] burn the bodies, try to cover up the evidence, and intimidate the witnesses, all while claiming normalcy.[106] Denial of this kind is already taking place, and while the BJP insist their policies aim to bring prosperity and development, every socio-economic indicator has fallen in Kashmir over the last two years.[107]

CONCLUSION

Due to the seriousness and grave implications of India's settler-colonial project and unilateral, illegal, and immoral abrogation of Articles 370 and 35A, the region has been thrown into disarray. This chapter aimed to explore the implications of the decision in a four-fold manner. First, it explained the origins of Articles 370 and 35A, closely scrutinizing the circumstances under which both articles were written and how its acceptance was between two sovereign entities: the state of India and the state of Jammu and Kashmir. It is important to recognize that Sheikh Abdullah was soon very disillusioned with the entire process of negotiations between his team and the Indian government. Eventually, he would be imprisoned. Once he had served his purpose of providing a veneer of indigenous Kashmiri support for Indian colonial aspirations, he was jailed. Next, this chapter explained the immediate impact of its abrogation on the Simla Agreement—a treaty between India and Pakistan, which now stands nullified. This fundamentally alters the status quo in the region, and, as the subsequent chapter will explain, brings China into the conflict. Third, this chapter details how the abrogation has led to a flurry of Indian settler-colonial policies in Kashmir. Those strategies include demographic change, invented residency certificates, land forfeiture, and cultural onslaught, among other tactics. Fourth, due to the extreme steps being taken by the extremist Hindutva Indian government, the reputable NGO Genocide Watch, led by Dr. Gregory Stanton, has issued two genocide alerts for Kashmir. Overall, the implications of these policies are likely heightening instability in the region and increasing the likelihood of war.

Lastly, the actions of the Indian government have been condemned worldwide; reputable NGOs such as Amnesty International and Human Rights Watch have strongly chastised India. Recently, the UN has convened two emergency Security Council Meetings, the first on Kashmir in over 50 years, on the deteriorating situation in the disputed territory that also called for respecting the relevant UN resolutions. More specifically, UN Secretary-General António Guterres expressed concern at the ongoing human rights situation. And, David Kaye, the UN's special rapporteur on freedom of expression, described the situation in Kashmir as "draconian." Still, nothing happens. The disputed territory of Kashmir remains the longest unresolved conflict on the agenda of the UN. It remains the most militarized space on the planet and has the atrocious appellation of being a nuclear flashpoint. Worse, as this chapter has highlighted, there is the very real possibility of genocide in Kashmir. In spite of all this, no matter how terrifying, we see no progress. Crime upon crime, threat upon threat, gross violations of human rights continue to be committed, and nothing comes of it. That needs to change and change fast.

8

Nuclear Flashpoint:
Sino-Indian Rivalry and Kashmir

On Monday, June 15, 2020, on a desolate patch of land nestled between some of the highest mountain passes in the world, pandemonium erupted. Chinese and Indian soldiers patrolling the Line of Actual Control (LAC)—the undemarcated borderlands between the two nuclear powers, fought a grueling, bloody battle referred to as the Galwan Valley clash. Goldman explains, "[t]he clash on Monday night, fought in one of the most forbidding landscapes on the planet, was a startling culmination of months of mounting tension and years of dispute."[1] Actually, for months preceding the clash, tensions had been rising. There were sporadic fistfights; both sides were accusing each other of patrolling no-go areas, violating agreements, and making provocations. "[M]elees broke out several times. In one clash at the glacial lake Pangong Tso, Indian troops were badly injured and had to be evacuated by helicopter."[2] Even former president Trump offered to mediate what he called the "raging border dispute."[3] Then, a couple of weeks later, an all-out brawl erupted, with the use of baseball bats wrapped in concertina wire and bamboo sticks with protruding nails. The intent was to kill. It was the climax of months of verbal threats and physical escalations, especially by India's forward policy of incrementally taking disputed lands between them and China. In the end, 20 Indians[4] and four Chinese soldiers[5] were killed.

Ultimately, what took an even worse beating than India's hubris was Sino-Indian relations. Chinese academics Hu Shisheng and Wang Jue referred to it as the "lowest point since the border war between them in 1962."[6] On the one side, China insisted the altercation was a response to aggressive land theft by India. Contrarily,

India complained of a hostile out-of-control China. The impact of the so-called Galwan Valley clash is much more than regional instability. This is what is lost within much of the commentary of the conflict—it occurred in Kashmir. Or, more specifically, a region of the disputed territory of Jammu and Kashmir known as Ladakh.[7] The conflict is now global.

THE HISTORY OF THE SINO-INDIAN BORDER DISPUTE

The Chinese–Indian border conflict begins in the late nineteenth century during the period of British imperialism. Zongyi writes, "the border area has never been formally demarcated and this issue was originally created by British colonialists."[8] Actually, both China and India have vastly different conceptualizations of their border regions. The history of these borderland regions reflects a complex interplay of British colonial interests, fear of Russian expansionism, and trepidation towards the Chinese Qing government. It was in this context that the border established by the British dissected what China considered its "traditional customary boundary ... which runs along the Karakoram mountains."[9] India does not acknowledge that as China's natural border. Instead, they insist that it has inherited the borders of the British Raj.[10] China does not accept this.

Kang reveals that the Sino-Indian conflict has its roots in meetings held as early as 1865 when British surveyor William H. Johnson proposed the "Johnson Line" that included the Aksai Chin region with Ladakh.[11] Importantly, the Aksai Region has never been controlled by the British. So, for the Chinese, it was pure colonial arrogance to claim Aksai Chin. Still, for geopolitical reasons the British claimed it. Afterwards, in 1897, there was the slightly modified "Ardagh-Johnson" line, then in 1899 another "Macartney-Macdonald" line.[12] Finally, in 1914, representatives from Britain, China, and Tibet gathered to negotiate a treaty that would demarcate the boundaries between the British Empire and China.[13] At that meeting, British Colonial official Henry McMahon established the infamous McMahon Line that essentially bifurcated Tibet to create a buffer zone between the British and China. Since then,

"India maintains that the McMahon Line, a 550-mile frontier that extends through the Himalayas, is the official legal border between China and India. But China has never accepted it."[14]

With the end of the British Raj, in 1947, the newly formed country of India inherited border tensions with the Chinese. According to Indian scholar Ipsita Chakravarty, there seems to have been a deliberate policy of so-called cartographic aggression, by the British towards a troubled China.[15] Yet, rather than negotiate in good faith, India refused to acknowledge Chinese claims to territory when the British left. This poisoned relations. In 1959, Premier Zhou Enlai flew to India to compromise and find a solution to the longstanding border dispute. Eventually, the two countries agreed on a de facto border—the LAC—but India flatly refused to negotiate a permanent settlement. Maxwell explains India's attitude as delusional: "there was no boundary dispute with China, that is, there could be no question about the alignment of India's boundaries ... there could be no negotiation."[16] Sawhney confirms this by saying: "To be fair to China, twice—in 1959 and in 1960—Zhou offered a give and take compromise to settle the boundary question."[17] Keep in mind, the Sino-Indian border can be neatly divided into western, middle, and eastern sectors. So, China was willing to accept India's claim in the eastern sector and hoped for acceptance of its claims in the western sector. However, Nehru's "rigid stance of non-recognition of the Chinese viewpoint and non-negotiation made headway impossible."[18]

It is not surprising that war broke out in 1962.[19] For India, it was a total disaster. They lost thousands of soldiers, with thousands more taken prisoner. In addition, China regained considerable territory. Yet, in a calculated move, China did not press ahead. Their aim was to force India to the negotiating table, not pummel India into a stupor.[20] Chinese troops crossed the McMahon Line and took over large swathes of disputed territory, including mountain passes, towns, and villages. Then, by November, Premier Zhou declared a unilateral ceasefire along a new de facto LAC. This, in hindsight, was a miscalculation by the Chinese. They could have taken the entire area but stopped themselves from over-reach. That fateful decision has come back to haunt them.

Within India, the 1962 military defeat did not lead to deep intro-spection on what went wrong. Nor was there a genuine effort to resolve the ongoing border dispute with China. Sawhney explains how, in a remarkable show of foolishness, the Indian parliament passed a resolution after the 1962 war "to recover Aksai Chin from China. Indira's government thus found it difficult to accept China's post-1962 status quo offer which would imply accepting Aksai Chin as Chinese territory .... For a defeated nation to demand more than the status quo was unrealistic."[21] While India plays to stereotypes of Chinese aggression, it conveniently whitewashes its own actions. Gardner explains that the perception of Chinese hostility is not accurate and details about the Sino-Indian rivalry are described in the Henderson Brooks-Bhagat report, written after the 1962 war. That report

> noted that the Army General Staff had failed to apprise the gov-ernment of the inability to effectively support a "forward policy" in Ladakh and the North-East Frontier Agency (NEFA), a policy largely inherited from the British. This top-secret report, one that the Indian government still refuses to release, suggested that the war was hardly a case of a pure Chinese aggression.[22]

INDIA'S FORWARD POLICY

In early 1962, prior to Sino-Indian hostilities, a document shared in official Indian government circles elaborated on India's "forward policy."[23] It was a central reason for the 1962 war and is as import-ant today. On November 2, 1961, "the Indian Government issued a directive for the implementation of what it called 'the forward policy.' This directive was passed on by Army HQ to the area com-manders concerned (after a crucial emendation) on 5 December."[24] In that directive was the following critical paragraph, which Maxwell quotes in his best-selling book, *India's China War*:

Ladakh: We are to patrol as far forward as possible from our present positions towards the International Border as recognized by us. This will be done with a view to establishing additional posts located to prevent the Chinese from advancing further and also to dominate any Chinese posts already established in our territory.[25]

The forward policy is an incremental way of India forcing a change to the status quo, provoking China, and doing so while claiming to be non-aggressive. Of course, this by no means absolves China of its role in heightening tensions by its military patrols in undemarcated areas. However, as Maxwell writes, the "forward policy was designed to evict China from territory India claimed, by 'dominating' Chinese positions and thus forcing their withdrawal."[26] India's justification for this policy is their insistence that the boundaries of the former British imperial power have been inherited by them. No neighbor of India is willing to accept this.

Moreover, even after the debacle of the 1962 war, India continued to raise tensions with its forward policy. Interestingly, Shisheng and Jue (2020) claim that this policy existed as early as Nehru's rule:

New Delhi, benefitting from topographic conveniences and the inheritance of colonial legacies from the British Empire, has been implementing the Forward Policy with great fanfare, willfully revising the border line between China and India in accordance with its own security needs and repeatedly intruding into, gnawing at, and seizing areas controlled and claimed by China in order to test its bottom line of tolerance.[27]

Zongyi concurs, stating that

India continued to force a fait accompli by snatching territory and strategic mountain heights in the undemarcated borderland, and through encroachment and aggression, India edged over the LAC to the Chinese side to occupy strategic commanding heights of the border area. The Nathu La and Cho La clashes in 1967, the

Tulung La skirmish in 1975, and the Sumdorong Chu confrontation in 1986 were all related to India's policy of encroachment.[28]

Considering this, is there any wonder why border confrontations keep erupting?

After 1986, China decided to meet the Indians more than halfway. China was willing to change strategy and hoped to re-engage with India. Hongwei writes that China acknowledged "disputes in the eastern, middle and western sectors of the Sino-Indian border, and the eastern section is the most controversial ... only when India makes adjustments in the eastern border area will China make corresponding corrections to the western section."[29] Both sides blamed each other for not committing to a negotiated settlement of their border dispute, but it seems that India kept insisting on a maximalist position. In contrast, the Chinese made a number of attempts to resolve all outstanding issues. Moreover, an overwhelming majority of Chinese academics, thinkers, and analysts insist on friendly Sino-Indian relations.[30] This in contrast to a vast majority of Indian academics/scholars targeting China. Simply by perusing official documents, and pro-government academics, it seems China has been consistently interested in resolving the border issue. However, India's unwillingness to negotiate territory or alter its "absolute security paradigm" inherited from British colonialists inhibited resolution.[31]

The concept of absolute security is important to consider when understanding a major reason for India's forward policy. It holds that India needs to ensure no strategic advantages to China, or anyone else for that matter, in regard to its borders. This is a tightly held belief in India's decision-making and strategic circles and "the fundamental reason why India has been obsessed with the Forward Policy over the past decades, even at the risk of going into military confrontation ... with China."[32] It is as powerful an ideological paradigm for India today as it ever was. And China has noticed its significance. On September 30, 2021, the Chinese foreign ministry spokesperson Hua Chunying said, "India has long been following the forward policy and illegally encroached upon China's territory across the border ... this is the root cause of the tension."[33] Similarly, Maxwell blames India for provoking tensions along the Sino-Indian border.[34] Gardner also agrees but sheds light on how India "imagines" its land as living and borders as sacred as another variable that motivates its forward policy.[35] Actually, there is much to be gathered from that. Post-colonial Indian intelligentsia manipulate the attachment to land in the national imaginary in order to rationalize geopolitical maneuverings. There is an enduring Indian mentality at work that refuses to negotiate land in their possession—even if it doesn't belong to them. This is related to the way Indian culture incarnates land, which makes any land negotiation practically impossible. India has become a victim of its own post-colonial propaganda, which prevents it from making concessions on its border with China or recognizing the rights of Kashmiris. For to do so invites shame. This has all become worse with the growing nationalist rhetoric of India under the BJP-led Hindutva government.

HINDUTVA BRAVADO

Following the 2014 election of a BJP-led Hindutva government, India's relations with all its neighbors began to decline. This is because the support base of the BJP comprises several Hindutva organizations such as the "RSS, BJP, VHP, Bajrang Dal and Shiv Sena ... all of them work together under the philosophy of Hindutva (i.e. Hindu-ness), which is hyper-aggressive and thin-skinned based on perceived historic ridicule of their unmanliness and cowardice."[36] In response, Hindutva ideologues overcompensate with absurd bellicosity and chest-thumping. Indian scholar Apoorvanand mirrors that opinion and writes, "India is changing in significant ways."[37] Undoubtedly, the domestic/internal transformations inside India are troubling and undeniable. However, another key by-product of Hindutva bravado is in how it impacts India's foreign policy. Especially, in heightening tensions with China.

Truschke notes that the Hindutva social imaginary is heavily militaristic and aggressive: "Already, the once religious sounding phrase 'Jai Shri Ram' is often heard as a cry of hate that has filled the ears of many Muslims in their final moments before being murdered by Hindu mobs."[38] Now, as Arndt explains, this aggressiveness has impacted India's foreign policy. As soon as Modi's government took power it began altering "Indian foreign policy to a new level of assertiveness."[39] This was especially evident during Modi's visit to China in May 2015, when he stressed "the need for China to reconsider its approach on some of the issues that hold us back from full potential of our partnership."[40] Then, during the same official trip, at a lecture at Tsinghua University, Modi repeated the assertion that bilateral relations were suffering as a result of China's policies.[41] Basically, Modi traveled to China, blamed it for their tense relations, and completely failed to mention India's forward policy.

India's newfound aggression was unsettling, but China was not rattled. China made several peace overtures to India and officially asked them to join their ambitious Belt and Road Initiative (BRI). They even tried to convince the Indians to abandon hostility, mend relations, and continue their policy of strategic autonomy. Several Indian academics and policymakers considered this a watershed opportunity and openly advocated joining the initiative. Arguably, this would have brought tremendous benefit to India, not least with huge Chinese investments. Yet, China's olive branch to India was spurned, since India was concerned about coming under China's economic influence and its relationship with Pakistan. Key Indian decision-makers remained unconvinced, especially due to BRI's flagship bilateral project the China–Pakistan Economic Corridor.[42] Outrageously, India complained to China that their project passes through an area it claims. Namely, the Gilgit-Baltistan region—an area that is entirely Muslim and defeated the Dogra Maharaja's army to raise the Pakistan flag in 1947. The commitment of Hindutva India to claiming land that is not its own continues, now with the added impetus of the desire to frustrate China's economic strategy.

Not joining China's BRI is one thing, but actively working against it is quite another. In a direct challenge to the BRI, India created alternative economic corridors and participated in the containment of China's power.[43] Also, it launched the "Indo-Korean axis" and "India Japan Act East Forum," both in an attempt to pursue its own version of an economic corridor. However, it is questionable whether India has the manufacturing, industrial, and economic clout and know-how to undertake such a massive response against the BRI. Understandably, many in India see the BRI as a major shift in China's global economic power, and this is why India might seek to resist it. Admittedly, "the BRI will fundamentally tilt the geopolitics of Asia in China's favor" from India's perspective, so resistance to it is acknowledged. Yet the question is does India have the organizational capacity and reach to impact it? Or should it negotiate terms that address some of its major concerns?

Ironically, the BJP-led Hindutva government has among its main agenda a "neighborhood first" policy. Yet, India's good-neighbor policy is pure fantasy. It promotes a facade of good neighborliness and instrumentalizes ambitions of becoming an economic powerhouse and global leader. It is a policy that weaponizes India's Western darling status to seek to dominate smaller neighbors. Admittedly, in a first, the Indian government invited the entire South Asian Association for Regional Cooperation (SAARC) together for Prime Minister Modi's inauguration.[44] Yet, what the gesture masked was the condescending way that India began behaving with its neighbors, including China. Ironically, India's relations with its neighbors have never been worse than under its so-called good-neighbor policy. Now, "India is facing tensions with its northern neighbors— Nepal, Pakistan, China and Myanmar."[45] And, as Hu Shisheng and Wang Jue point out, since 2019, "India [has] trespassed China's line of actual control [LAC] 1,581 times, of which 94 percent occurred in the western section of the China-India border."[46] Also, during this time, India has even managed to raise tensions with Nepal[47] and antagonize a former pliable ally such as Bhutan.[48] India's good-neighbor policy masks its disruptive actions in the region.

INDO-PACIFIC CONTESTATION

Perhaps no issue is as problematic for Sino-Indian relations than the way Modi's government has tethered its geopolitical horse to US Indo-Pacific strategy. Gokhale writes, the "Indo-Pacific is one area where India is becoming more of a factor in China's foreign policy making since 2017 because of its association with America."[49] While the debate is ongoing whether India must forsake its strategic advantage, its policy and rhetoric against China is quite clear. For China, it is becoming obvious where India stands. Claiming territory inside China, militaristic language used by leading Indian politicians, and the belief that Sino-US rivalry presents a unique window of opportunity for India are motivating factors. Such is the cold, calculating nature of realpolitik that another's misfortune presents one with an opportunity. Zongyi explains India's belief that "the strategic competition between China and the United States and the 'de-sinicization' of the U.S. economy provides a rare opportunity for its rise."[50] This is further substantiated by the words of Indian Minister of External Affairs Jaishankar, who said, speaking of US–China rivalry: "Frankly, in every clash, there is an opportunity. There are risks also. I don't deny that. And, obviously, my job will be to manage the risks and maximize the opportunity."[51] Similarly, in April 2019, Jaishankar went to great lengths to impress upon India's Western allies how important and committed India is to "manage" China.[52] Even Indian academics are openly advocating for an aggressive US response to China's insubordination.[53] In other words, it seems that India hopes to benefit from an intensification of US–China rivalry.

Clearly, the Indo-Pacific region is fast becoming a major source of international contestation. The reasons are clear: Both the South China Sea and Indian Ocean region are of unparalleled importance to China. The South China Sea is referred to by the Chinese as

the "second Persian Sea" for its oil reserves. It has 1,367,000 barrels of oil production a day. The Chinese have calculated that the South China Sea will ultimately yield 130 billion barrels of oil. If these calculations are correct then it contains more oil than any other area of the globe except Saudi Arabia.[54]

This is incredibly important considering China is energy driven and it "consumes ten percent of world oil production and over twenty percent of all energy on the planet."[55] Furthermore, the Indo-Pacific is immensely important for international trade and commerce.

> It is evident from the fact that out of the total trade conducted over the Indian Ocean, only 20 per cent of it is counted between the littoral countries of the region, whilst 80 per cent of extra-regional maritime traffic with some 120,000 ships traversing the Indian Ocean every year.[56]

Taken together, the South China Sea and Indian Ocean are the economic lifeline of China. Naturally, then, are the US and India taking such an interest in it. Of course, with India as America's "strategic partner," as evidenced in the US Department of Defense's 2019 report on the Indo-Pacific, is it any wonder why China is concerned about Indian intentions?[57] They believe "the US-Led Indo-Pacific strategy aims to contain China's rise."[58]

Prior to the BJP-led Hindutva government, India maintained a policy of strategic autonomy. This meant it would cleverly play both sides—US and China—against one another to maximize its advantage. In fact, China has been urging India to recommit to Manmohan Singh's "Non-Alignment 2.0" and develop a "cautious balance" between the US and China.[59] By deftly doing so, it could reap immense rewards. However, it is now engaged in a zero-sum game focused on isolating China.[60] In response, China is appealing for India to rethink its strategy of supporting the aggressive designs of the QUAD. But India has rebuffed those efforts and thrown its lot in with those aiming to contain China.[61] In a devastating move for Sino-Indian relations, India has joined the QUAD—an alliance formed for security cooperation in the Asia-Pacific region. It is a group of four countries—the United States, Australia, India, and Japan—who have formed an alliance to tackle security, economic, and health issues, but built around shared concerns "about China's increasingly assertive behavior in the region and [who] are more willing to define a constructive agenda of cooperation."[62] Bilal and Akhtar write that it was originally conceptualized in "2007 and revived in 2017 against the backdrop of

China's assertiveness in the South China Sea and its growing influence in the region. The US with QUAD members also initiated a new concept of 'Free and Open Indo-Pacific' (FOIP) which aims to improve connectivity between Asia and Africa."[63] However, what binds all QUAD members together is their critical opposition to and uneasiness with China's growing geopolitical and economic clout.

In the QUAD security arrangement, Chinese strategists consider India the weakest link. However, even with its limited capabilities, the US is encouraging India to play a pivotal role in constricting China. Since 2017, the US has been pressuring India to formally ask Australia to join its Malabar military exercises. Until recently, India refused. Now, they've agreed: "A decision (was) made by the Modi administration to officially invite Australia to join the India–US–Japan annual Malabar military exercise."[64] For many years India was reluctant to indulge in something that China blatantly considered a threat. However, India's policy of strategic autonomy has been discarded. Resultantly, "all four navies participated in their first joint navy exercise in over a decade in November 2020."[65] In other words, India has now entered a de facto alliance against China.

Another important aspect of the Indo-Pacific region is the role China plays in the global supply chain. United States discussions on "supply-chain resilience" indicate their intent on replacing/reducing China's international supply-chain role. Zongyi explains an unwritten aspiration of India's Indo-Pacific strategy is to "conspire(s) with the United States, Japan, Australia and other countries to transfer the global industrial chain and supply chain from China to India."[66] Here, India perceives an opportunity to benefit from heightened US–Chinese animosity. However, as Wu Lin reveals, there have been limited economic advantages to India, even as it capitulates to US demands vis-à-vis China. Indian gains on the economic front have been negligible.[67] Moreover, the Indian government has been unable to transform Western support to significant domestic or international geostrategic revitalization "as they are still constrained by multiple institutional bottlenecks at home."[68] Admittedly, there has been an opening of global diplomatic space for India which has contributed to boosting its image globally. Unfortunately, however, India has used that newfound geopolitical and diplomatic space provided by Western countries to present "an increasingly tough, uncompromising and even bold mentality ... toward China. Through its tough diplomacy, India is constantly testing China' s strategic bottom line."[69]

It would be a strategic mistake for India to be aggressive against China, especially considering the negligible economic advantage and illusory geopolitical leverage such a position has offered. A seat at the table is not necessarily influence. And this militaristic Hindutva thinking completely erases a rational understanding of international relations and security. Meanwhile, the US expects India to "adopt more aggressive policies in line with the Indo-Pacific Strategy."[70] And, no matter how much they do, America will press India to do more. In other words, India will begin to feel the crunch of constantly expecting to do more for its US benefactor. This was forcefully displayed by Indian American political strategist Ashley J. Tellis during an online seminar entitled "Sino-India Border: Escalation and Disengagement," organized by Carnegie India. He stated that the "US wanted India to be a little less subtle" and it was up to India "to set the pace for the intensity of the relationship it seeks."[71] And, as India moves in that direction, it risks putting itself at the forefront of military confrontation, being the only QUAD country that borders China.

THE ABROGATION OF ARTICLE 370 AND CHINA

The abrogation of Articles 370 and 35A has significantly escalated tensions with China, compelling it to intervene in Kashmir,[72] where it can no longer afford to remain neutral. China responded to the abrogation of Articles 370 and 35A by officially denouncing the action as illegal, null, and void. What followed was a diplomatic conflict between both countries. Not only had India unilaterally altered the disputed territory's status but split it into two federal union territories directly controlled by New Delhi and reiterated land claims against China. Controversially, India began distributing new maps that included areas in Chinese territory. In response, during the Chinese Foreign Ministry Spokesperson Geng Shuang's Regular Press Conference on October 31, 2019, he stated that

[t]he Indian government officially announced the establishment of the so-called Union Territory of Jammu and Kashmir and Union Territory of Ladakh, placing part of Chinese territory under Indian administration. China deplores and firmly opposes this. India is challenging China's sovereign rights and interests by unilaterally revising domestic law and administrative division. This is illegal, null and void. It will neither change the fact that the relevant region is under China's actual control nor produce any effect.[73]

Looking closely, the area India includes in its newly issued maps is Aksai Chin. India's home minister categorically declared in parliament that Aksai Chin was part of Ladakh and was Indian territory.[74] This was a direct threat to China and, obviously, would elicit a response. China expert Professor M. Taylor Fravel, from the Massachusetts Institute of Technology, said the

[c]reation of Ladakh as a federally administered union territory last August had a pretty strong impact on how China viewed Indian resolve in the dispute because the new state of Ladakh included all of Aksai Chin. That wasn't a new claim on the part of India. But then by publishing new maps and making strong statements in the Parliament about recovering this territory, it certainly got China's attention.[75]

By abrogating Articles 370 and 35A and claiming Chinese territory, India has sent a direct message to China and the US. To China, it is invalidating all previous treaties and understandings. To the US, who did not support the abrogation, the point is to please them by indicating willingness to take unilateral action in the region despite Chinese opposition. Yet, as the Galwan Valley clash reveals, China will retaliate, and India should be under no illusions of the potential consequences of this.

Lastly, India's reckless abrogation of Articles 370 and 35A has renewed expansionist claims against Pakistan vis-à-vis Gilgit-Baltistan and Azad Kashmir.[76] This has accelerated in recent years after the emergence of the China–Pakistan Economic Corridor, which passes through the disputed territory.[77] While India has never given up its claim to regions in China or Pakistan, such claims were defended by these regions being parts of the former princely state of Jammu and Kashmir, as it is hardly credible for Hindutva India to claim areas that are entirely in the socio-cultural and religious ambit of Pakistan or China. Especially in the case of Pakistan, the people in these areas revolted and defeated the foreign Dogra rulers. India's logic relies on the continued legacy of British colonialism, seeking as it does to rule areas by force with no consideration of the desires of the people.

CONCLUSION

This chapter explored the reasons for Sino-Indian rivalry and how they have been aggravated by Modi's government. Granted, there is a long history to the border disputes between both countries. However, those disputes were largely dormant until the Hindutva-led BJP took over. Since then, tensions have risen dangerously. With its newfound bravado—and US benefactor—India has been more eager, and willing to take more risks, pursue its forward policy, and heighten regional tensions. This positions it as the frontline state in the conflict with China. Moreover, most crucial was India's abrogation of Articles 370 and 35A, which directly impacted China. Not only did India vocally begin to claim Chinese territory but it passed a law in its parliament declaring the same claim. India's actions in the disputed territory of Kashmir have infringed on the sovereignty of both Pakistan and China, canceled bilateral agreements, and irrevocably set the tone for war. They have placed India on a direct collision course with both countries—neither of whom are under any illusions about the implications of the act. The Galwan

Valley clash was just a sample of the type of escalation that the world will witness. India's callous treatment of Kashmiris, its occupation and repression, and its machinations against China demonstrate the arrogance of Hindutva policy. The Indians can hardly contain the Pakistanis—by what stretch of the imagination do they think they can contain China?

Moreover, when reviewing the literature—academic articles and official statements by China and India on their relations over the last three years—a clear, downward trajectory is discernible. As US–China rivalry intensifies, India mistakenly believes to have found a niche, although it seems oblivious to the considerable risk that position poses. The policies that India is adhering to are placing it as a frontline country for any military action against China. And, while Indian protestations are loud, its actions speak louder on the choices it is making. If it wishes to join the Western club, it must target China. If it targets China, it must be ready for retaliation, which it fears. Thus, India finds itself in the unenviable position of a double bind. Rightly, Indian scholar Sawhney has cautioned India to not take on China and avoid being used as bait by the Americans. So far, Sawhney's advice is being ignored.

Furthermore, when considering recent developments between China and India, from the Galwan Valley clash to January 2022, a few key issues come to the fore. First, on September 23, 2021, India was alleged to have crossed the Chinese border, which elicited a response by China, sending 100 troops across the border, in a tit-for-tat move. Conveniently, this incident coincided with the QUAD meeting on September 24, 2021. This means tensions have not receded since the bloody Galwan Valley clash. Second, as recently as October 4, 2021, both countries are increasing their border patrols, troop activity, and war preparations. This means both countries are preparing for worst-case scenarios. Third, there have been 14 military-to-military engagements—specifically between respective military personnel—that have not produced any serious reduction of tension in the border areas. Actually, at the time of completing this book, a fifteenth session of military-to-military engagement was being planned with no headway in sight. Both China and India blame each other for their inflexibility.

Lastly, since August 5, 2019, every major international institution, especially the UN, has recognized the global threat emanating from Kashmir being pitched between three nuclear powers. Now, the broader US-Sino rivalry clearly adds another dimension to this complex territorial dispute. It is for this reason that the description of Kashmir as a nuclear flashpoint is so critical. In response, and "to stabilize the situation, China and Pakistan urged the UN Security Council to resume closed doors consultations to discuss the Kashmir issue." Actually, since August 5, 2019, the UN has discussed the Kashmir issue, behind closed doors and in a virtual meeting, three times. While the UNSC was blocked for taking any action or from formally issuing a statement, the message was clear, as stated by Pakistan's former foreign minister Shah Mahmood Qureshi: "Jammu and Kashmir is an international dispute firmly on the agenda of the Security Council and has nullified, yet another time, the Indian self-serving claim that it is an 'internal matter.'" All this points to the seriousness of the situation. This is what is so alarming and justifies the international community's elevated interest in the region: The threat of nuclear war under the macro-level US–China rivalry cannot be ruled out.

9

Conclusion

Freedom comes not with roses, but with sincerity and patience, sacrifice and commitment, bullets and graveyards. From there, the corpses in the graveyards call out to the living. Algeria had Larbi Ben Mhidi (executed by the French in 1957), Libya had Omar Mukhtar (executed by the Italians in 1931), Pakistan had Muhammad Ali Jinnah (d. 1948), and Kashmir had Syed Ali Shah Geelani (b. 1929) who recently passed away on September 1, 2021. The beloved *Peer Sahib* (Saintly Person) was no ordinary person. He heard the corpses. The inhumane way that the Indian occupation army snatched his body, desecrated it, and hurriedly buried it without recourse to last rites or family presence is unforgiveable.[1] Now, they have charged family members with treason for placing a Pakistani flag on his coffin.[2] It is of such magnitude that the very thought of it should shake you to the core. It is callous, demeaning, and criminal. And, most of all, it is a direct violation of Article 17 of the Geneva Conventions.

Yet, make no mistake. The legendary Syed Ali Shah Geelani was not diminished by this indignity. A better man cannot be harmed by a worse person, even if he has been killed. His stature has only risen. Now, more than ever before, he inspires people. His sacrifices are praised. His resilience admired. Under house arrest for nearly a decade, he never tired of protesting India's cruel occupation of Kashmir. For that reason, India is most afraid of people like him who are symbols of courage, honesty, and dedication. He could not be bought and would never bow. Because of that, he chose to be a prisoner in his own home, and that is where he died. For that was the only way a man living under occupation could truly be free. Amusingly, among his most viral videos is when he bravely argues with

Indian soldiers who were preventing him from leaving his house. He blasted them by saying: "Let me out, I want to attend the funeral of India's democracy."[3] That was the uncanny wit of the martyr Syed Ali Shah Geelani.

Today, his death imitates his life. Indian army soldiers are guarding his grave round the clock, preventing people from visiting or even congregating nearby. Such is the frightened way in which India claims to own Kashmir. Even with his passing, India continues to try and disempower the corpse of the martyr Syed Ali Shah Geelani. As Ferrara recognizes, democratic polities face "exemplary expansions of political identity with the goal of better accommodating hyper-pluralism."[4] Yet, what becomes of a society when it coerces homogeneity or is no longer open to accommodate that plurality? It resorts to nativism and enforced homogenization. This is the reality of Hindutva nationalism in India, where not a single civil society organization stands for the rights of Kashmiris to choose their own future. Where are the voices of condemnation against India's brutalization of Kashmiri society?

Above all, the life and times of Shaheed Syed Ali Shah Geelani taught us three important components of any revolutionary, anti-colonial struggle: vision, courage, and continuity. First, removing the chains of oppression is no easy task. It requires clarity of vision. Syed Ali Shah Geelani accurately presented Kashmir not as a separatist movement, since it has *never* been part of India, but as a legitimate struggle for self-determination. No matter what the Indian state offered him, he never accepted the Indian narrative. He refused to be coerced into accepting that identity.[5] He was principled and, notwithstanding his inclination for Pakistan, promised to abide by the results of any free, fair plebiscite. He acknowledged the rights of minorities and championed them. Still, he refused to accept that India had any rights over Kashmir, any more than the occupier has over the occupied. He knew, all too well, how the post-colonial Indian state has deliberately poisoned Kashmiri culture, history, and identity.

The nature of resistance against overwhelming military power requires courage: fearlessness in confronting the inevitability of death. Today, Kashmir suffers from the unbearable presence of nearly a million soldiers. It is a military occupation.

WHAT IS IT TO DIE?

What is it to die? Is it not contingent on how one lives? To either melt in His eternal warmth—that infinitely loving, tender embrace—or to wallow in the icy depths of unsightly darkness and frightening isolation. As for those who kill others unjustly, do they not forfeit their life? And what shall we make of the corpses of those murdered? Seize their breath if you will, but in death their everlasting words soothe us. Suffocate their voices in life, yet in death they shall indeed sing. You, the violator of another's rights, may have taken their eyes, but it is you who is blind. So even as the ground adoringly welcomes their twisted, contorted bodies back, they are now dancing. And how does this reflect on you? The martyr's death is a symbol of your end and the beginning of their reign. That is why corpses terrify you. You cannot even bear to look upon their bodies. Or is it that their faces seem wicked, since it is you who is unwanted?

Your covetousness, misery, and unrequited obsession—all are causes to lash out. You desecrate their corpses and secretly bury them in unmarked graves without allowing the presence of their families or the performance of their final rites. Just as the depraved weakling who throws acid in response to spurned desire: "If not me, then no one." This cruel, unusual form of punishment is a reflection of you. Thus, as the Indian government, led by the extremist BJP, revels in the monstrosity of snatching the bodies of innocent Kashmiris and burying them in forlorn graves, it is you and your ilk who are alone. Worse, know this: The unseen mourning leads to the riot you fear in the hearts of millions. This is how corpses resist. The dead have awoken the living. You may have spread poison in Kashmir, but you have also caused the cure. Truly, revolutions are fought in the heart; the battlefield is for the novice warrior.

The disputed territory of Jammu and Kashmir (Kashmir) remains the longest unresolved conflict on the agenda of the UN.[6] It is also the most militarized space on the planet.[7] Even worse, this international conflict—certainly not bilateral, since it involves Kashmir, Pakistan, India, and China—has the frightening description of being a *nuclear flashpoint*. Now, the reputable NGO Genocide Watch has issued two genocide alerts over Indian government designs/machinations in Kashmir.[8] In spite of the severity of the situation, so little is understood about this conflict. Thus, the motivation for this book: to tell the story of Kashmir through the eyes of its primary religious/ethnic demographic—the Kashmiri Muslims. More often than not, the history, culture, identity, and, most importantly, the will of the people of Kashmir has been deliberately obscured. Using a sophisticated network of misinformation, deflection, and self-righteous bravado, the post-colonial Indian state exhausts every effort to control and misdirect the narrative on Kashmir. All this, to conceal the ongoing human rights violations and program of settler-colonialism. To project an illusory normalcy in Kashmir.

But truth cannot be suffocated by lies indefinitely. It has a way of resurfacing. In Indian-Occupied Kashmir, Reuters reports that over the last 30 years alone the Indian occupation forces have killed nearly 100,000 people.[9] Moreover, India's occupation of Kashmir has led to thousands of rapes/molestations, over 6500 unmarked graves—the tip of iceberg—and created over 90,000 orphans.[10] And, as if this were not enough, the *Washington Post* reported that thousands of political prisoners, including children, are held without charge, with credible reports of their sexual abuse.[11] Recently, on October 11, 2021, the Indian government unleashed another wave of mass arrests targeting nearly 1000 Kashmiri youth.[12] This while over 600 *habeas corpus* cases are still pending in Indian courts.[13] Now, consider how these atrocious acts are being committed while millions of Kashmiris continue to suffer due to the lack of health preparedness, heightened during the coronavirus pandemic. Not only does New Delhi ignore the inalienable rights of Kashmiris but it has passed the "Jammu and Kashmir Reorganization Order 2020," a clumsy attempt at altering the disputed territory's demographics. So far, nearly 4.1 million fake citizenship certificates have been made.[14] With what contempt do they hold the people of Kashmir? If you will not be mine, then I will erase you, and invent others in your name. And the pain and suffering does not stop there, it has led to a mental health crisis impacting nearly half the population.[15]

Every struggle for freedom is beset by both poison and cure. The Hindutva settler-colonialist uses violence to pummel the fighting spirit of the people.[16] Then it sanitizes language, using false/mythical histories and discordant narratives to control their minds. Yet the people of Kashmir are defiant. And it is in this way that every revolutionary society is born. For it must be made ready to be free.

This book is an authentic attempt to challenge the dominant and inaccurate narratives that obscured the reality of the disputed territory of Kashmir. Actually, for Kashmiri Muslims the wretched 1846 Treaty of Amritsar launched the real oppression in their homeland. That is the date of their foreign occupation. When the British "sold" Kashmir, its land, people, and livestock to a non-Kashmiri Hindu Dogra family and thereafter provided them military support. That culminated in the cruelest era in Kashmir's history because the foreign Hindu Dogra rulers treated the indigenous people worse than slaves. They tried very hard to create a Hindu state out of an overwhelmingly Muslim-majority land. They did so by forced labor, forcible confiscation of land and agricultural produce, and intentional impoverishment. As a result, hundreds of thousands of Kashmiris fled their beloved homeland to Afghanistan and adjacent lands. From that tyranny, though, grew resistance, eventually leading to a popular revolt against the Dogras. In other words, the ebb and flow of resistance in Kashmir emerges as a direct response to Dogra tyranny. A longing for freedom that has never waned, even if quieted. Without doubt, this is Kashmir's story—desired, yet scorned; adored, but reviled; praised, but denigrated. Yet, above all, it resists. No matter how seemingly indiscernible, resistance to India's occupation is alive. For oppression cannot last. And crimes against humanity cannot be ignored. No matter how long it takes, Kashmir will be free. As proudly spoken by Ho Chi Minh, "You will kill ten of us, we will kill one of you, but in the end, you will tire of it first."[17]

To reiterate, with Dogra power weakening and the British quitting India, Maharaja Hari Singh thought of ways to carve out a small empire for himself. Kashmiris were revolting, so he knew that the state of Jammu and Kashmir, which was propped up by the British, would no longer hold. So, he decided to do the unthinkable. An unforgiveable crime against humanity—a genocide—took place. With delusions of creating their own fiefdom, the Dogras murdered at least 237,000 Muslims of Jammu. This was a painful chapter to write, considering what the Jammu genocide means to me on a personal level, and how it killed several members of my family— both paternal and maternal. It uprooted us from our ancestral homes and property. More troubling, this massive orgy of genocidal violence is hardly talked about. It slipped through the proverbial cracks. But how? The only explanation is the latent Islamophobia that dismissed Muslim deaths as unworthy of reporting. Very much like Afghan or Palestinian lives not being considered as important as Ukrainian lives. Because of that, this book carefully explored the conditions in the erstwhile state of Jammu and Kashmir prior to the massacre. I wanted to understand how violence was operational- ized and the systematic and state-sponsored nature of the genocide. Finally, I wanted to explain how the genocide continues to impact the memory of Kashmiri Muslims—not just in Indian-Occupied Kashmir but especially for the millions of Kashmiri descendants in Sialkot, Gujranwala, and Wazirabad and elsewhere throughout the world. Among the first words spoken to me by my maternal grand- mother Sughra Butt—a survivor—was "they stole everything."

After that, this book explored the deep-seated, pathological obsta- cles for peace in Kashmir. It did so by deconstructing the partition and uncovering the demonizing narratives embedded in it. There is a sophisticated process involved in the perpetuation of what I described as the partition industry that includes myth, demoniza- tion, and dispossession. Myth involves writing false history, claiming a monolithic ancient India, and appropriating the Indus civilization or ancient Kashmir. Demonization of Islam, and Muslims, constructs prejudicial stereotypes of violent Muslim foreigners who forcibly dispossessed Hindus of their land and wealth, and now threaten the same will happen again. Finally, the partition industry works to justify the dispossession of Kashmir by disregarding and erasing the primary ethnic religious demographic—the Kashmiri Muslims. Altogether, each variable of the partition industry interconnects to deny agency, demonize, and erase alternative identities in order to possess coveted territory. Moreover, it normalizes violence, making understanding of the partition industry vital for the current conflict.

Furthermore, it is crucial to recognize that the partition industry becomes imaginable as a reaction to the last days of the British Raj. It was during that time when questions of partition arose. After all, the idea of partition presumed a whole nation that preceded the British, but the British had "imagined" India—an imaginary that was and remains useful to Hindutva myth. Hence, they ask: what was partitioned? This brings forth a contentious assertion: that there was no partition of India in 1947. Instead, the British Raj was divided, creating two new, political entities—India and Pakistan— led by dominant and competing identities/ideological trajectories.[18] This part of South Asian history has not been judiciously explored. There are pervasive narratives that spread disinformation and that are used to disempower and appropriate. How does such a vast land as India with hundreds of languages and creeds become presented as "a monolithic" nation? Even the word India itself is not of Indian origin. It is a British distortion of the Persian word *Hind*. Creating one's own identity is fine but forcing it upon another is not. And the post-colonial Indian imaginary found it impossible to reconcile alternative identities. Whether by incarnating land or concocting past injustices, Hindutva India could not accept any negotiation of identity or land. Consequently, it had to disavow the Kashmiri right to self-determination, implement its forward policy with China, and claim land that doesn't belong to it.

Next, the book turned to focus on more recent events, focusing on the electoral victory of the BJP in 2014.[19] This victory represented a turn to Hindu nationalism, which fostered Islamophobia, internally in India, in the treatment of Kashmir, and in foreign policy generally. For Kashmir this led to the flouting of international laws, the Indian constitution, procedural regulations, or ethics of any sort. As a result, existing Islamophobia became emboldened and legitimized. Today, Islamophobia in India is a monstrosity that bodes ill for the world. All pretenses to respect the sentiments of the people of Kashmir, or other minorities like Christians, Sikhs, and Dalits, have been thrown away.[20] This has led to hundreds of documented cases of lynching and rape, and reignited the tinderbox of Kashmir in dangerous and, as of yet, unknown ways. But rather than just describe what is happening throughout India, I wanted to explore the contours of the Hindutva narrative. This is relevant in that it not only led to the rationalization of the Jammu genocide but continues to inform post-colonial Indian intelligentsia and policymakers. Moreover, I explained how Islamophobia is weaponized in India. Christophe Jaffrelot describes this as "the strategy of stigmatization and emulation of 'threatening Others' based on a feeling of vulnerability born of a largely imaginary threat posed by 'aliens,' principally Muslims and Christians."[21] Specifically, the act of "protecting" the Hindu majority results in well-documented criminal and Islamophobic acts. These include the following: 1) cow vigilantism, also known as *gau rakshak*; 2) *ghar vāpasī*—forced conversion; 3) love jihad—hatred against Muslim males wedding Hindu females; and 4) *Bahu lao, Beti Bachao*—bring a (Muslim) daughter-in-law and save your daughter (from Muslim men). All in all, there is a carefully orchestrated strategy, supported at the highest levels of government, to demonize Islam and Muslims in order to rationalize crimes against them.

In Kashmir, the Hindutva playbook is slightly different. It pursues three contradictory, irreconcilable strategies: weaponizing pluralism to enforce homogenization; utilizing a rhetoric of upholding the law to apply various punitive measures including mass arrest, cordon and search operations (CASOs), and murder; and, lastly, claiming to champion freedom of speech, assembly, and dissent while labeling Kashmiri Muslims who express their voice as guilty of terror. The policy lures unwitting targets out in order to punish them. This way the Indian occupation forces can claim to allow dissent but conceal the harsh, punitive measures taken against those who speak out. Admittedly, that playbook is becoming harder and harder to hide. The ongoing arrests of journalists, academics, and even those who make simple WhatsApp comments have been exposed. For that reason, the Indian narrative on Kashmir has crumbled both inside the disputed territory and with regard to the international community.

In Chapter 7, I explored the significance of the abrogation of Articles 370 and 35A, doing do so by dissecting the issue four-fold. First, by providing the background and origins of Articles 370 and 35A, explaining how it was written by two sovereigns and cannot legally be undone by any one side. Second, I explained that immediate impact of its abrogation is the nullification of the Simla Agreement—the treaty agreement signed between India and Pakistan on July 2, 1972. That treaty has been used by India to justify its insistence on restricting Kashmir to bilateral discussions. However, India's unilaterally alteration of the status of the disputed territory clearly violates the Simla Agreement. This means India cannot insist on bilateralism. Third, I described the ways the abrogation has led to a flurry of Indian settler-colonial policies in Kashmir operationalized through seven aspects: 1) inventing Kashmiris through issuance of domicile/citizenship certificates (so far, nearly 4.1 million fake citizenship certificates have been issued);[22] 2) land theft; 3) altering maps, changing names of public institutions, schools, and places of interest to enforce "Indianization"; 4) misrepresenting Kashmir on official government websites to falsely show it as having a Hindu majority; 5) coercive patriotism; 6) removing all Kashmiris from top bureaucratic positions to solidify the occupation; and 7) a delimitation process to project normalcy. Collectively, India's policies aim to pursue a settler-colonial path in the disputed territory, and its machinations have led to a serious rekindling of regional instability.

The last chapter explores the complex intersections of China–India border relations, the Galwan Valley clash, and the future of their rivalry regarding Kashmir, along with the broader discussion of Sino-US contestation. This will, in all likelihood, lead to elevated regional/global instability—even a nuclear flashpoint. India's illegal annexation of Kashmir directly brought China into the conflict. Driven by an aggressive foreign policy of "forward," India began to claim land in China and even to distribute newly made maps that included Chinese territory. Of course, China took notice. They responded firmly and made it clear that unilateral changes to maps do not change the ground reality. But the message was clear: India was provoking China, setting both countries on a war path of which the world must take notice. And that is what happened when both countries squared off during the infamous Galwan Valley clash. Twenty Indian and four Chinese soldiers were killed in a bloody melee using makeshift weapons and baseball bats wrapped in barbed wire. The whole world watched as videos of the altercation were uploaded on social media.

For that reason, the final chapter explained how Sino-Indian relations reached this point. It answers that by exploring five variables: 1) the history of the Sino-Indian border—a problem since British colonial times; 2) India's forward policy—which assumes borders that the British Raj imagined, even if they were not in possession of the land; 3) Hindutva Bravado—a renewed assertiveness that projects the idea of absolute security; 4) Indo-Pacific rivalry—India has decided to closely ally with the QUAD in direct threat to China; and 5) the impact of the abrogation of Articles 370 and 35A—which now forces China into the Kashmir conflict. Together, these five factors explain how Sino-Indian relations have deteriorated, the current pulse of their rivalry, and its impact on Kashmir. It does not look good. As of today, there have been 14 military-to-military engagements, which have not produced any serious reduction in tension.[23] Also, on September 23, 2021, India was alleged to have crossed the Chinese border, which elicited the response from China of sending 100 troops across the border in a tit-for-tat move.[24] Conveniently, this incident coincided with the QUAD meeting on September 24, 2021.[25] Now, as recently as October 2022, both India and the US are planning to hold military exercises near the Chinese border.[26] This is deeply troubling. It is imperative that the world takes notice and compels all sides—Pakistan, China, Kashmir, and India—to come to the negotiating table. If not, the alternative is most assuredly a war that will engulf not only the region, but the world.

Kashmiris need to document their own history. Champion their own heroes. Tell their own story. That is how this book has been written. To center the primary religious-ethnic/demographic in Kashmir—the Kashmiri Muslims. By doing so, it offers a detailed explanation of historical and contemporary sources, favors Kashmiri Muslim oral tradition, and confronts the false history, myths, and misleading narratives that continue to plague research on Kashmir. Any precursory glance at the literature on Kashmir reveals it is dominated by Indians. This is not to say that only those from a community may research it, but many post-colonial Indians have a political/ideological viewpoint that is complicit in cultural and structural violence, and in whitewashing the ground reality. They have flooded social media, academia, and media outlets with fictitious discourses on Kashmir that rationalize India's presence. This book exposes that. Whether by inventing religious pilgrimages such as Amarnath, mistranslating Persian texts on Kashmir or "Hinduizing" names, roads, and landmarks. All this is done to fabricate a dubious Sanskrit/Indic past and inaccurately connect Kashmir to India. I wanted to undo that. To unravel those fictitious narratives, false history, and deliberate misrepresentations, in order to reveal the reality of Kashmir as understood by the majority of its people. And what do we learn from that? Kashmir is not India. It is neither a separatist nor anti-national movement but a *bona fide* freedom movement.

Notes

CHAPTER 1   INTRODUCTION

1. Ather Zia and Javaid Iqbal Bhat (eds.), "Introduction," in *A Desolation Called Peace: Voices from Kashmir* (Harper Collins: India, 2019), 33.
2. Samreen Mushtaq and Mudasir Amin, "Why Has Kashmir Been Forgotten?" *Aljazeera Online*, March 2, 2019, www.aljazeera. com/indepth/opinion/kashmir-forgotten-190301213038382.html [accessed March 2, 2019].
3. Liu Zongyi, "Boundary Standoff and China–India Relations," in *China Quarterly of International Strategic Studies*, 6.2 (2020), 223–248, 240.
4. Gregory Stanton, "Kashmir Earns Genocide Alert," *Genocide Watch*, August 15, 2019, www.genocidewatch.com/single-post/2019/08/15/ genocide-alert-for-kashmir-india [accessed September 21, 2020].
5. Arundhati Roy et al., "Azadi: The Only Thing Kashmiris Want," in *Kashmir: The Case for Freedom* (London: Verso, 2011), 71.
6. Ather Zia, "The Haunting Specter of Hindu Ethnonationalist-Neocolonial Development in Indian Occupied Kashmir," in *Development*, 63 (2020), 60–66.
7. Chayan Kundu, "Fact Check: Kashmiri Images False," *India Today*, www.indiatoday.in/fact-check/story/fact-check-viral-images-of-kashmiris-smiling-at-security-forces-are-years-old-1579852-2019-08-11 [accessed August 27, 2019].
8. "Congress Ask Home Minister to Explain 'Final Solution.'" *Economic Times*, https://economictimes.indiatimes.com/news/politics-and-nation/congress-asks-home-minister-to-explain-final-solution-for-jammu-and-kashmir/articleshow/58902110.cms?from=mdr [accessed May 30, 2017].
9. Anik Joshi, "India Has Handed China a Way to Interfere in Kashmir," *Foreign Policy*, https://foreignpolicy.com/2020/06/16/china-kashmir-himalayas-pakistan-conflict/ [accessed June 20, 2020].
10. "Repression Persists in Jammu and Kashmir," *Human Rights Watch*, www.hrw.org/news/2022/08/02/india-repression-persists-jammu-and-kashmir [accessed August 2, 2022].
11. Richard Roth, "United Nations Security Council Meets on Kashmir," *CNN*, https://edition.cnn.com/2019/08/16/asia/un-security-council-kashmir-intl/index.html [accessed August 16, 2019].

12. Mona Bhan et al., "Introduction. 'Rebels of the Streets': Violence, Protest, and Freedom in Kashmir," in *Resisting Occupation in Kashmir*, ed. by Haley Duschinski, Mona Bhan, Ather Zia, and Cynthia Mahmood (Philadelphia: University of Pennsylvania Press, 2018), 1–41.

13. Gowhar Geelani, *Kashmir: Rage and Reason* (New Delhi: Rupa Publications India, 2019), 9.

14. Syma Mohamed, "Meet the Americans Who Give a Voice to Silenced Kashmiris," *TRT World Online*, August 20, 2019, www.trtworld. com/magazine/meet-the-americans-who-give-a-voice-to-silenced-kashmiris-29144 [accessed August 20, 2019].

15. Ather Zia, "Straw Man Arguments in Removal of Article 370," *Asia Dialogue*, September 27, 2019, https://theasiadialogue. com/2019/09/27/the-long-read-straw-man-arguments-and-the-removal-of-article-370/ [accessed September 27, 2019].

16. Christopher Snedden, *Understanding Kashmir and Kashmiris* (London: Hurst & Company, 2015), 21.

17. Naseer Ganai, "India Issues 41.05 Lakh Citizenship Certificates in Two Years," *Outlook India*, August 3, 2021, www.outlookindia. com/website/story/india-news-jk-govt-issued-4105-lakh-domicile-certificates-in-two-years/390368 [accessed August 20, 2021].

18. Zia (2020).

19. Usaid Siddiqui, "Kashmiri Cartoonist Taking a Dig at Indian Rule," *Aljazeera Features*, www.aljazeera.com/features/2020/8/13/meet-kashmiri-cartoonist-taking-a-dig-at-indian-rule [accessed August 20, 2020].

20. *United Nations Human Rights: Office of the High Commissioner*, July 8, 2018, www.ohchr.org/Documents/Countries/IN/KashmirUpdate Report_8July2019.pdf [accessed July 10, 2019].

21. Ian Stephens, *Pakistan* (London: Ernest Benn, 1963), 200. See, Iffat Rashid, "Theatrics of a 'Violent State' or 'State of Violence': Mapping Histories and Memories of Partition in Jammu and Kashmir," in *South Asia: Journal of South Asian Studies*, 43.2 (2020), 215–231.

22. Sudheendra Kulkarni, "Defying the Maharaja," *The Wire*, 2020, https://thewire.in/diplomacy/how-and-why-gilgit-baltistan-defied-maharaja-hari-singh-and-joined-pakistan [accessed September 25, 2020].

23. Ibid.

24. Yaqoob Khan Bangash, *A Princely Affair: The Accession and Integration of the Princely States of Pakistan 1947–1955* (Oxford: Oxford University Press, 2015), 7.

25. Ibid., 7–9.

26. Khalid Bashir Ahmad, *Kashmir: Exposing the Myth behind the Narrative* (Thousand Oaks, CA: Sage Publications, 2017), 3–11.

27. Geelani (2019), 19.

28. Krishna Prasad, "The Drumbeaters of Dystopia," *The Hindu*, www.thehindu.com/opinion/lead/the-drumbeaters-of-dystopia/article29385937.ece [accessed August 23, 2019]. Also, Samuels, Else, "Kashmir: Indian Government Vs. Facts," *Washington Post*, www.washingtonpost.com/politics/2019/08/23/kashmir-indian-government-versus-facts-ground/ [accessed August 23, 2019].

29. Muhammad Tahir Tabassum, "Political Situation in Kashmir and the Role of the United Nations," in *Studies of Changing Societies: Comparative and Interdisciplinary Focus*, 1.2 (2012).

30. Hilal Mir and Muhammad Raafi, "Torture in Disputed Kashmir," *TRT World*, August 20, 2019, www.trtworld.com/magazine/india-s-torture-methods-new-claims-emerge-from-disputed-kashmir-29879 [accessed September 18, 2019].

31. Judd Yadid, "Israel's Iron Lady," *Haaretz*, www.haaretz.com/2015-05-03/ty-article/.premium/17-golda-meir-quotes-on-her-117th-birthday/0000017f-db2a-d3a5-af7f-fbaef8be0000 [accessed October 4, 2022].

32. See, Audrey Truschke, "Hindutva's Dangerous Rewriting of History," in *South Asia Multidisciplinary Academic Journal*, 24/25 (2020), 1–2.

33. Christopher Snedden, *Independent Kashmir: An Incomplete Aspiration* (Manchester: Manchester University Press, 2021), 317.

34. Mangeet Negi, "Top Indian Muslim Body Supports Removal of Article 370," *India Today*, www.indiatoday.in/india/story/jamiat-ulama-i-hind-kashmir-integral-part-india-article-370-1598372-2019-09-12 [accessed April 4, 2020].

35. Aditya Menon, "Why Madani Supports Modi?" in *The Quint*, www.youtube.com/watch?v=xrIr_mAaNvQ [accessed December 4, 2019].

36. H. L. Erdman, *The Swatantra Party and Indian Conservatism* (Cambridge: Cambridge University Press, 2007), 55.

37. "Why a Map in India's New Parliament Has Riled Its Neighbors," *Aljazeera Explainer*, www.aljazeera.com/news/2023/6/7/why-a-map-in-indias-new-parliament-has-riled-its-neighbours [accessed June 7, 2023].

38. Homi Bhabha, "The Other Question: Difference, Discrimination and the Discourse of Colonialism," in *Literature, Politics and Theory*, ed. by Francis Baker et al. (London: Routledge, 2013), 155.

39. John Lee, "Unrealized Potential: India's Soft Power Ambition in Asia," *Foreign Policy Analysis Report*, Centre for Independent Studies, June

30, 2010, www.cis.org.au/app/uploads/2015/07/fpa4.pdf [accessed June 30, 2022].

40. Akbar S. Ahmed, *Jinnah, Pakistan and Islamic Identity: The Search for Saladin* (London: Routledge, 1997).

41. *United Nations Human Rights: Office of the High Commissioner*, July 8, 2019, www.ohchr.org/Documents/Countries/IN/KashmirUpdate Report_8July2019.pdf.

42. Christophe Jaffrelot, "The Fate of Secularism in India," *Policy Report*, Carnegie Endowment for International Peace, April 4, 2019, https://carnegieendowment.org/2019/04/04/fate-of-secularism-in-india-pub-78689 [accessed April 30, 2019].

43. Audrey Truschke, "Hindutva's Dangerous Rewriting of History," in *South Asia Multidisciplinary Academic Journal*, 24/25 (2020), 1–2.

44. Paula Thompson, Rhonda Itaoui, and Hatem Bazian, "Islamophobia in India: Stoking Bigotry," Policy Report in *Islamophobia Research and Documentation Project*, Center for Race and Gender at the University of California, Berkeley, April 2019, https://irdproject.com/wp-content/uploads/2019/04/Islamophobia-in-India-Web-Spread.pdf [accessed April 10, 2019].

45. Truschke (2020), 1–2. Italics mine.

46. Thompson, Itaoui, and Bazian (2019).

47. Interview with Kuldip Nayar on Friday, July 30, 2011, at Rayburn Gold Room #2168. Washington, DC, USA.

48. Rafi Samad, *The Grandeur of Gandhara: The Ancient Buddhist Civilization of the Swat, Peshawar, Kabul and Indus Valleys* (New York: Algora Publishing, 2013), 5–17.

49. François Bernier, *Travels in the Moghul Empire, 1656–58*, ed. by A. Constable (Paris, 1891).

50. Ahmad (2017), 3.

51. Jeremiah Morelock, "Introduction: The Frankfurt School and Authoritarian Populism: A Historical Outline," in *Critical Theory and Authoritarian Populism*, ed. by Jeremiah Morelock (London: University of Westminster Press, 2018), xiii–xxxviii.

52. Geelani (2019), 239.

53. Helen Regan et al., "Pakistan Downs Two Indian Fighter Jets," *CNN*, February 27, 2019, https://edition.cnn.com/2019/02/27/india/india-pakistan-strikes-escalation-intl/index.html [accessed February 28, 2019].

54. Ibid.

55. Laura Seligman, "Pakistan Shoots Down Two Indian Aircraft, Missing None," *CNN*, April 4, 2019, https://foreignpolicy.com/2019/04/04/

did-india-shoot-down-a-pakistani-jet-u-s-count-says-no/ [accessed April 4, 2019].

56. Michael Safi and Mehreen Zahra-Malik, "Pakistan Returns Captured Indian Pilot," *Guardian*, March 1, 2019, www.theguardian.com/world/2019/mar/01/pakistan-hands-back-indian-pilot-shot-down-over-kashmir-in-peace-gesture [accessed March 1, 2019].

57. Michelle Bachelet, "Opening Statement by UN High Commissioner for Human Rights," *Office of the High Commissioner of Human Rights*, www.ohchr.org/EN/NewsEvents/Pages/DisplayNews.aspx?LangID=E&NewsID=26806 [accessed March 1, 2021].

58. "Kashmir Report: UN Biased, Hasn't Done Homework, Says BJP," *Times of India*, https://timesofindia.indiatimes.com/india/kashmir-report-un-biased-hasnt-done-homework-says-bjp/articleshow/64594347.cms [accessed June 15, 2018].

59. Richard Bucher, *Diversity Consciousness: Opening Our Minds to People, Cultures, and Opportunities* (London: Pearson, 2015), 9.

60. Rebecca Ratcliffe, "Kashmir: India's Draconian Blackout Sets Worrying Precedent, Warns UN Envoy," *Guardian*, August 8, 2019, www.theguardian.com/world/2019/aug/08/kashmir-communications-blackout-is-draconian-says-un-envoy [accessed August 8, 2019].

61. Farhan Mujahid Chak, "On How Corpses Resist," *Daily Sabah*, February 3, 2021, www.dailysabah.com/opinion/op-ed/on-how-corpses-resist-in-kashmir [accessed February 4, 2021].

62. Rifat Fareed, "Pro-Indian Kashmiri Leaders Arrested," *Aljazeera*, September 19, 2019, www.aljazeera.com/news/2019/09/farooq-abdullah-arrest-leaves-india-allies-kashmir-190918153854815.html [accessed September 19, 2019].

63. Shilpa Shaji, "Indian Women on Fact-Finding Mission on Kashmir," *Newsclick India*, September 24, 2019, www.newsclick.in/50-days-lock-down-kashmir-women-activists-release-fact-finding-report [accessed September 24, 2019].

64. Ibid.

65. Peerzada Ashiq, "Now, Revolving-Door Arrests in Kashmir," *The Hindu*, www.thehindu.com/news/national/now-revolving-door-arrests-in-kashmir/article29310428.ece [accessed September 24, 2019].

66. Tariq Mir, "India–China Clash in Kashmir," *Aljazeera*, July 5, 2020, www.aljazeera.com/opinions/2020/7/5/what-was-the-deadly-india-china-border-clash-really-about [accessed July 5, 2020].

67. Pankaj Mishra, "Silence over Kashmir Conflict," *Guardian*, August 14, 2019, www.theguardian.com/theguardian/2010/aug/14/silence-over-kashmir-conflict [accessed August 14, 2019].

68. Vikram Sharma, "1 Million Indian Forces Guard Kashmir Valley," *Asian Age*, August 18, 2019, www.asianage.com/india/all-india/180819/forces-deploy-1-million-to-guard-kashmir-valley.html [accessed August 18, 2019].

69. "There Should Be a Plebiscite in Kashmir," *Indian Express*, July 21, 2016, https://indianexpress.com/article/india/india-news-india/plebiscite-in-kashmir-jyotiraditya-scindia-2926490/ [accessed July 28, 2019].

70. Roy (2011), 38.

71. Ather Zia, Mona Bhan, Haley Duschinski, and Cynthia Mahmoud, "Rebels of the Streets: Violence, Protest and Freedom in Kashmir," in *Resisting Occupation in Kashmir* (University of Pennsylvania Press, 2017), 2.

72. "India Fires Officers for Accidental Missile Launch into Pakistan," *Aljazeera English*, www.aljazeera.com/news/2022/8/23/india-fires-officers-for-accidental-missile-launch-into-pakistan [accessed August 23, 2022].

73. Ahmed (1997), 3–6.

74. Christophe Jaffrelot, "A Defacto Ethnic Democracy? Obliterating and Targeting, Hindu Vigilantes, and the Ethno-State," in *Majoritarian State: How Hindu Nationalism Is Changing India*, ed. by Angana P. Chatterji, Thomas Blom Hansen, and Christophe Jaffrelot (Oxford: Oxford University Press, 2019), 41.

75. Ganai (2021).

76. Swati Bhasin et al., "Chinese Troops Deployed in Considerable Numbers in Ladakh," *New Delhi Television Limited Broadcasting Channel*, October 2, 2021, www.ndtv.com/india-news/india-china-standoff-army-chief-manoj-mukund-naravane-on-increase-in-deployment-of-chinese-troops-in-eastern-ladakh-2561261 [accessed October 2, 2021].

77. "India Matching Chinese Troop Buildup on Disputed Border," *Dawn*, October 3, 2021, www.dawn.com/news/1649913/india-matching-chinese-troop-build-up-on-disputed-border-says-indian-army-chief [accessed October 4, 2021].

78. "Chinese PLA Soldiers Cross Border with India? Indian Media Habitual in Hyping the Topic," *Global Times*, October 2, 2021, www.globaltimes.cn/page/202109/1235502.shtml [accessed October 3, 2021].

79. "India Matching Chinese Troop Buildup on Disputed Border," *Dawn*, October 3, 2021, www.dawn.com/news/1649913/india-matching-chinese-troop-build-up-on-disputed-border-says-indian-army-chief [accessed October 4, 2021].

80. Vedika Sud, Barbara Starr, Sahar Akbarzai, and Kathleen Magramo. "US War Games near Chinese Border," *CNN*, August 7, 2022, www. cnn.com/2022/08/06/india/india-us-military-exercise-line-of-actual-control-china-intl-hnk/index.html [accessed August 7, 2022].

CHAPTER 2   WHO ARE THE KASHMIRIS? RESISTING POST-COLONIAL IDENTITY THEFT AND FALSE NARRATIVES

1. Eric Larson and Ron Aminzade, "Nation-Building in Post-Colonial Nation-States: The Cases of Tanzania and Fiji," in *International Social Science Journal*, 59.192 (June 2008), 169–182.
2. Benedict Anderson, *Imagined Communities: Reflections on the Origins and Spread of Nationalism* (London: Verso, 2006).
3. Eric Hobsbawm, *The Invention of Tradition* (Cambridge: Cambridge University Press, 2012).
4. M. S. Kumar and L. A. Scanlon, "Ireland and Irishness: The Contextuality of Postcolonial Identity," in *Annals of the Association of American Geographers*, 109.1 (2019), 202–222. https://doi.org/10.1080/2469445 2.2018.1507812.
5. Tariq Ali, "Afterword: Not Crushed, Merely Ignored," in *Kashmir: The Case for Freedom*, ed. by Tariq Ali et al. (London: Verso, 2011), 132–137.
6. Shantanu Kishwar, "The Rising Role of Buddhism in India's Soft Power Strategy," *Observer Research Foundation Policy Report (ORF)* (2018). The ORF is a major think-tank based in Mumbai, India. www. orfonline.org/wpcontent/uploads/2018/02/ORF_IssueBrief_228_ Buddhism.pdf [accessed May 1, 2021].
7. Ahmed Hasan Dani and Omar Khan, "An Interview with Ahmed Hasan Dani," *Harappa*, January 6, 1998, https://live harappacom. pantheonsite.io/script/danitext.html [accessed August 1, 2021].
8. Rupam Jain and Tom Lasseter, "By Rewriting History, Hindu Nationalists Assert Dominance," *Reuters*, March 6, 2018, www.reuters. com/investigates/special-report/india-modi-culture/ [accessed March 6, 2018].
9. Truschke (2020).
10. Samant Subramanian, "How Hindu Supremacists Are Tearing India Apart," *Guardian*, February 20, 2020, www.theguardian.com/ world/2020/feb/20/hindu-supremacists-nationalism-tearing-india-apart-modi-bjp-rss-jnu-attacks [accessed February 20, 2020].
11. Arundhati Roy, "Kashmir Was Never an Integral Part of India," *The Hindu*, www.thehindu.com/news/national//article59924835.ece [accessed October 10, 2010].

12. Arundhati Roy, "Kashmir Was Never Integral Part of India," *The Hindu*, October 28, 2020, www.thehindu.com/news/national/Kashmir-was-never-integral-part-of-India-Arundhati/article15794308.ece [accessed October 28, 2020].
13. Truschke (2020).
14. Nilanjana Bhowmick, "Meet the Militant Monk Spreading Islamophobia in India," *Washington Post*, March 24, 2017, www.washingtonpost.com/news/global-opinions/wp/2017/03/24/meet-the-militant-monk-spreading-islamophobia-in-india/ [accessed March 24, 2017].
15. Farhan Mujahid Chak, "Kashmir and the Myth of Indivisible India," *Aljazeera Online*, September 2016, www.aljazeera.com/opinions/2016/9/28/kashmir-and-the-myth-of-indivisible-india/ [accessed September 2016].
16. Mridu Rai, "Kashmiris in the Hindu Rashtra," in *Majoritarian State: How Hindu Nationalism Is Changing India*, ed. by Angana P. Chatterji, Thomas Blom Hansen and Christophe Jaffrelot (Oxford: Oxford University Press, 2019), 259–260.
17. Bernier (1891), 393.
18. Snedden (2015), 21.
19. Ahmad (2017), 25.
20. Rashid (2020).
21. Snedden (2015), 21.
22. Ganai (2021).
23. P. N. K. Bamzai, *Culture and Political History of Kashmir*, Vol. 1 (New Delhi: M. D. Publications, 1994), 4.
24. Ahmad (2017), xxii, footnote 10.
25. Bernier (1891), 397.
26. Ram Lal Kanilal and Pandit Jagadhar Zadoo, "Introduction," in *Nilmatapuranam* (Lahore: Moti Lal Banarsi, Punjab Sanskrit Book Depot, 1924), 4.
27. Ibid., 4.
28. Ibid., 4–5.
29. K. M. Pannikar, "Introduction," in Ved Kumari (1968), *The Nilamata Purana: A Cultural and Literary Study of a Kashmiri Purana*, Vol. 1, vi (Delhi: J. & K. Academy of Art, Culture and Languages).
30. Ahmad (2017), 27. See, Pannikar, vi.
31. Ram Lal Kanilal and Pandit Jagadhar Zadoo, "Introduction," in *Nilmatapuranam*, 6 (Lahore: Moti Lal Banarsi, Punjab Sanskrit Book Depot, 1924).
32. Trilokinath Raina, *A History of Kashmiri Literature* (New Delhi: Sahitya Akademi, 2002), 2.

33. Chitralekha Zutshi, "Translating History: Rajatarangini and the Making of India's Past," *Library of Congress Video*, July 10, 2008, www. loc.gov/today/cyberlc/feature_wdesc.php?rec=4351.

34. Gulshan Majeed, "No Naga Presence in Ancient Kashmir," in *Approaches to Kashmir Studies*, ed. by G. M. Khawaja and Gulshan Majeed (Srinagar: Gulshan Books, 2011), 39.

35. M. A. Stein, (translator), *Kalhana's Rajatarangini*, Vol. 2 (Delhi: Motilal, 1961), 377.

36. Ibid., 377–379.

37. Ahmad (2017), xxii, footnote 10.

38. Stein (1961), 377.

39. Ahmad (2017), xvi.

40. Mohibul Hasan, *Kashmir under the Sultans* (Calcutta: Iran Society, 1959), 19.

41. Ahmad (2017), xvi.

42. *Baharistan-i-Shahi*, trans. by K. N. Pandit (Calcutta: Firma KLM, 2022), footnotes 7–8.

43. Muhammad Ali Kashmiri, *Tofhatul-Ahbab*, trans. by K. N. Pandit (New Delhi: Voice of India, 2018), 253.

44. Ibid., 253, footnote 2.

45. Shonaleeka Kaul, *The Making of Early Kashmir: Landscape and Identity in the Rajatarangini* (Oxford: Oxford University Press, 2018), 7–10.

46. Ahmad (2017), 11.

47. Ibid., xviii.

48. See, Sisi Kumar Das, *A History of Indian Literature, 500–1399: From Courtly to the Popular* (Delhi: Sahitya Akademi Publications, 2005), 193. Also, Kaul (2018), 5–11.

49. M. Ashraf Bhat, *The Changing Language Roles and Linguistic Identities of the Kashmiri Speech Community* (Newcastle upon Tyne: Cambridge Scholars Publishing, 2017).

50. Ahmad (2017), 9.

51. Ibid., 343.

52. Ibid., 343–348.

53. Ibid., 344.

54. Stein (1961), 79.

55. J. N. Ganhar and P. N. Ganhar, *Buddhism in Kashmir and Ladakh* (New Delhi: Karol Bagh, 1957), 15.

56. Upinder Singh, *Political Violence in Ancient India* (Cambridge, MA: Harvard University Press, 2017), 240.

57. René Grousset, *In the Footsteps of the Buddha* (1929; trans. 1932). See, Ganhar and Ganhar (1957), 15.

58. Ahmad (2107), 307.
59. Stein (1961), 43.
60. Ganhar and Ganhar (1957), 15.
61. Tukan D. Somi, "Kanishka's Buddhist Council in Kashmir," in F. Hassnain, *Heritage of Kashmir* (Srinagar: Gulshan Publishers, 1980), 34.
62. Edward C. Sachau, *Alberuni's India*, Vol. 1 (London: Kegan Paul, Trench, Trubner & Co., 1910), 206.
63. Antonio Monserrate, *The Commentary of Father Monserrate: On His Journey to the Court of Akbar* (Oxford: Oxford University Press, 1922), 111.
64. Ibid., 111.
65. Bernier (1891), 430.
66. Ibid., 342.
67. Hasan (1959), 37–39.
68. Ibid., 38.
69. Ibid., 39.
70. Ibid., 39–41.
71. Ibid., 40.
72. Khalid Bashir Ahmad, "The Hill and the History," *Greater Kashmir*, March 14, 2015, https://kbahmad05.medium.com/the-hill-and-the-history-342d11a180a5 [accessed March 14, 2015].
73. Ibid.
74. Godfrey Thomas Vigne, *Travels in Kashmir, Ladak, Iskardo* (London: Henry Colburn Publishers, 1842), 395.
75. G. M. D. Sufi, *Kashir: A History of Kashmir*, Vol. 1 (Lahore: University of Punjab, 1948), 15.
76. Ibid., 18.
77. Ibid., 18–20. See, Hasan (1959), 62–64.
78. J. M. Downie, T. Tashi, F. R. Lorenzo, J. E. Feusier, H. Mir, J. T. Prchal, et al., "A Genome-Wide Search for Greek and Jewish Admixture in the Kashmiri Population," in *PLOS One* (2016), 1–4.
79. Farrukh Hussain, *Afghanistan in the Age of Empires: The Great Game for South and Central Asia* (Afghanistan: Silkroad Books, 2018), 12–15.
80. Ghulam Qadir Bhat, "The Emergence and Development of the Muslim Political Identity in Kashmir 1846–1947," in *Journal of South Asian Studies*, 7.1 (2019), 9–18.
81. Ahmad (2017), xv.
82. "Kandahar's Qizilbash," *Kashmir Life*, November 2017, https://kashmirlife.net/kandahars-qizilbash-issue-35-vol-09-157293/ [accessed November 30, 2017].

83. Mridu Rai, *Hindu Rulers, Muslim Subjects: Islam, Rights and the History of Kashmir* (London: Hurst & Company, 2004), 39.
84. Mona Bhan, "Divide and Rule," *Kindle Magazine: Politics and Society*, April 2, 2016, http://kindlemag.in/divide-and-rule/ [accessed April 2, 2016].
85. Ibid.
86. Shahid Tantray, "India Trying to Create a Shia–Sunni Divide in Kashmir," *Caravan Magazine*, https://caravanmagazine.in/video/is-india-trying-to-create-a-shia-sunni-divide-in-kashmir [accessed September 20, 2021].
87. Census of India, 2011. The Registrar General and Census Commissioner, India. Religious Affiliation, www.census2011.co.in/data/religion/state/1-jammu-and-kashmir.html [accessed August 2021].
88. Siddhartaa Gigoo, "Subjects of a Lost State," *Live Mint Online*, October 18, 2019, www.livemint.com/mint-lounge/features/subjects-of-a-lost-state-11571390952620.html [accessed October 18, 2019].
89. Ganai (2021).
90. Chandel, Nitin, "State Subject: The Evolution," *Kashmir Life Online*, April 10, 2019, https://kashmirlife.net/state-subject-the-evolution-story-issue-02-vol-11-207016/ [accessed April 10, 2019].
91. Sehla Ashai, "The Jammu and Kashmir State Subjects Controversy Of 2004," in *Drexel Law Review*, 2 (2010), 537–555, 537.
92. Ghulam Shah and G. N. Reshi, *State Subjectship in Jammu and Kashmir* (Srinagar: Jupitor Press, 1988), 24.
93. Ibid., 24–25.
94. Ashai (2010), 537–538.
95. Ibid., 539.
96. Ibid., 539–540.
97. Shah and Reshi (1988), 8–14.
98. Zia (2020).
99. Umar Lateef Misgar, "Young Kashmiris Want Indians to Leave," *Aljazeera English Online*, March 12, 2020, www.aljazeera.com/news/2020/3/12/young-kashmiris-want-indian-forces-to-leave-survey [accessed March 12, 2020].
100. Alastair Lamb, *Birth of a Tragedy: Kashmir 1947* (Hertford: Roxford Books, 2008), 143.
101. Claude Rakisits, "Diplomacy in South Asia: A Four-Step Grand Plan for Kashmir," in *Australian Journal of International Affairs*, 75 (2021), 1–9. doi: 10.1080/10357718.2020.1787334.
102. Ibid., 5.
103. Rai (2019), 259–260.

104. George Grierson, *Dictionary of the Kashmiri Language* (Illinois: Advent Books, 1986), 14–21.

105. Ahmad (2017), xviii.

106. Swathi Seshadri, "Deification of Land and the State: Industry-Military Complex in Kashmir," *Jammu Kashmir Public Policy and Law*, August 7, 2020, https://jklpp.org/deification-of-land-and-the-state-industry-military-complex-in-kashmir/ [accessed August 20, 2020].

107. Zulfiqar Majid, "India Compels Jammu and Kashmir to Fly Indian Flag," in *Deccan Herald*, March 11, 2021, www.deccanherald. com/national/north-and-central/schools-in-jk-asked-to-put-up-signboards-with-national-flag-960724.html [accessed March 11, 2021].

108. Sufi (1948), 3–7.

109. Census of India, 2011. The Registrar General and Census Commissioner, India. Religious Affiliation, www.census2011.co.in/data/religion/state/1-jammu-and-kashmir.html [accessed June 20, 2021].

110. Alastair Lamb, *Kashmir: A Disputed Legacy 1846–1990* (Hertford: Roxford Books, 1991), 7–9.

111. Zia (2020).

CHAPTER 3   THE LONG LIFE CYCLE OF RESISTANCE

1. Farhan Mujahid Chak, "The Grave of Kashmir's Last King," in *Free Press Kashmir Online*, January 30, 2019, https://freepresskashmir. news/2019/01/30/debate-continues-now-yusuf-shah-chaks-qatar-based-descendent-offers-his-myth-busting-account/ [accessed January 30, 2019].

2. Sufi (1948), 15.

3. Ibid., 32.

4. *Baharistan-i-Shahi* (trans. by K. N. Pandit), 144.

5. Nizamuddin Wani, *Kashmir under Muslim Rule* (Jammu and Kashmir: Jay Kay Book House, 1987), 118–124, 137.

6. *Baharistan-i-Shahi* (trans. by K. N. Pandit), 156.

7. Hasan (1959), 193.

8. "Grave of Kashmir's Exiled King Lies in Ruins," *Greater Kashmir*, www.greaterkashmir.com/todays-paper/grave-of-kashmirs-exiled-king-yusuf-shah-chuk-in-bihar-lies-in-ruins [accessed, January 20, 2019].

9. Nizamuddin Wani, *Kashmir under Muslim Rule* (Jammu and Kashmir: Jay Kay Book House, 1987), 141.

10. Ibid., 142–145. See, Emperor Jehangir, *Tuzuk-i-Jehangiri*, Vols. 1–2, trans. by A. Rodgers, ed. by Henry Beveridge (London Royal Asiatic Society: 1909–1914).
11. Lamb (1991), 13.
12. Rai (1988), 17.
13. F. M. Hassnain, *The Heritage of Kashmir* (Srinagar, Kashmir: Gulshan Books, 1980), 210.
14. Ibid., 211.
15. Khalid Bashir Ahmad, *Kashmir: Exposing the Myth behind the Narrative* (Thousand Oaks, CA: Sage Publications, 2017), 66.
16. G. M. D. Sufi, *Islamic Culture in Kashmir* (New Delhi: Light and Life Publishers, 1979), 118.
17. Ibid., 119.
18. See, Nile Green (ed.), *Afghan History through Afghan Eyes* (2016; online edition, Oxford Academic, May 19, 2016), https://doi. org/10.1093/acprof:oso/9780190247782.001.0001 [accessed 12 June 2023].
19. P. N. K Bamzai, *Culture and Political History of Kashmir*, Vol. 1: Ancient Kashmir (New Delhi: M. D. Publications). See, Chitralekha Zutshi, "Translating History: Rajatarangini and the Making of India's Past," *Library of Congress Video*, July 10, 2008; Shonaleeka Kaul, *The Making of Early Kashmir: Landscape and Identity in the Rajatarangini* (Oxford: Oxford University Press, 2018).
20. See, Birbal Kachru, *Majmuat Tawarikh* (Srinagar: Per. Ms. Research & Publication Department, 1835); R. K. Parmu, *A History of Muslim Rule in Kashmir (1320–1819)* (New Delhi: Peoples Publishing House 1969); Anand Koul, *The Kashmiri Pandit* (Delhi: Utpal Publications, 1991); and P. N K. Bamzai, *Cultural and Political History of Kashmir*, Vol. 2 (Srinagar: Gulshan Books: 1994).
21. Baron Charles Hugel, *Travels in Kashmir and the Punjab* (London: John Petheran, 1845), 220.
22. Aushaq Hussain Dar, "Reinterpreting Afghan Rule in Kashmir," in *The Communications*, 27.1 (2019), 178–192.
23. Showkat Sheikh, *Interview*, June 13, 2021.
24. Ibid., 221. See, Sufi (1948), 15.
25. Dar (2019).
26. See, R. K. Parmu, *A History of Muslim Rule in Kashmir (1320–1819)* (New Delhi: Peoples Publishing House 1969), 351.
27. Owais Gul, "Historic Bridges Losing Their Sheen," *Kashmir News Observer*, February 15, 2021, www.kashmirnewsobserver.com/ jammu-and-kashmir/srinagar%E2%80%94-historic-seven-bridges-losing-sheen-gradually-kno-61165 [accessed February 15, 2021].

28. Ibid.
29. Amar Jahangir, Mirwais Kasi, and Muhammad Alam, "Cultural Impact of Afghan Rule in Kashmir," in *Takatoo*, 17 (June 2017). http://web.uob.edu.pk/uob/journals/takatoo/data/2017/jan-june/English/8-14.pdf [accessed June 10, 2021], 1–7, 2.
30. Masood Hussain, "The Man Who Purchased Kashmir," *Kashmir Life*, https://kashmirlife.net/the-man-who-purchased-kashmir-issue-15-vol-07-81400/ [accessed April 20, 2021].
31. J. S. Grewal, *The Sikhs of the Punjab* (Cambridge: Cambridge University Press, 1990), 99–101.
32. Rupali Mishra, *A Business of State: Commerce, Politics, and the Birth of the East India Company* (Cambridge, MA: Harvard University Press, 2018), 17–21.
33. Lamb (1991), 7–8.
34. Sufi (1979), 305.
35. Sufi (1948), 3–7.
36. Muhammad Iqbal as cited in Prem Nath Bazaz, *The History for Struggle of Freedom in Kashmir* (New Delhi: Kashmir Publishing Co., 1954), 123.
37. Robert Thorp, *Cashmere Misgovernment* (Calcutta: Wyman Books, 1868), 54.
38. Rai (2004), 7.
39. Ibid., 13.
40. Walter Lawrence, *The Valley of Kashmir* (Pune: Chinar Publishing House, 1992), 284.
41. India. Office of the Commissioner of the Census. *Census of India 1941: Vol. 22. Jammu and Kashmir. Parts I & II.* Essay and tables by Capt. R. G. Wreford (1943).
42. Census of India, 2011. The Registrar General and Census Commissioner, India. Religious Affiliation, www.census2011.co.in/data/religion/state/1-jammu-and-kashmir.html [accessed June 20, 2021].
43. Khalid Bashir Ahmad, "Changing Place Names in Kashmir," *Counter Currents*, December 2018, https://countercurrents.org/2018/12/changing-place-names-in-kashmir/ [accessed December 28, 2018].
44. Showkat Ahmad Naik, "Land Reform Measures in Kashmir During Dogra Rule," in *Proceedings of the Indian History Congress*, 72.1 (2011), 587–603.
45. Suhail Rehman Lone, "Begār (Forced Labour) In Kashmir during the Dogra Period (1846–1947 A. D.)," in *Proceedings of the Indian History Congress*, 73 (2012), 861–871.
46. Seshadri (2020).

47. Rai (1988).
48. Tariq Ahmad Sheikh, "Popular Unrest and State Response in Kashmir (1846–1947)," in *Proceedings of the Indian History Congress*, 74 (2013), 522–531.
49. Showkat Ahmad Naik, "Land Reform Measures in Kashmir During Dogra Rule," in *Proceedings of the Indian History Congress*, 72.1 (2011), 587–603, 588.
50. Ibid., 588.
51. Ibid., 587.
52. Suhail Rehman Lone, "Begār (Forced Labour) in Kashmir during the Dogra Period (1846–1947 A. D.)," in *Proceedings of the Indian History Congress*, 73 (2012), 861–871, 861.
53. Ibid., 861.
54. Rai (1988), 155.
55. Ibid., 155–156.
56. Ibid., 861–862.
57. Muzammil Rashid, "Begar in Kashmiri History," *Kashmir Life*, November 7, 2018, https://kashmirlife.net/begar-in-kashmir-history-issue-32-vol-10-191243/ [accessed November 17, 2018].
58. Lone (2012), 862.
59. Rashid (2018).
60. Sheikh (2013).
61. Anderson (2006), 3–11.
62. See, the Shri Amarnathji Shrine Board, www.shriamarnathjishrine.com/the-holy-shrine.html [accessed February 2020].
63. Seshadri (2020).
64. Showkat Sheikh, "History of Kashmir," Personal Interview, June 13, 2021.
65. Ibid.
66. M. A. Stein (trans.), *Kalhana's Rajtarangini: A Chronicle of the Kings of Kashmir* (Westminster: Archibald Constable and Company, 1900), 282, note 183.
67. Seshadri (2020).
68. Parvez Imroz, Khurram Parvez, Kartik Murukutla, and Swathi Seshadri, *Amarnath Yatra: A Militarized Pilgrimage*, Jammu Kashmir Coalition of Civil Society (JKCCS) (Bengaluru: National Printing Press, 2017), 200–201, https://jkccs.files.wordpress.com/2017/05/amarnath-report-2017.pdf [accessed July 11, 2021].
69. Seshadri (2020).
70. Ibid.
71. Sheikh (2021).

72. Hakim Sameer Hamdani, *Shi'ism in Kashmir: A History of Sunni–Shia Rivalry and Reconciliation* (London: I. B. Tauris, 2022), 1–2. The history of Sunni–Shia rivalry is deliberately exaggerated often to serve a greater political agenda. As the author describes, much of it based on rumors, without evidence.

73. Mona Bhan, "Divide and Rule," in *Kindle Magazine: Politics and Society*, April 2, 2016, http://kindlemag.in/divide-and-rule/ [accessed July 20, 2021].

74. Ibid.

75. F. Bethke. "The Consequences of Divide and Rule Policy in Africa," *Peace Economics, Peace Science and Public Policy*, January 2012, 1–25, 2.

76. A. J. Christopher. "Divide and Rule: The Impress of British Separation Policies," in *Area*, 20.3 (September 1988), 233–240.

77. Rai (1988).

78. Agha Iqbal Ali and Oliver Ali Agha, *The Agha Family of Kashmir*, August 5, 2015, https://aghafamilyofsrinagarkashmir.wordpress.com/tag/history-of-the-agha-family-of-srinagar/ [accessed August 11, 2021].

79. "Kandahars Qizilbash," *Kashmiri Life*, November 30, 2017, https://kashmirlife.net/kandahars-qizilbash-issue-35-vol-09-157293/ [accessed November 30, 2017].

80. Lawrence (1992), 87.

81. Showkat Sheikh, "History of Kashmir," Personal Interview, June 13, 2021.

82. Bhan (2016).

83. Ibid.

84. Fayaz Wani, "No Eid Prayer in Srinagar Eidgah in Kashmir," *New Indian Express*, www.newindianexpress.com/nation/2023/jun/29/for-fourth-year-in-a-row-no-eid-prayer-at-eidgah-in-srinagar-2589635.html [accessed June 29, 2023].

85. Irshad Hussain, "Ruhulluh Mehdi Raises Questions on Lifting Ban on Shia Processions," *Kashmiriyat*, August 1, 2021. http://thekashmiriyat.co.uk/ruhullah-mehdi-raises-questions-over-lifting-of-ban-over-muharram-processions-after-30-years/ [accessed August 1, 2021].

86. Ibid.

87. Snedden (2015), 96–97.

88. Lamb (1991), 88.

89. Kulbhusan Warikoo, *Central Asia and Kashmir: A Study in the Context of Anglo-Russian Rivalry* (New Delhi: Gian Publishing House, 1989), 134.

90. Snedden (2015), 96.

91. Ahmad (2017), 95.
92. Hamaad Habibullah, "July 13: Kashmir Martyr's Day," *Maktoob Media Online*, July 13, 2022, https://maktoobmedia.com/2022/07/13/13-july-kashmirs-martyrs-day-india-wants-to-forget/ [accessed July 13, 2022].
93. Frantz Fanon, *The Wretched of the Earth*, (New York: Grove Press, 2015), 97–101.
94. Ibid., 178.
95. Ibid., 236.
96. Snedden (2015), 96–97.
97. Ibid., 96–97.
98. Ashraf Zain, "July 13: A History of Martyr's Day," *Kashmir Reader*, July 17, 2020, https://kashmirreader.com/2020/07/17/july-13-1931-a-history-of-martyrs-day/ [accessed July 17, 2020].
99. Ghulam Hassan Khan, *Freedom Movement in Kashmir (1931–1940)* (New Delhi: Light and Life Publishers, 1980), 126.
100. Huma Dar, "Martyr's Day," Personal Interview, December 22, 2021.
101. Sheikh Muhammad Abdullah, *The Blazing Chinar*, trans. by Muhammad Amin (Srinagar, Kashmir: Gulshan Books, 2013), 61.
102. Ahmad (2017), 99.
103. Zia and Bhat (2019), 7.
104. Ahmad (2017), 100–101.
105. Snedden (2015), 96–97.
106. Ibid., 97.
107. Anuradha Bhasin Jamwal, "Indian Policies in Kashmir Making Youth More Defiant," *Newsline Magazine*, September 2010, https://newslinemagazine.com/magazine/indian-policies-making-youth-in-kashmir-more-defiant-and-fearless/ [accessed September 1, 2010].
108. Sheikh (2013), 522–531.

CHAPTER 4   JAMMU GENOCIDE

1. Rashid (2020), 217.
2. Ibid., 222.
3. Christopher Snedden, *The Untold Story of the People of Azad Kashmir* (London: Hurst & Co., 2012), 239–240. Census of India 1941.
4. Henry R. Huttenbach, "The Psychology and Politics of Genocide Denial: A Comparison of Four Case Studies," in *Studies in Comparative Genocide* (London: Palgrave Macmillan, 1999), 216–229.
5. Ibid., 217–218.

6. Nasar Meer, "Islamophobia and Postcolonialism: Continuity, Orientalism and Muslim Consciousness," in *Patterns of Prejudice*, 48.5 (2014), 500–515, 501.
7. Rashid (2020), 218–220.
8. Gregory Stanton, "10 Stages of Genocide," *Genocide Watch*, 2013, www.scasd.org/cms/lib5/PA01000006/Centricity/Domain/1482/ TenStages.pdf [accessed August 19, 2019].
9. See, Waltraud Ernst and Biswasmoy Pati (eds.), *India's Princely States: People, Princes and Colonialism*. (London: Routledge, 2010).
10. Aijaz Ashraf Wani, *What Happened to Governance in Kashmir?* (Oxford: Oxford University Press, 2018), 27.
11. Jawaharlal Nehru, *Selected Correspondence between Jawaharlal Nehru and Karan Singh* (Delhi: Penguin India, 2006), 132.
12. Bhan (2016).
13. Kulkarni (2020).
14. Bazaz (1954), 127.
15. Census of India, 2011. The Registrar General and Census Commissioner, India. Religious Affiliation, www.census2011.co.in/ data/religion/state/1-jammu-and-kashmir.html [accessed July 20, 2020].
16. Ibid.
17. Kulkarni (2020).
18. Interview with Ved Bhasin on Friday, July 30, 2011, at Rayburn Gold Room #2168. Washington, DC, USA.
19. Ibid.
20. Saeed Naqvi, *Being the Other: The Muslim in India* (New Delhi: Aleph Book Company, 2016), 358.
21. Naqvi (2016), 358.
22. Fareed, Rifat, "The Forgotten Massacre," *Aljazeera English*, November 6, 2017, www.aljazeera.com/news/2017/11/6/the-forgotten-massacre-that-ignited-the-kashmir-dispute [accessed November 6, 2017]. Professor Idrees Kanth, a Jammu specialist, is quoted in the opinion piece.
23. Khalid Bashir Ahmad, "Circa 1947: A Long Story," *Kashmir Life*, November 5, 2014, https://kashmirlife.net/circa-1947-a-long-story-67652 [accessed July 1, 2020].
24. Rashid (2020), 222.
25. Naqvi (2016), 358.
26. Zafar Choudhary, *Kashmir Conflict and the Muslims of Jammu* (Srinagar: Gulshan Books, 2015).
27. Snedden (2015), 119.
28. Ibid., 51–53.

29. Alastair Lamb, *Birth of a Tragedy: Kashmir 1947* (Hertford: Roxford Books, 2008), 68–69. Italics Mine.
30. Ibid., 68–69.
31. Ahmad (2014).
32. Ahmad (2014).
33. Ibid.
34. Rashid (2020), 224.
35. Muhammad Yusuf Saraf, *Kashmiris Fight for Freedom*, Vol. 1 (1819–1946); Vol. 2 (1947–1978) (Lahore: Ferozsons Publishers, 1979), 818–819.
36. Shabir Ahmad Salahria, interviewed in Ahmad (2014).
37. Ibid.
38. Qudratullah Shahab, *Shahab Nama* (Lahore: Sang-e-Meel Publications, 1987), 376.
39. Naqvi (2016), 382.
40. Ibid., 382–383.
41. Ahmad (2014).
42. Ibid.
43. Karan Singh, *Karan Singh: Autobiography* (Oxford: Oxford University Press, 1995), 47.
44. Balraj Puri, *Kashmir: Insurgency and After*. Third Edition (Hyderabad: Orient Blackswan, 2008), 29.
45. Ilyas Chattha, "Terrible Fate: Ethnic Cleansing of Jammu Muslims," in *Journal of Pakistan Vision*, 10.1 (2009), 117–140, 126.
46. Lamb (1991), 154.
47. Ibid., 155.
48. Robert Wirsing, Robert, *Pakistan and the Kashmir Dispute: On Regional Conflict and Its Resolution* (New York: St. Martin's Press, 1994), 52.
49. Ahmad (2014).
50. Ibid.
51. Rashid(2020), 223–224.
52. Rashid(2020), 224.
53. Christopher Snedden, "What Happened to Muslims in Jammu? Local Identity, '"the Massacre" of 1947' and the roots of the 'Kashmir problem,'" *South Asia: Journal of South Asian Studies*, 24.2 (2001), 111–134, 111.
54. Ahmad (2014).
55. Rashid (2020), 224.
56. Stephens (1963), 200.
57. Chattha (2009), 117.

58. "Elimination of Muslims from Jammu: Part II," *T h e Times*, August 10, 1948.
59. Ibid.
60. Ahmad (2014).
61. Rashid (2020), 224.
62. Paul Brass, "The Partition of India and Retributive Genocide in the Punjab, 1946–1947: Means, Methods," in *Journal of Genocide Research* (2003) 5.1, 71–101.
63. India. Office of the Commissioner of the Census. *Census of India 1941: Vol. 22. Jammu and Kashmir. Parts I and II*. Essay and tables by Capt. R. G. Wreford (1943).
64. Ilyas Chattha, "The Long Shadow of 1947: Partition, Violence and Displacement in Jammu & Kashmir," in *Revisiting India's Partition: New Essays on Memory, Culture and Politics*, ed. by Amritjit Singh et al. (Washington DC: Lexington Books, 2016), 145.
65. Rashid (2020), 224.
66. Ibid., 225.
67. Urvashi Butalia, *The Other Side of Silence: Voices from the Partition of India* (Durham, NC: Duke University Press, 2000), 72–73.
68. Muharram Hashmi, *Memory Lane to Jammu*, ed. by Rehmat-Ullah-Rad and Khalid Hasan (Lahore: Sang-e-Mahal Publishers, 2004), 107.
69. Ved Bhasin. "Jammu 1947: Interview with Ved Bhasin," *Kashmir Life*, November 17, 2015. https://kashmirlife.net/jammu-1947-issue-35-vol-07-89728/ [accessed November 17, 2015].
70. Huttenbach (1999).
71. Ahmad (2014).
72. Ibid.
73. Ilyas Chattha, "The Long Shadow of 1947: Partition, Violence and Displacement in Jammu and Kashmir," in *Revisiting India's Partition: New Essays on Memory, Culture and Politics*, ed. by Amritjit Singh et al. (Washington DC: Lexington Books, 2016), 149.
74. Ibid., 150.
75. Ibid., 150–151.
76. Ritu Menon and Kamla Bhasin, *Borders and Boundaries: Women in India's Partition* (New Delhi: Kali for Women, 1998), 43.
77. Rashid (2020), 226.
78. Ahmad (2014).
79. Josef Korbel, *Danger in Kashmir* (Princeton, NJ: Princeton University Press, 1954), 23.
80. Ibid.
81. Snedden (2001), 120.

CHAPTER 5   THE MYTH OF PARTITION

1. Norman Fairclough, *Language Is Power*. Third Edition (London: Routledge, 2014), 3.
2. Ahmed (1997).
3. Crispin Bates, "The Hidden Story of Partition and Its Legacies," *BBC Network Video*, March 3, 2011, www.bbc.co.uk/history/british/modern/partition1947_01.shtml [accessed March 3, 2011].
4. Yogesh Snehi, "Hindutva as an Ideology of Cultural Nationalism," in *Social Change*, 33.4 (2003), 10–24, 14. See, Yasmin Khan, *The Great Partition: The Making of India and Pakistan* (New Haven, CT: Yale University Press, 2007).
5. Interview with Kuldip Nayar on Friday, July 30, 2011, at Rayburn Gold Room #2168. Washington, DC, USA.
6. Penderel Moon, *Divide and Quit* (Oxford: Oxford University Press, 1998), 32.
7. Ahmed (1997), 3–6.
8. See, "India's Strategies against Separatism in Assam, Punjab and Kashmir," in *Secession and Security: Explaining State Strategy Against Separatists* (Ithaca, NY: Cornell University Press, 2017), 83–124.
9. Yasmin Khan, *The Great Partition: The Making of India and Pakistan* (New Haven, CT: Yale University Press, 2007). Khan admits that part of her family migrated to Pakistan. Yet, she mistakenly assumes this as a majority experience.
10. Gyanendra Pandey, *Remembering Partition* (Cambridge: Cambridge University Press, 2001), 13–15.
11. Arundhati Roy, "The Silence Is the Loudest Sound," *New York Times*, August 15, 2019, www.nytimes.com/2019/08/15/opinion/sunday/kashmir-siege-modi.html [accessed August 15, 2019].
12. "Abrogation of Article 370," *Bhartiya Janata Party YouTube Channel*, August 2019, www.youtube.com/watch?v=UHVIM_osIZs.
13. See, Mobeen Khan, *Partition, Pakistan and the Legacy of Destruction* (Denver, CO: Outskirts Press, 2013). This book presents an absurd argument that the suffering of India's Muslims should be blamed on Pakistan.
14. Kajol Bhattacharjee, "Partition Horrors Remembrance Day," *The Hindu*, August 14, 2021, www.thehindu.com/news/international/partition-horrors-remembrance-day-people-of-india-will-reject-it-says-pakistan/article35918734.ece [accessed August 17, 2021].
15. Interview with Kuldip Nayar on Friday, July 30, 2011, at Rayburn Gold Room #2168. Washington, DC, USA.

16. "Protest against Pakistan: Narendra Modi," *Telegraph Online*, January 1, 2020, www.telegraphindia.com/india/protest-against-pakistan-narendra-modi/cid/1732461 [accessed January 1, 2020].
17. Leonard Mosley, *The Last Days of the British Raj* (London: Weidenfeld and Nicholson, 1960), 4.
18. A. G. Noorani, *The RSS and the BJP: A Division of Labour* (New Delhi: Leftword Books, 2017), 11.
19. Chak (2016).
20. Vikram Sampath, *Echoes from a Forgotten Past: 1883–1924* (New Delhi: Penguin, 2019).
21. Susan Bayley, "Imagining 'Greater India': French and Indian Visions of Colonialism in the Indic Mode," in *Modern Asian Studies*, 38.3 (July 2004), 703–744.
22. Manu Baghavan, "The Hindutva Underground: Hindu Nationalism and the Indian National Congress in Late Colonial and Early Post-Colonial India," in *Economic and Political Weekly*, 43.37 (2008), 39–48.
23. Hazem Bazian, Rhonda Itaoui, and Paula Thompson, *Islamophobia in India: Stoking Bigotry* (Berkley, CA: Islamophobia Research and Documentation Project, Center for Race and Gender, at the University of California, Berkeley, 2019), 38.
24. Edward C. Moulton, "Allan O. Hume and the Indian National Congress: A Reassessment," in *South Asia: Journal of South Asian Studies*, 8.1–2 (1985), 9–12.
25. Richard Sisson, "Congress and Indian Nationalism: Political Ambiguity and the Problems of Social Conflict and Party Control," in *Congress and Indian Nationalism: The Pre-Independence Phase*, ed. by Richard Sisson and Stanley Wolpert (Oakland, CA: University of California Press, 1988), 3.
26. Ahmed (1997), 44.
27. Thomas Blom Hansen, "Democracy against Law: Reflections on India's Illiberal Democracy," in *Majoritarian State: How Hindu Nationalism Is Changing India*, ed. by Angana P. Chatterji, Thomas Blom Hansen, and Christophe Jaffrelot (Oxford: Oxford University Press, 2019), 24.
28. Ishtiaq Ahmed, *Jinnah: His Successes, Failures and Role in History* (New Delhi: Penguin, 2020), 6–11.
29. R. J. Tomlinson, *The Indian National Congress and the Raj* (Cambridge: Cambridge University Press, 1976), 32.
30. Ibid., 32–34.
31. Lee (2010).

32. James Rennel, *Memoir of a Map of Hindoostan, or the Mogul Empire* (London, 1788), xl.
33. James Mill, *The History of British India,* six vols. Third edition (London: Baldwin, Cradock, and Joy, 1826).
34. Mosley (1960), 4.
35. B. R. Ambedkar, *Pakistan or the Partition of India* (Bombay: Thackers, 1945), chapter 2.
36. Mosley (1960), 6.
37. Baghavan (2008).
38. Ahmed (1997), 138.
39. Charles Taylor, *Modern Social Imaginaries* (Durham, NC: Duke University Press, 2004), 23.
40. Ibid., 24.
41. Ibid., 25.
42. Snehi (2003), 10.
43. Sampath (2019).
44. Vinayak Savarkar, *Essentials of Hindutva: Who Is a Hindu?* (1923), http://savarkar.org/en/encyc/2017/5/23/2_12_12_04_essentials_of_hindutva.v001.pdf_1.pdf [accessed June 2020].
45. Shamsul Islam, *Hindutva: Savarkar Unmasked.* (Kozhikode: Media House, 2016), 30.
46. Ibid., 31–34.
47. Bazian et al. (2019), 11–14.
48. Sampath (2019).
49. Janaki Bakhle, "Country First? Vinayak Damodar Savarkar (1883–1966) and the Writing of *Essentials of Hindutva,*" in *Public Culture,* 22.1 (2010), 152–156. doi: https://doi.org/10.1215/08992363-2009-020.
50. Sudha Ratan, "Hindutva: The Shaping of a New Hindu Identity," in *Southeastern Political Review,* 26.2 (1998), 201–217, 203.
51. Ambedkar (1945).
52. Bakhle (2010), 152–156.
53. J. Kuruvachira, *The Roots of Hindutva: A Critical Study of Hindu Fundamentalism and Nationalism* (Delhi: Delhi Media House, 2005), 121.
54. Sampath (2019), 473.
55. Ibid.
56. Romila Thapar, *The Penguin History of Early India: From the Origins to AD 1300.* (London: Penguin, 2015), 133.
57. Ibid., 176.
58. See, Adriana G. Proser, *The Buddhist Heritage of Pakistan: Art of Gandhara* (New York: Asia Society, 2011).

59. Snigdhendu Bhattacharya, "From Hindu Ocean to Sindhu Sea: Here's What RSS-Backed Schools Are Teaching Children about History," *Newslaundry*, August 24, 2021, www.newslaundry.com/2021/08/24/from-hindu-ocean-to-sindhu-sea-heres-what-rss-backed-schools-are-teaching-children-about-history?\ [accessed August 24, 2021].

60. Harriet A. Harris, *Fundamentalism and Evangelicalism* (Oxford, Oxford University Press, 2007), v.

61. Angana P. Chatterji, Thomas Blom Hansen, and Christophe Jaffrelot, "Introduction," in *Majoritarian State: How Hindu Nationalism Is Changing India*, ed. by Angana P. Chatterji et al. (Oxford: Oxford University Press, 2019), 2.

62. Islam (2016), 23–29.

63. Kuruvachira (2005), 122.

64. Ibid., 122.

65. Thapar (2015), 14.

66. Ibid., 14–15.

67. Kuruvachira (2015), 123.

68. Ratan (1998), 202.

69. Ibid.

70. Audrey Truschke, "Hindutva's Dangerous Rewriting of History," in *South Asia Multidisciplinary Academic Journal*, 24/25 (2020), 1–2.

71. Bazian et al. (2019), 91.

72. Ibid.

73. Farhan Mujahid Chak, "Kashmir and India's Settler Colonial Project," *TRT World*, December 2019, www.trtworld.com/opinion/india-s-settler-colonial-project-in-kashmir-should-force-the-world-to-act-31848 [accessed December 9, 2019].

74. Hilal Mir, "Indian Government Website Shows Kashmir as Hindu," *Anadolu Agency*, May 11, 2021, www.aa.com.tr/en/asia-pacific/govt-website-declares-97-muslim-kashmir-predominantly-hindu/2236765 [accessed May 11, 2021].

75. Truschke (2020).

76. Thapar (2015), 57.

77. Ibid.

78. Sukhadeo Thorat, "Dalits in Post-2014 India: Between Promise and Action," in *Majoritarian State: How Hindu Nationalism Is Changing India*, ed. by Angana P. Chatterji et al. (Oxford: Oxford University Press, 2019), 217.

79. Ibid.

80. Eviane Leidig, "Hindutva as a Variant of Right-Wing Extremism" *Patterns of Prejudice*, 54.3 (2020), 215–237. https://doi.org/10.1080/0031322X.2020.1759861 [accessed July 2021].

81. Thapar (2015), xxiii.
82. Rosalind O'Hanlon, *Caste, Conflict and Ideology: Mahatma Jotirao Phule and Low-Caste Protest in Nineteenth Century Western India* (Cambridge: Cambridge University Press, 1985), 141–145.
83. Sampath (2019), 473.
84. Savarkar (1923).
85. Truschke (2020), 2–4.
86. Sushant Singh, "The World Ignored Russia's Delusions. It Shouldn't Make the Same Mistake with India," *Foreign Policy*, May 8, 2022, https://foreignpolicy.com/2022/05/08/india-akhand-bharat-hindu-nationalist-rss-bjp/ [accessed May 8, 2022].
87. Tanika Sarkar, "How the Sangh Parivar Writes and Teaches History," in *Majoritarian State: How Hindu Nationalism Is Changing India*, ed. by Angana P. Chatterji et al. (Oxford: Oxford University Press, 2019), 151.
88. O'Hanlon (1985), 141–145.
89. Abdullah Yusuf Ali, *The Making of India* (Delhi: Sang-e-Meel Publications, 2006). Another Indian author who claims the arrival of Muhammad bin Qasim made India.
90. Ismail Kazi, *Chachnama: The Ancient History of Sind*, trans. by Kalichbeg Fredunbeg Mirzabeg (Karachi: Commissioners Press, 1900), 3.
91. Thapar (2015), xxix. Kindly note that, arguably Brahmanism, though referred to as proto-Hindu, is distinct from it.
92. O'Hanlon (1985), 145–148.
93. Kazi (1900), 3.
94. Ibid., 6.
95. Savarkar (1923).
96. Truschke (2020), 5.
97. Mosley (1960), 4.
98. Ahmed (2020), 21.
99. Ian Talbot, *Inventing the Nation: India and Pakistan* (London: Bloomsbury, 2000), 3–6.
100. Kitu Reddy, *A Vision of United India: Problems and Solutions* (Scotts Valley, CA: CreateSpace, 2014), 9–17.
101. Rai (2019), 264–244.
102. Arkotong Longkumer, "Playing the Waiting Game: BJP, Hindutva and the Northeast," in *Majoritarian State: How Hindu Nationalism Is Changing India*, ed. by Angana P. Chatterji et al. (Oxford: Oxford University Press, 2019), 288.
103. Truschke (2020), 5–7.
104. Ahmed (1997), 57.

105. Ahmed, I. (2020), 47–52.
106. Khurram Shafique, *Jinnah: The Case for Pakistan* (Nottingham: Libredex Publishers, 2018), 7.
107. Ratan (1998), 203–205.
108. Dia Da Costa, "Memories of Colonial Unknowing," in *ARCGIS*, February 2, 2020, www.arcgis.com/apps/Cascade/index.html?appid= 905d3055675049f593290428102ea55f [accessed February 2, 2020].
109. Ratan (1998), 203–205.
110. Ibid., 203.
111. Ahmed (1997), 4–6.
112. Suhas Palshikar, "Toward Hegemony: The BJP beyond Electoral Dominance," in *Majoritarian State: How Hindu Nationalism Is Changing India*, ed. by Angana P. Chatterji, Thomas Blom Hansen, and Christophe Jaffrelot (Oxford: Oxford University Press, 2019), 104.
113. Fayaz Dar and Amit Kumar, "Marginality and Historiography: The Case of Kashmir's History," in *Economic & Political Weekly*, 50.39 (2015), 37–44.
114. Johann Galtung, "Cultural Violence," in *Journal of Peace Research*, 27.3 (1990), 291–305.
115. Hansen (2019), 23–24.
116. Chak, "Kashmir and India's Settler Colonial Project" (2019).
117. Stanley Wolpert, *Shameful Flight: The Last Years of the British Empire in India* (Oxford: Oxford University Press, 2006).
118. Zia, Ather, "Resistance: A Way of Life for Kashmiri Youth," *Aljazeera Online*, April 26, 2017, www.aljazeera.com/indepth/opinion/2017/04/resistance-life-kashmiri-youth-170425081937812.html [accessed April 26, 2017].
119. Ambedkar (1945).
120. Ibid.
121. Chak (2016).
122. Ibid.

CHAPTER 6 INDIA, ISLAMOPHOBIA, AND THE HINDUTVA PLAYBOOK

1. "Elimination of Muslims from Jammu: Part II," *The Times*, August 10, 1948.
2. Wirsing (1994), 2.
3. Ahmed (1997), 138.

4. Aijaz Ashraf Wani, *What Happened to Governance in Kashmir?* (Oxford: Oxford University Press, 2018), 1.
5. Ibid., 2–4.
6. Altaf Hussain Para, *The Making of Modern Kashmir: Sheikh Abdullah and the Politics of the State* (New York: Routledge, 2019), 197.
7. Ibid., 198–200.
8. Wani (2018), 138.
9. Shahla Hussain, *Kashmir in the Aftermath of Partition* (Cambridge: Cambridge University Press, 2021), 134. Hafsa Kanjwal, "Reflections on the Post-Partition Period: Life Narratives of Kashmiri Muslims in Contemporary Kashmir," in *Himalaya*, 38.2 (2018), 40–60.
10. See, Ather Zia and Javaid Iqbal Bhat, "Introduction," in *A Desolation Called Peace: Voices from Kashmir*, ed. by Ather Zia and Javaid Iqbal Bhat (London: Harper Collins, 2019), 1–33.
11. Sumantra Bose, *Kashmir: Roots of Conflict, Paths to Peace* (Cambridge, MA: Harvard University Press, 2005), 7.
12. See, Tariq Ali et al., *Kashmir: The Case for Freedom* (Verso, 2011).
13. See, Sanjay Kak, *Until My Freedom Has Come: A New Intifada in Kashmir* (London: Penguin Books, 2011).
14. Jaffrelot, "A Defacto Ethnic Democracy?" (2019), 41.
15. Snedden (2021), 314–317.
16. Wirsing (1994), 39–41.
17. P. N. Jalali, "Accession of Kashmir and the Role of the Muslim League," in *Kashmir Tourism to Terrorism*, ed. by Yatish Mishra et al. (Columbia, MO: South Asia Books, 1996), 32.
18. Akbar S. Ahmed (1997), 138.
19. M. J. Chitkara, *The Kashmir Imbroglio: Diagnosis and Remedy* (New Delhi: APH Pub. Corp, 1996), 27.
20. Lamb (1991), 51.
21. Government of India, *White Paper on Jammu and Kashmir* (Government of India Press, 1948), 23.
22. Wirsing (1994), 46.
23. Lamb (1991), 120.
24. Ibid.
25. Mehr Chand Mahajan, *Looking Back: Autobiography of Mehr Chand Mahajan* (New Delhi: Har-Anand Publications, 2018), 126.
26. V. Shankar, *Sardar Patel's Select Correspondence 1945–1950* (New Delhi: Navajivan Publishers, 1974), 46–47.
27. Lamb (1991), 154.
28. Ibid., 155.
29. Wirsing (1994), 52.
30. Ibid., 53.

31. See, B. L. Sharma, *The Kashmir Story* (Bombay: Asia Publishing House, 1967). Indian account of the so-called "tribal invasion."

32. Lamb (1991), 159.

33. Salman Sayyid, *A Fundamental Fear: Eurocentrism and the Emergence of Islamism* (London: Zed Books, 1997), 33.

34. J. Krieger, "After Empire," in *The Oxford Handbook of British Politics*, ed. by M. Fliners et al. (New York: Oxford University Press, 2011), 590.

35. Fozia Lone, *Historical Title, Self-Determination and the Kashmir Question* (Leiden: Brill Publishers, 2018), 315.

36. Ibid.

37. Muhammad Sultan Pampori, *Kashmir in Chains: 1819–1992* (Srinagar: Srinagar Publishers, 1992), 119.

38. Ahmed (1997), 178.

39. A. H. Suhrawardy, *Tragedy in Kashmir* (Lahore: Wajidalis, 1983), 123.

40. Bangash (2015), 7.

41. M. J. Akbar, *Nehru: The Making of India* (New York: Viking, 1988), 448.

42. M. Abdullah, "Kashmir, India and Pakistan," in *Foreign Affairs*, 43.3 (1965), 528–535.

43. Sumantra Bose, *The Challenge of Kashmir: Democracy, Self-Determination and a Just Peace* (New Delhi: Sage Publications, 1997), 31.

44. Ibid., 27–32.

45. A. Khan, "The Kashmir Dispute: A Plan for Regional Co-operation," in *Columbia Journal of Transnational Law*, 31 (1994), 495–550, 495.

46. L. H. Miller, "The Kashmir Dispute" in *International Law and Political Crisis: An Analytical Casebook*, ed. by Lawrence Shienman and David Wilkinson (Boston, MA: Little Brown, 1968), 51.

47. United Nations Security Council Resolution 47.

48. Lamb (1991), 183.

49. Miller (1968), 61.

50. Zia and Bhat (2019), 8.

51. Bose (2005), 7.

52. Victoria Schofield, *Kashmir in Conflict: India, Pakistan and the Unending War* (London: Bloomsbury, 2003), 150.

53. Zia and Bhat (2019), 9.

54. Ibid.

55. Bose (2005), 7.

56. Zia and Bhat (2019), 9.

57. Ibid., 41–43.

58. Bazian et al. (2019), 3–10.

59. Suparna Chaudry, "India's New Law May Leave Millions of Muslims without Citizenship," *Washington Post*, December 13, 2019, www.washingtonpost.com/politics/2019/12/13/indias-new-law-may-leave-millions-muslims-without-citizenship/ [accessed December 18, 2020].

60. "Who Is the Hindu Hard-Liner Running India's Most Populous State," *BBC*, March 29, 2017, www.bbc.com/news/world-asia-india-39403778 [accessed March 20, 2019].

61. Ranjai Singh, "Muslim Man Beaten in Front of Police," *India Today*, August 8, 2021, www.indiatoday.in/india/story/muslim-man-beaten-up-in-kanpur-in-police-presence-over-charges-of-forced-conversion-1840196-2021-08-12 [accessed August 8, 2021].

62. Truschke (2020).

63. Bazian et al. (2019), 11–14.

64. Truschke (2020), 5–6.

65. Christophe Jaffrelot, *The Hindu Nationalist Movement and Indian Politics: 1925 to the 1990s—Strategies of Identity-Building, Implantation and Mobilisation* (Delhi: Viking Penguin in Association with C. Hurst & Co., 1996), 522.

66. Ibid.

67. "India: Cow Protection Groups Attack Minorities," *Human Rights Watch*, February 18, 2019, www.hrw.org/news/2019/02/19/india-vigilante-cow-protection-groups-attack-minorities [accessed February 18, 2019].

68. Bazian et al. (2019), 78.

69. "India: Cow Protection Groups Attack Minorities," *Human Rights Watch*.

70. "Hate Crimes against Muslims," *Amnesty International Online*, June 2017, www.amnesty.org/en/latest/press-release/2017/06/india-hate-crimes-against-muslims-and-rising-islamophobia-must-be-condemned/ [accessed June 30, 2017].

71. Bazian et al. (2019), 74–84.

72. Special Report, "In Modi's India, Cow Vigilantes Deny Muslim Farmers Their Livelihood," *Reuters*, November 6, 2017, www.reuters.com/investigates/special-report/india-Politics-Religion [accessed August 20, 2021].

73. Ibid.

74. Arundhati Roy, "Our Battle for Love," *Siasat Daily*, www.siasat.com/our-battle-for-love-must-be-militantly-waged-and-beautifully-won-arundhati-roy-2079894/ [accessed November 20, 2022].

75. Charu Gupta, "Allegories of 'Love Jihad' and 'Ghar Wapsi:' Interlocking the Socio-Religious with the Political," in *Rise of Saffron Power*, ed. by Mujibur Rehman (London: Routledge, 2018), 84–110, 100.
76. Bazian et al. (2019), 92.
77. Ibid.
78. Gupta (2018), 85.
79. Ibid., 85–86.
80. Ibid, 97.
81. Truschke, (2020), 1.
82. Mishra, Ishita, "Hindu Right-Wing Organization Launches New Campaign," *Times of India*, December 29, 2014, https://timesofindia. indiatimes.com/city/agra/Bajrang-Dal-to-launch-bahu-laao-beti-bachao-in-February/articleshow/45669704.cms? [accessed December 29, 2014].
83. Simon George, "Why Narcissistic Bullies Really Taunt," www. drgeorgesimon.com [accessed August 11, 2019].
84. Susan M. Swearer and Shelly Hymel, "Understanding the Psychology of Bullying: Moving Toward a Social-Ecological Diathesis–Stress Model," in *Educational Psychology Papers and Publications*, 344 (2015), https://digitalcommons.unl.edu/edpsychpapers/175 [accessed August 25, 2021].
85. Kancha Ilaiah Shepherd, "In Mohan Bhagwat's India, Everyone Is Hindu," *Wire*, December 31, 2019, https://thewire.in/religion/mohan-bhagwat-rss-hindu-rashtra [accessed January 11, 2020].
86. *Jammu and Kashmir Bank*, www.jkbank.com/others/common/board. php.
87. Kaiser Mir, "A Viral Photo Evokes Kashmir Occupation under Dogras," *Kashmir Observer*, April 10, 2020, https://kashmirobserver. net/2020/04/10/when-a-viral-photo-evoked-dogra-raj/ [accessed April 10, 2020].
88. See, Timothy White, "Catholicism and Nationalism: From Fusion in the 19th Century to Separation in the 21st Century," in *Westminster Papers in Communication and Culture*, 4.1 (2007), 47–64.
89. Amnesty International, *Tyranny of A "Lawless Law": Detention without Charge or Trial under the J&K Public Safety Act*, 2019, https:// amnesty.org.in/wp-content/uploads/2019/06/Tyranny-of-A-Lawless-Law.pdf [accessed 23 March 2020].
90. M. A. Bhat, "Preventative Detention in Counter-Insurgencies: The Case of Kashmir," in *Insight Turkey*, 21.4 (2019), 53–68.
91. Jitendra Bahadur Singh. "100 Terrorists Killed in Kashmir in 2022," *India Today*. June 12, 2022, www.indiatoday.in/india/story/100-

terrorists-killed-in-jammu-and-kashmir-this-year-1961476-2022-06-12 [accessed 23 June 2022].

92. See, S. N. Ghosh and H. Duschinski, "The Grid of Indefinite Incarceration: Everyday Legality and Paperwork Warfare in Indian-controlled Kashmir," in *Critique of Anthropology*, 40.3 (2020), 364–384.

93. "Muslims Not Equal in India," *The Week*, April 4, 2020, www.theweek.in/news/world/2020/04/03/muslims-not-in-equal-category-imran-tweets-subramanian-swamy-video.html [accessed April 20, 2020].

94. Robina Khan, Muhammad Zubair Khan, and Zafar Abbas, "Moving Towards Human Catastrophe: The Abrogation of Article 370 in Kashmir Valley," in *Journal of Muslim Minority Affairs*, 41.1 (2021), 78–85.

95. "Demographic Flooding: India Introduces New Domicile Law," *Aljazeera English*, April 1, 2020, www.aljazeera.com/news/2020/4/1/demographic-flooding-india-introduces-new-kashmir-domicile-law [accessed September 4, 2020].

96. Mir, K. (2020).

97. Ibid.

98. Samreen Mushtaq and Mudassir Amin, "To Invoke Allah or Not," *Caravan Magazine*, 2019, https://caravanmagazine.in/politics/to-invoke-allah-or-to-not-secular-islamophobia-and-the-protesting-indian-muslim [accessed December 31, 2019].

99. Ibid.

100. Truschke (2020), 1–2.

101. Gupta (2018), 104.

102. Truschke (2020), 5.

103. Gupta (2018), 88.

104. Chatterji (2019), 411.

CHAPTER 7 THE "FINAL SOLUTION": ABROGATION OF ARTICLES 370 AND 35A

1. "Congress Ask Home Minister to Explain Final Solution," *Economic Times*, May 30, 2017, https://economictimes.indiatimes.com/news/politics-and-nation/congress-asks-home-minister-to-explain-final-solution-for-jammu-and-kashmir/articleshow/58902110.cms?from=mdr [accessed May 30, 2017]. The words "Final Solution" were used by Rajnath Singh when he was Home Minister in 2017. It has been invariably used several times by Hindutva leaders regarding Kashmir.

2. Azad Essa, "India Consul-General Calls for Israeli Solution in Kashmir," *Middle-East Eye*, November 26, 2019, www.middleeasteye. net/news/india-consul-general-united-states-calls-israeli-solution-kashmir [accessed November 28, 2019].

3. Ibid.

4. Ibid.

5. Sounak Mukherjee, "How the Right-Wing Unknowingly Compares Modi with Hitler," *Money Control*, August 6, 2019, www.moneycontrol. com/news/politics/article-370-kashmir-final-solution-how-right-wing-is-unknowingly-comparing-pm-modi-with-hitler-4295321. html [accessed August 6, 2019].

6. "Congress Asks Home Minister to Explain Final Solution for Jammu and Kashmir," *Economic Times*, May 20, 2017, https://economictimes. indiatimes.com/news/politics-and-nation/congress-asks-home-minister-to-explain-final-solution-for-jammu-and-kashmir/ articleshow/58902110.cms [accessed May 20, 2017].

7. Mona Bhan and Haley Duschinski, "Occupations in Context: The Cultural Logics of Occupation, Settler Violence, and Resistance," in *Critique of Anthropology*, 40.3 (2020), 285–297, 285–286.

8. Anuradha Bhasin, *A Dismantled State: The Untold Story of Kashmir after Article 370* (Gurugram: HarperCollins India, 2022), 11.

9. Gregory Stanton, "Kashmir Earns Genocide Alert", *Genocide Watch*, August 15, 2019, www.genocidewatch.com/single-post/2019/08/15/ genocide-alert-for-kashmir-india [accessed September 21, 2020].

10. Wirsing (1994), 46.

11. A. G. Noorani, *Article 370: A Constitutional History of Jammu and Kashmir* (Oxford: Oxford University Press, 2011), 2.

12. Ibid., 2.

13. Lone (2018), 317.

14. Snedden (2021), 186.

15. Noorani (2011), 9.

16. Ibid., 9–10.

17. Ibid., 10.

18. Sameer Lalwani and Gillian Gayner, "India's Kashmir Conundrum: Before and After the Abrogation of Article 370," in *Special Report for United States Institute of Peace*, 473 (August 2020), 3–24.

19. Bose (2005), 69.

20. Noorani (2011), 2.

21. Ibid.

22. "Article 370: What Happened with Kashmir and Why It Matters?," *BBC*, August 6, 2019, www.bbc.com/news/world-asia-india-49234708 [accessed August 6, 2019].

23. Ibid.
24. P. R. Chari and Pervaiz Iqbal Cheema, *The Simla Agreement 1972: Its Wasted Promise* (New Delhi: Manohar, 2001), 11.
25. Avtar Singh Bhasin, *India and Pakistan: Neighbors at Odds* (London: Bloomsbury, 2018), 258.
26. Eric Margolis, *War on Top of the World: The Clash for Mastery of Asia* (Toronto, Ontario: Key Porter, 1999), 72.
27. Wirsing (1994), 70.
28. Ibid., 71.
29. *Agreement on Bilateral Relations between the Government of India and the Government of Pakistan*, July 2, 1972, India–Pak., 858, U.N.T.S., Article 1(ii), at 72.
30. A. G. Noorani, "Shimla Scrapped," *Dawn*, August 2, 2019, www.dawn.com/news/1501373 [accessed August 30, 2019].
31. Ibid.
32. Ibid.
33. Zia and Bhat (2019), 9.
34. Lorenzo Veracini, "Introducing," in *Settler Colonial Studies*, 1.1 (2011), 1–12.
35. Ibid., 1.
36. Ganai (2021).
37. "From Domicile to Dominion: India's Settler Colonial Agenda in Kashmir," in *Harvard Law Review*, 134.7 (May 2021), 2530.
38. Ibid., 2530.
39. "Demographic Flooding: India Introduces New Kashmir Domicile Law," *Aljazeera English*, April 1, 2020, www.aljazeera.com/news/2020/4/1/demographic-flooding-india-introduces-new-kashmir-domicile-law [accessed April 1, 2020].
40. Mirza Saaib Beg, "J&K's New Citizenship Order: Disenfranchising Kashmiris One Step at a Time," *The Wire*, May 30, 2020, https://thewire.in/rights/kashmir-domicile-law [accessed May 30, 2020].
41. Hilal Mir, "UN Experts Express Grave Concern over New Kashmir Laws," *Anadolu Agency*, April 17, 2021, www.aa.com.tr/en/asia-pacific/new-kashmir-laws-matter-of-grave-concern-un-experts/2212325 [accessed April 17, 2021].
42. Ibid.
43. Ghulam Nabi Suhail Peer, *Pieces of Earth: The Politics of Land-Grabbing in Kashmir* (Oxford: Oxford University Press, 2018), 16, 174, 175.
44. P. G. Nabi and J. Ye, "Of Militarisation, Counter-Insurgency and Land Grabs in Kashmir," in *Economic and Political Weekly*, 50.46/47 (2015), 58–68, 58.

45. Rifat Fareed, "India Enacts New Laws in Kashmir for 'Land-Grab,'" *Aljazeera English*, October 28, 2020, www.aljazeera.com/news/2020/10/28/india-enacts-new-laws-in-kashmir-allowing-outsiders-to-buy-land [accessed October 30, 2020].

46. Zahoor Ahmed, "Book Review: Pieces of Earth," *in South Asia Journal*, August 20, 2020, http://southasiajournal.net/book-review-pieces-of-earth-the-politics-of-land-grabbing-in-kashmir/ [accessed August 20, 2020].

47. "Amarnath Board Gets Land in Srinagar," *Freepress Kashmir*, August 22, 2021, https://freepresskashmir.news/2021/08/22/at-rs-10-per-kanal-amaranth-board-gets-land-in-srinagar/ [accessed August 22, 2021].

48. Ibid.

49. Khalid Bashir Ahmad, "Changing Place Names in Kashmir," *Counter Currents*, December 2018, https://countercurrents.org/2018/12/changing-place-names-in-kashmir/ [accessed December 28, 2018].

50. Riyaz Bhat, "75 Roads and 75 Schools in Kashmir to Be Renamed," *Rising Kashmir*, August 5, 2021, www.risingkashmir.com/75-roads--75-schools-in-J-K-to-be-renamed-after-local--unsung-heroes---CS-Mehta [accessed August 30, 2021].

51. Ahmad (2018).

52. Ibid.

53. Mir, "UN Experts Express Grave Concern over New Kashmir Laws" (2021).

54. Ibid.

55. Ibid.

56. Safwat Zargar, "How August 15 Is Changing Colors in Centrally-Run Kashmir," *Scroll*, August 14, 2021, https://scroll.in/article/1002801/how-august-15-is-changing-colours-in-centrally-run-kashmir [accessed August 14, 2021].

57. Ibid.

58. Showkat Sheikh, "History of Kashmir," Personal Interview, June 13, 2021.

59. Aditi Tandon, "Burhan Wani's Father Hoists Indian Flag," *Tribune India*, August 15, 2021, www.tribuneindia.com/news/j-k/burhan-wanis-father-hoists-tricolour-at-govt-school-in-j-ks-tral-297903 [accessed August 15, 2021].

60. "Every Employee Must Be Loyal to India in J&K," *Kashmir Reader*, September 17, 2021, https://kashmirreader.com/2021/09/17/every-employee-must-maintain-allegiance-to-india-constitution-jk-govt/ [accessed, September 22, 20].

61. Ibid.

62. Irfan Malik, "Kashmir Administrative Posts to Non-Locals," *The Wire*, October 8, 2020, https://thewire.in/government/kashmir-administrative-posts-non-local-muslims [accessed August 30, 2021].
63. Ibid. Brackets mine.
64. Ibid.
65. Kaiser Andrabi and Zubair Amin, "Modi Is Trying to Engineer a Hindu Majority in Kashmir," *Foreign Policy*, August 11, 2021, https://foreignpolicy.com/2021/08/11/modi-is-trying-to-engineer-a-hindu-majority-in-kashmir/ [accessed August 11, 2021].
66. Ibid.
67. Ibid.
68. Stanton (2013).
69. Arshi Javaid, "A BJP Minister Threatens with Jammu Massacre," *Scroll*, May 29, 2016, https://scroll.in/article/808707/a-ministers-loose-remark-has-reopened-one-of-the-darkest-chapters-of-jammus-history [accessed September 10, 2021].
70. Binish Ahmed, "Call the Crime in Kashmir by Its Name: Ongoing Genocide," *Genocide Watch*, August 9, 2019, www.genocidewatch.com [accessed September 21, 2020].
71. Ibid.
72. Ibid.
73. "Congress Asks Home Minister to Explain Final Solution Comment," *Economic Times*, May 30, 2017, https://economictimes.indiatimes.com/news/politics-and-nation/congress-asks-home-minister-to-explain-final-solution-for-jammu-and-kashmir/articleshow/589 02110.cms [accessed May 30, 2017].
74. Truschke (2020), 5.
75. Stanton (2013).
76. Elsa Evangeline, "Ban on Kashmiri Pheran," *Gulf News*, December 19, 2018. https://gulfnews.com/world/asia/india/ban-on-kashmiri-pheran-cultural-onslaught-in-india-1.61021151 [accessed December 20, 2018].
77. Ibid.
78. Irfan Malik, "Kashmir Administrative Posts to Non-Locals," *The Wire*, October 8, 2020, https://thewire.in/government/kashmir-administrative-posts-non-local-muslims [accessed August 30, 2021].
79. Amnesty International, *Tyranny of a "Lawless Law": Detention without Charge or Trial under the J&K Public Safety Act* (2019), https://amnesty.org.in/wp-content/uploads/2019/06/Tyranny-of-A-Lawless-Law.pdf [accessed 23 March 2020].
80. Bhat, M. A. (2019).

81. Evangeline Elsa, "India Ban on Kashmiri Pheran Cultural Onslaught," *Gulf News*, December 19, 2018, https://gulfnews.com/world/asia/india/ban-on-kashmiri-pheran-cultural-onslaught-in-india-1.61021151 [accessed 2 March 2021].

82. Truschke (2020), 5–7.

83. Alex Traub, "India's Dangerous New Curriculum," *New York Review*, December 6, 2018, www.nybooks.com/articles/2018/12/06/indias-dangerous-new-curriculum/ [accessed December 8, 2018].

84. Prabhash Dutta, "Why Send More Troops?" *India Today*, August 2, 2019, www.indiatoday.in/news-analysis/story/-if-situation-has-improved-then-why-send-38-000-troops-to-j-k-1576436-2019-08-02 [accessed August 5, 2019].

85. Ajaz Ashraf, "Do You Need 700,000 Soldiers to Fight 150 Militants? Kashmiri Rights Activist Khurram Pervez," *Scroll*, July 21, 2016, https://scroll.in/article/812010/do-you-need-700000-soldiers-to-fight-150-militants-kashmiri-rights-activist-khurram-parvez [accessed July 25, 2016].

86. Vikram Sharma, "India Deploys 1 Million Soldiers," *Deccan Chronicle*, August 18, 2019, www.deccanchronicle.com/nation/current-affairs/180819/forces-deploy-1-million-to-guard-every-inch-of-kashmir-valley.html [accessed August 30, 2019].

87. Stanton (2013).

88. Rifat Fareed, "Interfaith Marriages Trigger Controversy between Muslims and Sikhs in Kashmir," *Aljazeera English*, July 1, 2021, www.aljazeera.com/news/2021/7/1/interfaith-marriages-trigger-controversy-between-muslims-sikhs [accessed July 7, 2021].

89. Ibid.

90. Stanton (2013).

91. Ibid.

92. "200 Paramilitary Companies Being Deployed in Jammu and Kashmir," *Kashmir Walla*, July 1, 2021, https://thekashmirwalla.com/200-paramilitary-companies-being-deployed-in-j-k-report/ [accessed July 20, 2021].

93. Zulfikar Majid, "Rumors Fly Thick and Fast Due to Large Troop Movement," *Deccan Herald*, June 7, 2021, www.deccanherald.com/national/north-and-central/rumours-fly-thick-and-fast-in-kashmir-due-to-large-troops-movement-994673.html [accessed June 8, 2021].

94. Stanton (2013).

95. Ahmed, B. (2019).

96. Ibid.

97. Ibid.

98. Bilal Kuchay, "Kashmiri Journalist Aasif Sultan Kept in Jail for 1000 days," *Aljazeera English*, May 31, 2021, www.aljazeera.com/news/2021/5/31/kashmiri-journalist-aasif-sultan-kept-in-jail-for-over-1000-days [accessed May 31, 2021].

99. "113 Kashmiris Killed So Far," *Free Press Kashmir News*, October 1, 2021, https://freepresskashmir.news/2021/10/01/113-militants-killed-in-kashmir-in-2021-so-far-july-deadliest-month-with-31-killings/ [accessed October 1, 2021].

100. Haley Duschinski, "Reproducing Regimes of Impunity," in *Cultural Studies*, 24.1 (2010), 110–132.

101. Ibid., 130.

102. "Bi-Annual Human Rights Review," *Jammu and Kashmir Coalition of Civil Society Organizations*, July 1, 2020, https://jkccs.net/bi-annual-hr-review-229-killings-107-casos-55-internet-shutdowns-48-properties-destroyed/ [accessed October 1, 2021].

103. Stanton (2013).

104. Ibid.

105. Umar Baba, "Will India Identify Kashmiri Mass Graves," *TRT World*, April 29, 2018, www.trtworld.com/magazine/will-india-identify-bodies-in-kashmir-s-mass-graves-like-it-did-in-iraq-17044 [accessed April 29, 2018].

106. Naseer Ganai, "Myth of Normalcy in Kashmir," *Outlook India*, April 16, 2021, www.outlookindia.com/website/story/india-news-sense-of-normality-in-kashmir-is-a-myth-says-yashwant-sinha-led-groups-report/380438 [accessed April 16, 2021].

107. Divya Chandra and Kritika Geol, "Omar Abdullah Slams Development Myth," *Quint*, August 4, 2021, www.thequint.com/news/india/omar-abdullah-cites-jammu-kashmir-development-data-in-interview-how-accurate-is-he [accessed August 5, 2021].

CHAPTER 8   NUCLEAR FLASHPOINT: SINO-INDIAN RIVALRY AND KASHMIR

1. Russell Goldman, "India–China Border Dispute: A Conflict Explained," *New York Times*, June 17, 2020, www.nytimes.com/2020/06/17/world/asia/india-china-border-clashes.html [accessed June 17, 2020].

2. Ibid.

3. Amy Kamzin, "Donald Trump Offers to Mediate in China–India Border Conflict," *Financial Times*, June 1, 2020, www.ft.com/content/ce361221-6f19-4e77-b83b-de6fa1bc2fob [accessed June 1, 2020].

4. Vijay Gokhale, "The Road from Galwan: The Future of India–China Relations," *Carnegie Endowment for International Peace (Working Paper)*, March 10, 2021, https://carnegieindia.org/2021/03/10/road-from-galwan-future-of-india-china-relations-pub-84019 [accessed March 10, 2021].

5. "China Admits It Lost 4 of Its Soldiers in 2020 India Border Clash," *Aljazeera English*, February 19, 2020, www.aljazeera.com/news/2021/2/19/china-admits-it-lost-four-soldiers-in-2020-india-border-clash [accessed February 19, 2020].

6. Hu Shisheng and Wang Jue, "The Behavioral Logic of India's Tough Foreign Policy Towards China," in *China International Relations*, 30.5 (September–October 2020), 37–65, 38.

7. Zongyi (2020), 240.

8. Zongyi (2020).

9. Ibid., 227.

10. Kyle Gardner, *The Frontier Complex: Geopolitics and the Making of the India–China Border 1846–1962* (Cambridge: Cambridge University Press, 2021), 218.

11. Minjun Kang, "Try to Analyze the Origin of the Johnson Line and Its Position in Sino-Indian Border Dispute," in *Journal of Beijing Normal University (Social Sciences Edition)*, 4 (2004), 19–27.

12. Ibid., 27.

13. Gardner (2021), 218.

14. Goldman (2020).

15. Ipsita Chakravarty, "How British Ambiguity about Frontier between India and China Paved Way for Post-Colonial Conflict," *Scroll*, June 27, 2020, https://scroll.in/article/965502/how-british-ambiguity-about-frontier-between-india-and-china-paved-way-for-a-post-colonial-conflict [accessed June 27, 2020].

16. Neville Maxwell, *India's China War* (Bombay: Jaico Publishing, 1970), 102.

17. Pravin Sawhney and Ghazala Wahab, *Dragon at Our Doorstep* (New Delhi: Aleph Book Company, 2021), 42.

18. Ibid., 42.

19. Ibid., 42.

20. Zongyi (2020), 232.

21. Sawhney and Wahab (2021), 44.

22. Gardner (2021), 249.

23. A. G. Noorani, "India's Forward Policy," in *The China Quarterly*, 43 (1970), 136–141, 136.

24. Neville Maxwell, and Noorani, A. G., "India's Forward Policy," in *The China Quarterly*, 45 (1971), 157–163.

25. Maxwell (1970), 221–224.
26. Maxwell and Noorani (1971), 158.
27. Shisheng and Jue (2020), 38.
28. Zongyi (2020), 232.
29. Ibid., 233.
30. See, Li Zhang, "China-India Relations: Strategic Engagement and Challenges (Policy Report)," *Center for Asian Studies* (2020), www.ifri.org/sites/default/files/atoms/files/asievisions34zhangli.pdf; Rong Ying and Zhang Lei, "The New India Vision and the Building of a Closer China-India Partnership," in *China International Studies*, 28.80 (January/February 2020), 28–41; Chao Xie, (2019). "How Status-Seeking States Can Cooperate: Explaining India–China Rapprochement After the Doklam Standoff," in *India Quarterly*, 75.2 (2019), 171–189.
31. Gardner (2021), 249.
32. Shisheng and Jue (2020), 40.
33. "India Hits Out at China: Rejects Fresh Allegations," *The Hindu*, September 30, 2021, www.thehindu.com/news/national/india-hits-out-at-china-rejects-fresh-allegations-over-eastern-ladakh-standoff/article36765787.ece [accessed October 1, 2021].
34. Maxwell (1970), 221–224.
35. Gardner (2021), 254.
36. Kalim Siddiqui, "A Critical Study of 'Hindu Nationalism' in India," in *Journal of Business & Economic Policy*, 3.2 (June 2016), 9.
37. Apoorvanand, "Umbrella Politics of Hindutva," *Aljazeera English*, April 23, 2021, www.aljazeera.com/opinions/2017/4/23/umbrella-politics-of-hindutva [accessed April 23, 2021].
38. Truschke (2020), 7. *Jai Shri Ram* translates to "long live the Hindu deity named Ram."
39. Michael Arndt, "India's Foreign Policy and Hindutva," in *Majoritarian State: How Hindu Nationalism Is Changing India*, ed. by Angana P. Chatterji, Thomas Blom Hansen, and Christophe Jaffrelot (Oxford: Oxford University Press, 2019), 74.
40. Ibid.
41. "Address by Prime Minister at the Tsinghua University Beijing," *Indian Ministry of External Affairs*, May 15, 2015, www.mea.gov.in/Speeches-Statements.htm?dtl/25242/Address_by_Prime_Minister_at_the_Tsinghua_University_Beijing_May_15_2015 [accessed August 10, 2020].
42. Sayantan Haldar, "Mapping Substance in India's Counter-Strategies to China's Emergent Belt and Road Initiative," in *Indian Journal of Asian Affairs*, 31.1/2 (June–December 2018), 75–90, 80–82.

43. Ibid., 80.
44. Sumit Ganguly, "India Is Paying the Price for Neglecting Its Neighbors," *Foreign Policy*, June 23, 2020, https://foreignpolicy.com/2020/06/23/india-china-south-asia-relations/ [accessed June 23, 2020].
45. Vidhi Bubna, "Is Bhutan Slowly Turning Tides against India because of India–China," *Modern Diplomacy*, September 13, 2020, https://moderndiplomacy.eu/2020/09/13/is-bhutan-slowly-turning-tides-against-india-because-of-india-china-tensions/ [accessed September 19, 2020].
46. Hu and Wang (2020), 38.
47. Karun Kishor Karki, "Nepal–India Relations: Beyond Realist and Liberal Theoretical Prisms," in *Journal of International Affairs*, 3 (2020), 84–102.
48. Bubna (2020).
49. Gokhale (2021), 17.
50. Zongyi (2020), 245.
51. Lin Wu, "India's Perception of and Response to China–US Competition," in *China International Studies*, 85 (November/December 2020), 130–155, 134.
52. Ibid., 135.
53. Rajesh Rajagopalan, "Evasive Balancing: India's Unviable Indo-Pacific Strategy," in *International Affairs*, 96.1 (2020), 75–94. See, Sanjana Mohan, "India Gears Up the Play Great Indo-Pacific Game," *Daily Pioneer*, December 29, 2019, www.dailypioneer.com/2019/sunday-edition/india-gears-up-to-play-the-great-indo-pacific-game.html [accessed August 10, 2020].
54. Nandini Jawli, "South China Sea and India's Geopolitical Interests," in *Indian Journal of Asian Affairs*, 29.1/2 (June–December 2016), 85–100, 86.
55. Ibid., 86.
56. Asma Bilal and Shaheen Akhtar, "India's 'Indo-Pacific' Strategy: Emerging Sino-Indian Maritime Competition," in *Strategic Studies*, 40.3 (2020), 1–21, 2.
57. "Indo-Pacific Strategy Report: Preparedness, Partnerships and Promoting a Networked Region," *United States Department of Defense*, Policy Report (June 2019), 1–65, 3.
58. Kai He and Mingjiang Li, "Understanding the Dynamics of the Indo-Pacific: US–China Strategic Competition, Regional Actors, and Beyond," in *International Affairs*, 96:1 (2020), 1–7, 2.
59. Wu (2020), 135.
60. Hu and Wang (2020), 63.
61. Ibid., 60–63.

62. Sheila Smith, "The QUAD in the Indo-Pacific," *Council on Foreign Relations* (2021), www.cfr.org/in-brief/quad-indo-pacific-what-know [accessed June 27, 2021].

63. Asma Bilal and Shaheen Akhtar, "India's 'Indo-Pacific' Strategy: Emerging Sino-Indian Maritime Competition," in *Strategic Studies*, 40.3 (2020), 1–21, https://issi.org.pk/wp-content/uploads/2020/10/5-SS_Asma-Sana-and-Shaheen-akhtar_No-3_2020.pdf [accessed October 21, 2020].

64. Hu and Wang (2020), 57–58.

65. Smith (2021).

66. Zongyi (2020), 245.

67. Wu (2020), 135–138.

68. Hu and Wang (2020).

69. Ibid., 61.

70. Ibid., 57.

71. Ashley J. Tellis, "Sino-Indian Border: Escalation and Disengagement," *Carnegie India Seminar*, June 24, 2020, https://carnegieindia.org/2020/06/24/sino-indian-border-escalation-disengagement-event-7369 [accessed June 24, 2020].

72. Anik Joshi, "Indian Has Handed China a Way to Interfere in Kashmir," *Foreign Policy*, June 16, 2020, https://foreignpolicy.com/2020/06/16/china-kashmir-himalayas-pakistan-conflict/ [accessed July 10, 2020].

73. "Foreign Ministry Spokesperson Geng Shuang's Regular Press Conference," *Ministry of Foreign Affairs of Peoples Republic of China*, www.fmprc.gov.cn/mfa_eng/xwfw_665399/s2510_665401/t1712371.shtml [accessed October 31, 2019].

74. Zongyi (2020), 242.

75. Ibid.

76. Gokhale (2021), 8.

77. Muhammad Faisal, "CPEC and Regional Connectivity," in *Strategic Studies*, 39.2 (Summer 2019), 1–17, 10.

CHAPTER 9   CONCLUSION

1. "India Locks Down Kashmir," *Aljazeera English*, September 2, 2021, www.aljazeera.com/news/2021/9/2/india-kashmir-lockdown-syed-ali-shah-geelani-death-burial [accessed September 2, 2021].

2. Ibid.

3. Sameer Yasir, "Kashmir Leader Dies," *New York Times*, September 2, 2021, www.nytimes.com/2021/09/02/world/asia/syed-ali-shah-geelani-dead.html [accessed September 2, 2021].

4. A. Ferrara, "Hyper-Pluralism and the Multivariate Democratic Polity," in *Philosophy & Social Criticism*, 38.4–5 (2012), 435–444, 436.

5. Mirza Waheed, "The Endurance of the Dead Kashmiri," *Caravan Magazine*, September 8, 2021, https://caravanmagazine.in/conflict/syed-ali-shah-geelani-endurance-dead-kashmir [accessed September 8, 2021].

6. Zia and Bhat (2019), 33.

7. Mushtaq and Amin, "Why Has Kashmir Been Forgotten?" (March 2019).

8. Gregory Stanton, "Kashmir Earns Genocide Alert," *Genocide Watch*, August 15, 2019, www.genocidewatch.com/single-post/2019/08/15/genocide-alert-for-kashmir-india [accessed September 21, 2020].

9. "India Revises Death Toll," *Reuters*, November 21, 2008, www.reuters.com/article/idINIndia-36624520081121?edition-redirect=in [accessed November 30, 2018]. Kashmiri Muslim organizations in the disputed territory use the number of upwards to 100,000 people killed since 1990.

10. "Bi-Annual Human Rights Review," *Jammu and Kashmir Coalition of Civil Society Organizations*, July 20, 2020, https://jkccs.net/bi-annual-hr-review-229-killings-107-casos-55-internet-shutdowns-48-properties-destroyed/ [accessed October 1, 2021].

11. Niha Masih and Joana Slater, "Thousands of Children Detained by India," *Washington Post*, August 29, 2019, www.washingtonpost.com/world/asia_pacific/among-the-3000-detained-by-indian-authorities-in-kashmir-children/2019/08/29/1616b5c0-c91c-11e9-9615-8f1a32962e04_story.html [accessed August 30, 2019].

12. "Tensions High as India Detains Hundreds in Kashmir," *TRT World*, October 10, 2021, www.trtworld.com/asia/tensions-high-as-india-detains-hundreds-in-kashmir-50638 [accessed October 10, 2021].

13. Apoorva Mandhani, "99% of Habeas Corpus Pleas Pending since Article 370 Removed," *Print*, June 28, 2020, https://theprint.in/judiciary/99-habeas-corpus-pleas-filed-in-jk-since-article-370-move-are-pending-hc-bar-tells-cji/450281/ [accessed June 30, 2020].

14. Ganai (August 2021).

15. Housen, T., Lenglet, A., Shah, S., Sha, H., Ara, S., Pintaldi, G., & Richardson, A. (2019). "Trauma in the Kashmir Valley and the Mediating Effect of Stressors of Daily Life on Symptoms of Posttraumatic Stress Disorder, Depression and Anxiety." *Conflict and Health*, 13(1), 1–9.

16. "Kashmir," *Human Rights Watch*, www.hrw.org/tag/Kashmir [accessed August 30, 2021].

17. Mitchell Hall, *The Vietnam War* (Harlow: Pearson Longman, 2000), 83.
18. Ahmed (1997), 3–6.
19. Jaffrelot, "A Defacto Ethnic Democracy?" (2019), 41.
20. Snedden (2021), 314–317.
21. Christophe Jaffrelot, *The Hindu Nationalist Movement and Indian Politics: 1925 to the 1990s: Strategies of Identity-Building, Implantation and Mobilisation* (Delhi: Viking Penguin in Association with C. Hurst & Co., 1996), 522.
22. Ganai (August 2021).
23. "Chinese Troops Deployed in Considerable Numbers in Ladakh," *New Delhi Television Limited Broadcasting Channel*, October 2, 2021, www.ndtv.com/india-news/india-china-standoff-army-chief-manoj-mukund-naravane-on-increase-in-deployment-of-chinese-troops-in-eastern-ladakh-2561261 [accessed October 2, 2021].
24. "India Matching Chinese Troop Buildup on Disputed Border," *Dawn*, October 3, 2021, www.dawn.com/news/1649913/india-matching-chinese-troop-build-up-on-disputed-border-says-indian-army-chief [accessed October 4, 2021].
25. "Chinese PLA Soldiers Cross Border with India? Indian Media Habitual in Hyping the Topic," *Global Times*, September 29, 2021, www.globaltimes.cn/page/202109/1235502.shtml [accessed October 3, 2021].
26. Vedika Sud, Barbara Starr, Sahar Akbarzai, and Kathleen Magramo. "US War Games Near Chinese Border," *CNN*, August 7, 2022. www.cnn.com/2022/08/06/india/india-us-military-exercise-line-of-actual-control-china-intl-hnk/index.html [accessed August 7, 2022].

Index

For topics related to India and Kashmir, *see* the topic, e.g. marriage; settler-colonialism

Dar, Aushaq Hussain 46
Dar, Feroza 63
Dar, Zubeida 63
Delhi Agreement (1952) 134
Dev, Rajguru Swami Sant 69
Devi, Tara 69
Disturbed Area Act (DAA) 122,
    141
Dixon Plan 38
Dogra regime 33, 34, 37, 41, 43–4,
    48–61, 64–70, 128–9, 169
Durrani, Ahmad Shah 46
Durrani empire 33, 45, 47
Duschinski, H. 122

East India Company 43, 47–8
European Union 3, 5

Fairclough, Norman 77
Faisal, Shah 13
Fanon, Frantz 57
Fareed, Rifat 136
Ferrar, A. 166
forced labor 49, 50–1
Fravel, M. Taylor 161
Free and Open Indo-Pacific (FOIP)
    159

Galwan Valley clash (2020) 1,
    148–9, 161–3, 173
Gandhi, Mohandas 83–4, 121
Gardner, Kyle 151, 154
Gayner, Gillian 130
Geelani, Syed Ali Shah 165–6
Geneva Conventions 54, 134
Geng Shuang 161
genocide: stages of 140–7
Genocide Watch 1, 128, 139–40,
    146, 168
Ghani, Mulla Tahir *Diwan* 45
Ghosh, S.N. 122–3
Gilgit Scouts 6, 122

Gilgit-Baltistan 4, 6, 23, 35, 38, 66,
    72, 108, 155, 162
Glancy, Sir Bertrand 59
Gokhale, Vijay 156–7
Goldman, Russell 148
Guardian 3
Gupta, Charu 118, 119, 124, 125
Guterres, António 147

Hansen, Thomas Blom 84, 103
Haq-i-Malikan (proprietary rights)
    49
Harris, Harriet A. 90
Hassnain, F.M. 44
Henderson Brooks-Bhagat report
    151
Hind 96, 97
Hinduness 92–3, 121
Hindus
    attitude to Muslims 92, 95,
        100–1
    prohibition on conversion to
        other religions 118–9
    prohibition on marriage to
        Muslims 117, 119–20, 143, 172
Hindutva ideology 2, 9–11, 82–3,
    85, 86–104, 116–26, 154–5,
    172–3
    insecurity of 125–6
Ho Chi Minh 169
Hu Shisheng 148, 152, 156
Hua Chunying 153–4
Human Rights Watch 3, 117, 146
Hume, Allan 83
Hussain, Shalah 106

Imroze, Parvez 145
India
    caste system in 84, 95
    Census (1941) 49, 62, 72
    Census (1961) 74
    creation of identity of 19–21

INDEX

Thanks to our Patreon subscriber:

Ciaran Kane

Who has shown generosity and
comradeship in support of our publishing.

Check out the other perks you get by subscribing
to our Patreon – visit patreon.com/plutopress.
Subscriptions start from £3 a month.

The Pluto Press Newsletter

Hello friend of Pluto!

Want to stay on top of the best radical books
we publish?

Then sign up to be the first to hear about our
new books, as well as special events,
podcasts and videos.

You'll also get 50% off your first order with us
when you sign up.

Come and join us!

Go to bit.ly/PlutoNewsletter